The Medieval Underworld

The Medieval Underworld

Andrew McCall

DORSET PRESS
New York

This edition published by Dorset Press,
a division of Marboro Books Corporation,
by arrangement with A.M. Heath & Company, Limited
1991 Dorset Press

ISBN 0-88029-714-X

Printed in the United States of America
M 9 8 7 6 5 4 3 2

Contents

Acknowledgments

For their encouragement, patience and generosity, I should like to thank Charles and Annette Barton, Professor Haim Beinart of the Hebrew University of Jerusalem, Anthony Blond, James Coats, Budwin Conn, Vanessa Fox, Richard Girouard, Anne Gray, Dr Hassell of the Bodleian Library, Anthony Heckstall-Smith, Michael Holroyd, The Trustees and Staff of the London Library, Judith Mackrell, the Trustees of the Phoenix Trust, Philippa Pullar, Simon Raven, Sir Steven Runciman, Joy Rutherford of the Bodleian Library, the late Miriam Sacher, Lady St Just, Christopher Sinclair-Stevenson, the Revd. Charles Sinnickson, Biddy Tucker and Professor Yigael Yadin.

The Author and Publishers wish to thank the following for permission to quote copyright material: G. G. Coulton and Cambridge University Press for quotation from *Medieval Panorama*; Charles Dahlberg and Princeton University Press for quotation from *The Romance of the Rose*; M. R. B. Shaw and Penguin Books for quotation from *Chronicles of the Crusades*; Leo Sherley-Price and Penguin Books for quotation from *A History of the English Church and People*; Geoffrey Brereton and Penguin Books for quotation from Jean Froissart's *Chronicles*; John T. McNeill, Helen M. Gamer and Columbia University Press for quotation from *Medieval Handbooks of Penance*; J. Bridsall and Columbia University Press for quotation from Jean de Venette's *Chronicle*; C. C. Swinton Bland and Routledge & Kegan Paul for quotation from Guibert of Nogent's *Autobiography*; Francesco Gabrielli, E. J. Costello and Routledge & Kegan Paul for quotation from *Arab Historians of the Crusades*.

Every effort has been made to trace the copyright holders of the quoted material. Should there be any omissions in this respect, we apologize and shall be pleased to make appropriate acknowledgment in future editions.

To my mother and father

1

The Middle Ages

THE MIDDLE AGES are often thought of as a stagnant interlude, a uniform and depressing hiatus in the progress of Western civilisation. So, especially, did they appear to the liberated Italian of the fifteenth century, who coined the term 'Middle Ages' expressly to dismiss the eleven dark centuries of bigoted ignorance which it seemed to him had supervened between the collapse of Rome beneath the invasions of the Northern barbarians and his own emergence into the bright new world of the Western European Renaissance. But between the 'Middle Ages' and the 'Renaissance' there was, in reality, no distinct break. Nor is either designation even precise; both are terms rather of convenience, and while in Italy the Renaissance could be said to have begun as early as the fourteenth century, it might just as accurately be said that in England the Middle Ages lasted long into the sixteenth. Others again would assert that the 'Dark Ages' preceeded the 'Middle Ages' and that the Middle Ages proper do not begin until the tenth or even the eleventh century.

For our purpose, however, which is to consider the fate of those people who were either unwilling or unable to comply with the laws of medieval society, the period must open with the barbarian triumphant amongst the ruins of the Roman Empire: a barbarian in some cases still pagan but who would in time be converted to Christianity; a barbarian who was greatly affected by the discovery of his immortal soul and whose code of behaviour was to be refashioned accordingly by the teachings of the Old and the New Testaments and the great 'Fathers' of his new faith.

The gradual fusion of Teutonic tribal custom with the doctrines of

Christianity and assorted pickings from the debris of what had been classical civilisation produced a society that came to consider itself, above all else, Christian but whose social structure was, nevertheless, essentially military in emphasis. For the internal organisation of the barbarian hordes had always been geared to warfare; and even when they began to settle down in their conquered territories, defining boundaries and becoming acquainted with the gentler ways of their subject populations, they were still compelled to defend their possessions against new waves of equally rapacious marauders. Amongst themselves, too, the strong attacked the weak. Dynasties rose by the sword, the club, the battleaxe, poison or the dagger; and fell the same way. In the prevailing atmosphere of violence and tumult, the sprawling Frankish Empire established over large tracts of continental Europe by Charlemagne in the early ninth century was but a flash in the pan; an ambitious dream, far ahead of its time, it had by the middle of the same century disintegrated.

The Christian West was, meanwhile, harassed from all sides by the heathen: Magyars threatened the eastern borders; Saracens and Moors attacked along the Mediterranean littoral and overland through Moslem Spain; the northern and western coasts and their rivers were ravaged by Vikings, whose longships raided as far up the Seine even as Paris. In the face of these attacks from without and the return to general lawlessness that followed the brief manifestation of a strong central authority, what remained of Charlemagne's dream was further fragmented as Christian Europe formed itself into thousands upon thousands of separate units—the units of feudalism, where men, who as individuals were powerless to defend themselves, placed themselves and their property under the protective authority of a local warlord or strongman.

Although the feudal relationship was, in theory, contractual, voluntarily entered into, with obligations due on both sides, it was not long before many descendants of those free men who had sworn loyalty to a potential protector found that their position had so far deteriorated, in a society which had more or less succeeded by now in preventing the ownership of at any rate Christian slaves, as to be virtually indistinguishable from servitude. For whereas the lord was all too often forgetful or even ignorant of his own duties, he was seldom slow in demanding his rights from his serfs, who became in effect little more than his personal chattels. Yet miserable as the lot of the serf or 'villein' may have been, he can in no sense be classed as an outcast or as an enemy of medieval society: he was, on the contrary, considered to be an integral and most necessary part of the feudal community.

While at this lowest level the peasant farmer bartered his labour and his smallholding—and, unwittingly, his freedom—in return for the promise of protection, at the higher level great magnates were 'enfeoffed' with grants of land, in return for service of arms, by Kings and Emperors to whom they swore fealty. Lesser magnates were enfeoffed by greater magnates, and so on down the scale. The old concept of direct loyalty to the tribal chieftain was thus replaced by an ascending series of personal allegiances, while authority, and hence the right to dispense justice, came to be thought of as descending through a corresponding series of ever-diminishing jurisdictions from the King's court, at the summit of the pyramid, down to that of the Lord of the Manor.

Since the feudal scheme of land tenure developed haphazardly, in response to the particular needs of time and place, there was considerable variety in its earlier forms. But, as feudalism spread gradually over more and more of Western Europe, it became more uniform in its application, and the idea began to emerge of a multi-tiered society which reflected a rigid and hierarchical system of descending authority: a system which was, through its affinity with the Christian hierarchy of Divine Beings, immediately attractive to the Church; which was to permeate the whole of medieval life with its ideals and formalities; which was to leave its mark upon the minds and the institutions of Europe for centuries after the circumstances that had called it into being had vanished.

During the course of the tenth and eleventh centuries, the Infidel threat was overcome. The Magyars, defeated by the Emperor Otto the Great at Lechfield in 955, were thereafter to be converted to Christianity. In Northern Europe, the Vikings, too, saw the Light: in the year 911, Rollo, a Viking chieftain, received the duchy of Normandy in fief from the French King and became a Christian; in 1027, Canute, King of England and Denmark, made the pilgrimage to Rome; and not long afterwards, King Olaf I of Norway, killed in battle at Stiklestad in 1030 by the pilgrim Canute, was actually canonised. To the South, the Moslem Saracens and Moors, while obstinately maintaining the superiority of their own religion, were, for the time being, held at bay.

By the end of the eleventh century Christianity was the established religion of Western Europe and feudalism the established social order. But almost immediately that order began to change. The trade routes were safer to travel and commerce revived. Towns which had lain in ruins, little more than villages, since their destruction at the time of the first barbarian invasions, were rebuilt and others were founded at strategic points along the trade routes, old and new. Money circulated and promissory bonds. The capital amassed from trade was invested in light manufacturing industries, such as weaving. For these labour was needed and there was a steady drift towards the towns. The villein who ran away, if he managed to stay a year and a day in a town without recapture, was deemed to have become a free man. Others bought their freedom. As the populations and the prosperity of the towns grew, so did the bargaining power of their town councils; many were able to purchase their independence from their feudal overlords and the right of jurisdiction over their own internal affairs. While some towns chose to place themselves under the direct authority of the King, others preferred to band together for their mutual assistance and defence in Associations and Leagues. Amongst the craftsmen and merchants similar associations were formed; the various craft and trade guilds, each with its own officers, emblem and patron Saint.

To the more far-sighted rulers of the period, the growing commercialism of the later Middle Ages offered a welcome opportunity to escape from their inhibiting dependence on their great feudal magnates. For by allying themselves to the new merchant class, by demanding taxes in lieu of knight service from their subjects, they could hope to accumulate enough money, not only to pay for a better equipped and a better trained army than the feudal levy could supply, but also to provide themselves with a more efficient bureaucracy, whose professional skills were vital to them if they were to succeed in wresting power from the feudal magnates and to concentrate it instead in the hands of a strong centralised monarchy.

To the feudal magnates, however, apart from those Bishops and Barons who sought to rival Kings and Emperors by playing the same game, to the lesser baronage and the knights, to the Church, to the poor and even to many merchants, the ever-increasing importance of money seemed to be the source of all evil and the reason why God had decided to punish the world by afflicting it with so many plagues, droughts and floods. What was needed, the cry echoed and re-echoed throughout the later Middle Ages, was a return to the 'Old days', when, untroubled by thoughts of money, everyone had performed, and had been content to perform, his appointed function in society.

The idea of a Chain of Being, and thence of an appointed place and function in the Christian hierarchy, was central to the medieval conception of the Universe. Known sometimes as the Golden

Chain, it was given its consummate theological expression in the mid-thirteenth century *Summa Theologica* of St Thomas Aquinas, who united the newly discovered Aristotelian system of physics and philosophy with Christian theology in constructing an Ideal Universe which was seen, by reason, to spring from the Christian faith and in which the various degrees of being were described as descending from the Ultimate Godhead, through the hierarchy of angels and through man, down to the meanest inanimate object. So long as every component part of the Divine Plan kept to its proper place and discharged its proper function, in accordance with Right Reason, here, said St Thomas, was Order. But let anyone try to step outside his appointed place, let anyone act in defiance of Right Reason and his proper function, then here was the seed of disaster.

Since the Universe was held to have been divinely ordered by God, if anything appeared to be wrong with the world, there could only be one possible reason for it. If men hankered after money rather than God, if the clergy was avaricious and corrupt, if comets or swarms of locusts flew through the sky, even those people who had never heard of St Thomas Aquinas or his *Summa Theologica* knew at once that somebody somewhere, and usually quite near at hand, was not fulfilling his function in the Divine Scheme and that Right Reason was disrupted. Yet in a world which knew nothing of the forward march of civilisation, but only of the journey of tainted souls 'on board of this Ship of Penitence' towards death and, just possibly, salvation, there was little chance of improvement. Indeed, since the world was generally reckoned to be in the sixth of its seven ages and awaiting the necessary prelude to the Day of Judgement, the terrible coming of Antichrist and the chaos of the Last Days, it seemed probable that matters would deteriorate still further.

The greater the materialism of the Middle Ages became and the more blatant the disparity between the actual world and the Ideal World, the more was the Ideal emphasised. From the twelfth century onwards, as new horizons were opened up by commerce and the Crusades, as a growing restlessness and curiosity took hold of men, as the Church became gradually more secularised and individuals came to think more in terms of a salvation which was to be achieved through the personal intercession of the Saviour or the Virgin Mary, rather than through the regular offices of the organised Church, so did the authorities, seeing the Ideal threatened, try to save it by making it ever more demanding. The only answer to unorthodoxy seemed to be insistence on still greater orthodoxy; the only answer to the failure of the feudal scheme to

1 *A twelfth-century* Ladder of Virtue. *Salvation of the immortal soul is the ultimate goal of the Christian, but demons and vices conspire to prevent him from securing a place in the Kingdom of Heaven.*

2 *The coming of Antichrist and the chaos of the Last Days.*

accommodate mercantile realities, to make that scheme even more unaccommodating.

As early as the twelfth century, then, medieval society had begun to close in on itself. And the results were disastrous. Stringent measures against heretics produced more heretics; an hysterical fear of witches produced hysterical witches; attempts to coerce the more restless elements in society made those elements more restive. At the intellectual level, meanwhile, since the Divine Synthesis of St Thomas Aquinas was held to have said all that was to be said, about both the visible and invisible worlds, by reducing them to one indivisible system dependent upon God, men like Duns Scotus and Ockham, who wished to take the investigation of natural phenomena a stage further, found it necessary, in the interests of orthodoxy, to declare that there were in fact two separate sorts of knowledge; on the one hand the purely physical or, as we might say, scientific, and on the other the theological or Divine.

It was this distinction between the physical nature of a thing and its divine nature, as it filtered through to all levels of society and came to be applied to every aspect of life, that gave rise in the later Middle Ages to the prevailing mental attitude of double-think or the simultaneous subscription to two separate and often directly opposed sets of standards; the one theoretical, the other ruthlessly egoistic and practical. Yet although such an attitude might seem to us mere hypocrisy, to the medieval way of thinking it did not. For however debilitating the subscription to two sets of standards may have been, to medieval people the theoretical or Divine nature of the world was just as real as the practical—if not, since the world below was but the imperfect reflection of the Divine World, even more so. Indeed, it was precisely because he and his forbears had for so long teetered on the tightrope of double-think, precisely because they had believed in the increasingly rigorous and therefore increasingly irrelevant Ideal Scheme, that the shattering of that Ideal Scheme seemed to Renaissance man to be of such cataclysmic significance.

But what of course Renaissance man could not see, considering himself a revolutionary, the saviour of civilisation and of Man's faith in his own humanity from over a thousand years of retrogression, was that the Middle Ages had in fact been, for all the talk of an Immutable Order, an age of evolution and flux; an age during which ideas and institutions, secular and ecclesiastical, had been developed, adapted and amended—initiated, even, and discarded; an age during which the whole fabric of Western European civilization had, in short, been in a state of continual metamorphosis.

The history of the changes which took place in Western Europe between the collapse of the Roman Empire of the West and the Renaissance, has been written in a variety of contexts. All of these accounts have, in their different ways, emphasised the debt we owe to the Middle Ages not only for castles and cathedrals and for picturesque little towns; for illuminated manuscripts, Giotto and Fra Angelico; for Dante, Boccaccio, François Villon, Chaucer, Copernicus and Erasmus; but also for that part of classical civilization which the Church managed to salvage from the barbarian holocausts and keep alive in the monasteries, the cathedral schools and, latterly, the Universities; for Shakespeare, in whom the medieval spirit lived on alongside the modern; for Martin Luther, Kepler, Galileo, Francis Bacon and many other besides. Yet still it is hoped that this present sketch, which looks at the period from the point of view of 'the outsider', or of those men and women who either could not or would not conform to the conventions of a society whose insistence upon conformity was finally to become obsessive, might perhaps add something to an understanding of a millenium that was so important to the development of Western civilization as we know it today.

2

Church, State and Sin

MEDIEVAL PEOPLE were subject to two sets of laws: the law of the land in which they lived and the law of God, or Canon law. In theory, Caesar and his representatives dealt with what concerned Caesar and God, as represented by the Church, with what concerned Him. But dispensing justice was a lucrative business; Canon law was in general more humane than the secular law; and there were areas in which it was difficult to say whether God or Caesar might have been the more affronted by the commission of a particular offence. The result of this confusion — and of the thirst for power, too, and of greed on both sides — was a running battle between Church and State, which was to reach its climax in the twelfth and thirteenth centuries, over those cases in which both claimed the right to adjudicate.

In the opening period of the Middle Ages, during those centuries when the spread and, perhaps, even the survival of Christianity in Western Europe had depended on the conversion of the new pagan rulers to the Faith, the Church had been wise enough not to encroach too far upon the ancient prerogatives of the tribal chieftains. The eventual holy alliance of barbarian might and the supernatural power claimed by the Church was achieved, therefore, in an atmosphere of give and take. In an illiterate world (the Emperor Charlemagne, we are told, 'used to keep writing-tablets and note-books under the pillows on his bed, so that he could try his hand at forming letters in his leisure moments; but, although he tried very hard, he had begun too late in life and he made little progress')[1] the royal administration came to be carried out largely by monks, whose book-learning may have been scoffed at by brutish warriors, but whose services were vital to the operation of the methods of government which the new Kings found in use among their conquered Roman subjects and the application of which they sought to extend to the government of their own unruly tribesmen. For these civil services and for the divine sanction with which the Church's theocratic view of all power as deriving from God endorsed their practical authority, the Kings of the barbarians were prepared to pay handsomely. As the frontiers of Catholic Christianity expanded, so were fat lands showered on the monasteries, which produced the civil servants, and on the bishoprics, with which the more favoured of the royal administrators were often rewarded. The Church became steadily richer, and more influential; and, for the time being, did not protest too loudly at the royal appointment of Bishops or Abbots.

No sooner did the triumph of Catholicism in the West seem assured, however, than ecclesiastical claims to an authority superior to all secular authority became more vociferous. For, if authority derived from God, the Church insisted, must it not then be transmitted through God's representatives on earth, the Church? And had not St Augustine of Hippo himself said that the Pope, as St Peter's successor, was the head of that Church? Some time during the course of the eighth century there appeared the spurious Donation of Constantine, a forgery which maintained that the Emperor Constantine had, upon his miraculous recovery from leprosy some four hundred years earlier, granted the Popes the right to crown a Roman Emperor of the West; and, in the year 800, King Charlemagne of the Franks tacitly acknowledged this claim by allowing Pope Leo III to crown him Emperor at Rome.

Although before the time of Charlemagne there had been a certain amount of movement from monastery to monastery and from one royal court to another, although missionaries had carried the Word of God deep into pagan fastnesses and pilgrims had set out on hazardous journeys to the Holy Places, yet still communications between one part of Christian Europe and another were poor. The times were violent and travel was dangerous. In these circumstances, the actual power of the Church in any given barbarian kingdom had depended not so much on the claims made for it at Rome but on the policy and the generosity of the local monarch with whom it had thrown in its lot. Briefly, under Charlemagne and his immediate successors, there was a spell of relative stability. Horizons widened. But with the collapse of a central authority they narrowed again. The Churches were forced back into the arms of their military protectors and it was not until the eleventh century,

3 God disposes, from the twelfth-century tympanum of the church of Ste Foy at Conques-en-Rouergue.

when the infidel threat had been stemmed by the new order of feudal monarchies, that the Papacy was able to make any significant capital out of the victory it had gained in 800 by establishing its claim to an authority superior to that even of the Emperor of the West.

As soon as there was some degree of security, then, in Western Europe and communications within its frontiers began to improve, the Church took advantage of the situation to try to disentangle the spiritual from the secular and so to free itself from its shameful dependence on the secular rulers. From the middle of the eleventh century, the papal throne was occupied by a succession of men whose ambition it was to establish the position of the Church as a separate entity, as a supranational organization, whose lands and whose officers, although distributed throughout the various Catholic kingdoms, were subject only to the authority of the ecclesiastical hierarchy, presided over by the Pope at Rome. To such advocates of the Church's independence as Popes Leo IX or Gregory VII it was unthinkable that laymen should be allowed to continue, as they had been in the habit of doing, to make ecclesiastical appointments: princes who persisted in claiming the right to do so were denounced from the pulpit, and before the close of the century, in 1088, the powerful German Emperor, Henry IV, was on his knees in the snow at Canossa, a penitent before Pope Gregory VII, craving papal forgiveness and the lifting of the ban of excommunication which had been placed upon him.

On the face of it, Canossa was a great victory for the Papacy and for the idealists who hoped to make the Church more spiritual by cleansing it of unseemly secular interference. But even as those goals for which the idealists had striven were being realised—as Rome became established as the legislative and administrative centre of the Church and the immunity of the clergy from secular jurisdictions came, for the most part, to be recognised—so did the system of ecclesiastical government have to be overhauled and expanded to cope with the increasing volume of business that found its way to Rome. In this process, the Papacy itself was gradually secularised; and Rome, which in the earlier Middle Ages had been generally thought of, whatever the sometimes sordid reality, as a sort of spiritual powerhouse, became instead the 'Great Whore, arrayed in purple and scarlet colour, and decked with gold and precious stones and pearls', the insatiable 'step-mother' who, not content with selling justice at home, despatched her loathsome agents into every corner of Catholic Europe to pry into people's lives and extort money from them.*

Once the ideal for which some churchmen claimed St Thomas à

---

* A particularly dreadful Pope of the earlier period would seem to have been John XII (955–64) who is reported to have turned the church of St John's Lateran into a brothel, and was accused at his trial of perjury, sacrilege, simony, adultery, incest and murder.

Becket had suffered martyrdom in 1170 had been so debased, the more powerful national monarchs of the later Middle Ages were able to use anti-papal sentiment to encourage the local development of the increasingly nationally-minded Churches characteristic of the last years of our period. For although successive attempts on the part of secular powers at turning the Popes into their own creatures—the attempts, for instance, of the Roman bandit Matteo Orsini in the thirteenth century or of the Kings of France during the fourteenth-century papal residence at Avignon—had all in the end failed, so, too, did the efforts of a series of reforming Church Councils, such as those of Constance in 1414–18 and Basle in 1431–49, fail to stimulate any appreciable resurgence of that popular respect which the Papacy had commanded in the eleventh or twelfth centuries.* The most accomplished of the fifteenth-century Popes were, significantly, accomplished administrators; at the Vatican, as elsewhere, internationalism was by now on the way out; local Farneses, Medicis, and Spanish Borgias vied with one another to secure their election, or that of a favourite relative, to the enjoyment of St Peter's valuable patrimony—and, slowly, the backdrop for the Reformation fell into place.

But while the concentration of ecclesiastical authority at Rome in the eleventh century was ultimately to result in the corruption of the Papacy and the alienation of the devout, it was also to bring the beginnings of system to the vast and amorphous body of Canon law. Already, in the earlier years of that century, men like Ivo of Chartres were busy collating the various regional selections from the Scriptures, writings of the Church Fathers, decretals of Bishops and Popes, decisions of Church Councils and other assorted opinions that were considered authoritative; in about 1140 came the publication of Gratian of Bologna's definitive *Decretum*; and in 1234 the *Decretum*, with the addition of subsequent papal decretals, was made official by the *Bull Pacificus* of Gregory IX.

It was through the work of Gratian and his fellow-students of ecclesiastical law that much of Roman law, to whose principles they looked for guidance when confronted by contradictory opinions, was absorbed into Canon law. And it was through this revival of

---

* In the early thirteenth century Matteo Orsini had the electing Cardinals locked up in a small ruined temple, without food or water. His soldiers were instructed to urinate and to 'empty their bowels' on their Eminences through the holes in the roof until such time as they should agree to nominate the candidate of his choice. But Orsini's victory, when it came, was short-lived: conditions inside the temple had become so appalling that the new Pope died two days after his election and two of the Cardinals followed soon after.

legal studies in the clerical world that the Church was encouraged to put forward claims to a jurisdiction in cases which had little or nothing to do with religion or God. For, in theory, as we have seen, the Church was supposed to concern itself with what concerned God: a theory which gave the ecclesiastical courts grounds for claiming exclusive judicial rights in cases involving clerics, both civil and criminal; over those people, such as pilgrims or crusaders, who were temporarily engaged in activities to do with the Church; and in all cases relating to Faith and to the Sacraments, to the property of the Church and the clergy, vows and obligations undertaken upon oath, sacrilege, witchcraft and heresy. But with this the reformed Papacy was not satisfied. The list was capable, obviously, of being extended by analogy—and, in the twelfth and thirteenth centuries, it was: although clerics were forbidden to submit to any form of lay jurisdiction, the Church claimed that in all 'personal actions' the layman might, if he chose, summon other laymen to appear before an ecclesiastical court.

At the time, in the middle years of the twelfth century, when the controversy between Church and State over rights of jurisdiction blew up into a major issue, the secular administration of justice was in general, and especially by comparison with the ecclesiastical, fairly haphazard. Papal prestige was at its height whereas the positions of the secular rulers, of whose support the Church no longer felt so much need, were still relatively weak. At first, therefore, the Papacy had the upper hand; many even of its most exaggerated claims were admitted, and it was not until the secular rulers had consolidated their positions and could provide more efficient justice that they were able to refute some at least of the papal claims.

If the dividing line between what concerned God's courts and what concerned Caesar's was an uncertain and, at times, a hotly disputed one, there was a sense, nevertheless, in which all crimes could be considered to have been committed against God. For, just as authority was generally conceived of as being God-given, so too, since it supplied the means of preserving that earthly order which was thought to reflect the Divine Order, was the whole corpus of the law.* To defy any law was hence to defy God. No matter in what

* The theocratic or descending conception of authority was, to a certain extent, challenged by the contractual theory of feudalism and by the jurisprudential view of customary law as deriving its force from the consent of the individuals to whom it applied. In countries, therefore, like England, whose Common law evolved out of custom and feudal practice, the rights of the individual were less purely theoretical than in, say, France or Germany, where Roman law had a greater influence on the development of the legal system.

4 *A dying man surrounded by demons who have come to confront him with his sins: 'You have fornicated, you have killed . . .*

court a person was tried—whether in an ecclesiastical court or a royal court, in the feudal court of the Lord of the Manor or that of a Bishop who, as a feudal lord would be represented in this his secular court by a 'vidame' or advocate—whosoever was found guilty of breaking the law was deemed also to have sinned.

Every crime was, thus, a sin and required that the sinner atone for it by doing penance. But, in practice, the Church was more interested in the sinful aspect of crimes committed against the Canon law or against other people—or even in the many sins such as vainglory and accidia, which were not crimes at all—than it was in crimes, such as coin-clipping, which were essentially crimes against the State. Nor indeed did anybody ever challenge the principle that the correction of sin, as such, should be the exclusive concern of the Church. Trouble arose only in those cases where Church and State claimed the right to adjudicate and the Church maintained that an ecclesiastical trial or the imposition of an ecclesiastical penalty precluded any possibility of a secular trial. For the rest, everyone recognised that sin was solely a religious matter, a matter between the sinner, the salvation of whose soul it jeopardized, and God, without the gift of whose supernatural Grace no soul could be saved. If the sinner died unshriven, he was supposed to proceed directly to Hell and the Church's ultimate purpose, therefore, in prescribing specific acts of atonement was not so much to punish the sinner as to help him to annul the consequences of his sin by some compensatory form of earthly suffering and so, it was hoped, to re-establish himself in God's good favour through the ineffable workings of His Divine Grace.

Throughout the Middle Ages, as today, the performance of penance involved three separate stages, or acts: first, the sinner had, with a contrite heart, to repent of his sin; secondly, he must confess it; and thirdly, he had to make some kind of satisfaction so that he might obtain absolution. But between early Christian practice and penance in its developed medieval form there was a difference. During the first few centuries of Christianity, the confession of sin was made in public. The penitent, who as a rule confessed only once in a lifetime and so generally left it until he felt close to the moment of death, was enjoined to kneel down in front of the congregation of 'those who are dear to God' and to beseech 'all the brethren to be his ambassadors to hear his deprecatory supplication before God'.[2] But as the list of offences for which penance might be required or accepted grew steadily longer and longer, so, gradually, did the idea of a single and all-embracing confession give way to a new system of repeated confessions— until, in 1215, we find the Fourth Lateran Council stipulating that every Christian must confess at least once a year—and so, too, did public confession come to be replaced by a private rite, in which the penitent confessed to, and was absolved by, a priest.

While private confession to a priest was slowly replacing the act of public confession, the public part of the older form of confession was sometimes incorporated instead into the punishment. Where this occurred, some sort of public act, or a series of them, would be enjoined on the penitent as atonement for his sin. And although, as the Middle Ages advanced, the whole process of penance became increasingly a private matter, the public performance of penance was never suppressed. Thus in England, for example, in the four-teenth century, when one Nicholas the Porter assisted in snatching some malefactors out of sanctuary in the Church of the Carmelites at Newcastle, as a result of which the wanted men were delivered into the hands of the civil authorities and executed, Bishop Richard wrote to the curate of St Nicholas at Durham ordering that, as penance, the porter 'on Monday, Tuesday and Wednesday of the Whitsun week just coming . . . shall receive the whip from your hands publicly, before the chief door of your Church, in his shirt, bareheaded and barefoot. He shall there proclaim in English the reason for his penance and shall admit his fault'; after which, he was to proceed 'these three days' with his scourger following behind him, to the cathedral church of Durham and, in front of that place, repeat the performance.[3]

To drag a person out of 'sanctuary', or in other words to violate the guarantee of protection that the Church offered to those sus-pected or even convicted criminals who managed to reach the safety of a church or any other place which custom authorized to afford immunity, was a serious offence. For, although the right of sanctuary was open to the most outrageous abuses, to defy it was nonetheless to commit sacrilege and called for the excommunica-tion of anyone who dared to do so.* Hence it had been in the case of

* The English *Statute Books* contain a petition (Statute 9 E II cap. 10, 1315–16) which complains that the personal enemies of those who have fled to sanctuary are disregarding the fugitives' right to protection by arming themselves and establish-ing themselves in the cemeteries of the churches so as to prevent the fugitives from getting food or even coming out to 'satisfy their natural wants'. More usual, though, are complaints about criminals who have taken advantage of the right of sanctuary. In the early fifteenth century, for example, the Commons of England complained to their King about the community of apprentices who had robbed their masters and left them, of tradesmen who had run into debt and even of seasoned robbers, who were all of them living together in the sanctuary of London's St Martin-le-Grand 'there forging by day charters, obligations and false quittances, on which they imitate the seals and signatures of honest city merchants while the murderers and brigands go out at night to commit new crimes'. Similarly, in the reign of Richard III, it had been said of Westminster Abbey that

Nicholas the Porter that before any penance could be prescribed for his offence, the intervention of the papal nuncio, representing the authority of the Supreme Pontiff, had been required to ensure that the porter might, after the performance of a suitable penance, be permitted a pardon.

If Nicholas's punishment for his part in handing over suspected criminals to the authorities may seem to us somewhat harsh, however, we may be fairly certain that had he been not a porter but a man of greater estate, his punishment would have been more severe. For it was characteristic of the Church's attitude to the correction of sin that not only the gravity of the sin but also the position of the sinner in society should be taken into account: an attitude which is to be found embodied in the earliest of the manuals, known as penitentials, for the guidance of confessors in prescribing penances and one which was, on the whole, to persist throughout the medieval period. In many cases, too, the rank of the injured party was taken into account—as in the collection of seventh-century Irish *Canons* which stipulated that if a man had pulled hairs out of a Bishop's venerable head, then the assailant's hairs were to be plucked from his own head at the ratio of twelve to one—but this in no way invalidated the general principle that a sin was more reprehensible when it was committed by a man of education or substance than if it was committed by, say, a youth or an illiterate labourer. While therefore crimes against the clergy were penalised especially heavily, so too were crimes committed by the clergy, as may be seen from an eighth-century penitential ascribed by Albers to Bede and recommending penances for capital sins, which it lists as 'Pride, envy, fornication, vainglory, anger of longstanding, worldly sadness [the dreaded accidia, from which apparently large numbers of medieval people suffered], avarice, gluttony, sacrilege, adultery, false witness, theft, robbery, con-

Continued from previous page

'thieves bring thither their stolen goods and live thereon. They devise there new robberies; nightly they steal out, they rob, they reave and kill and come in again'; while in 1427, at Rome, San Bernardino preached one of his famous sermons against a less hallowed local extension of the right which claimed that anyone who committed murder was immune from arrest as soon as he was safely back behind the iron gates or fence of his house—a sermon so stirring, apparently, that within a short time of its delivery many of the offending gates and fences were torn down. (For St Martin's: *Rotuli Parliamentorum*, Records Commission 1776–7, iii, 503–4. For Westminster Abbey, see *The History of King Richard III (unfinished) writen by Master Thomas More, than one of the undersheriffs of London: about the year of our Lorde, 1513*. London 1557. Reprinted by S. W. Singer, Chiswick, 1821, pp. 44–45.)

tinual drunkenness, idolatry, effeminacy, sodomy, evil-speaking and perjury'. 'For these,' the *Penitential* declares, 'liberal alms are to be given and prolonged fasting is to be kept. . . ; laymen three years, clerics five years, subdeacons six years, presbyters ten years, bishops twelve years', while if the sin was habitual, bishops were to do the same penance fourteen years, presbyters twelve years, deacons ten years, subdeacons nine, clerics seven and laymen five.[4]

The distinction between the occasional and the habitual offender is again typical of most penitentials, which often also take into consideration whether the sin involved was intentional or unintentional and whether it was premeditated or committed in a moment of anger. Thus the *Penitential of Cummean* (c.650) directs that 'he who commits murder through nursing hatred in his mind, shall give up his arms until death, and dead unto the world, shall live unto God. But if it is after vows of perfection [in other words, if the murderer be a monk] he shall die unto the world with perpetual pilgrimage. But he who does this through anger, not through premeditation, shall do penance for three years with bread and water and with alms and prayers. But if he kills his neighbour unintentionally, by accident, he shall do penance for one year'.[5] An earlier penitential, entitled *Certain Excerpts from a book of David*, and dating from the first quarter of the sixth century, deals in a similar fashion with a more personal sin: 'He who intentionally becomes polluted in his sleep shall get up and sing seven psalms and live on bread and water for that day; but if he does not do this he shall sing thirty psalms. But if he desired to sin in sleep but could not, fifteen psalms; if however he sinned but was not polluted, twenty-four; if he was unintentionally polluted, fifteen.'[6]

As may be imagined from the general tenor of even the few examples quoted above, the penitentials were the product of the monasteries—in particular the early Celtic monasteries, whose influence over the surrounding countryside, at a time when most of Northern Europe still bowed to pagan gods, was considerable. To these scattered strongholds of their Faith, Christians made their way to confess their sins, and it was in order that the monks might have rules-of-thumb to help them in prescribing penances for them that the application of the Celtic penitentials—the earliest of which tend to concentrate on matters of internal discipline within the monasteries themselves—came to be extended, first, to the Celtic Christian community at large and, later, to the whole of Western Christendom. For the role of the Celtic monks in converting many of the Northern barbarian tribes to Christianity was a leading one; where the Celtic monks went, naturally, the penitentials went also;

and, despite repeated attempts on the part of various religious authorities to do away with them—such, for instance, as a Synod of Paris, which in 829 ordered all penitentials to be burned 'that through them unskilled priests may no longer deceive men'—in the end the Bishops were forced to recognise their utility and, while seeking to modify them somewhat,to give to both their methods and to much of their material the stamp of episcopal authority.*

While the misuse of penitentials by 'unskilled priests' was obviously an important factor in marking them out for official disapproval, so too were some of the punishments that the manuals recommended. For, although the compilers were generally aware that penance was supposed to be a medicine for the afflicted Christian soul, a sort of purge whereby, according to the prevailing 'Methodist' view of medicine, contraries were cured by contraries, yet still many of the penitentials, and especially the earlier ones, all too clearly reflected their debt to pagan practices in the remedies they prescribed for effecting these cures. 'The sleepy man,' says a *Penitential of Columban* (c.600) 'is to be sentenced to watchfulness'[7] —a prescription with which nobody could have quarrelled. But an eighth-century Irish *Table of Commutations* is more specific on this subject of watchfulness, or in other words 'vigils', which it enjoins for a number of sins; to make sure that he performs his vigil properly, with unceasing prayer and without nodding off, the penitent is commanded to lie down not only in water, on nettles or on nutshells but also, on certain occasions, 'with a corpse in the grave.'[8]

---

* Official titivation and approval of the penitentials did not, however, render the administration of penance immune from misuse at the hands of 'unskilled' or even unscrupulous priests. To give but one example from many such 'misuses' that were actually reported, it is related in the *Chronicle of Lanercost* (trs. Sir Herbert Maxwell, Bart—*Scottish Historical Review* Vol.VI p. 177) of the parish priest of Inverkiethling, named John—who had already, in Easter week, 1282, scandalised decent people by reviving 'the profane rites of Priapus, collecting young girls from villages, and compelling them to dance in circles to [the honour of] Father Bacchus . . . carrying in front on a pole a representation of the human organs of reproduction, and singing and dancing himself like a mime . . . and stirring them to lust by filthy language'—that 'in the same year, when his parishioners assembled according to custom in the Church at dawn in Penance Week at the hour of discipline he would insist that certain persons should prick with goads [others] stripped for penance'. In this particular case—and it is here, perhaps, that it is unusual—the priest met with what the Chronicler thought to be his just deserts, since 'the burgesses, resenting the indignity inflicted upon them, turned upon its author; who, while he as author was defending his nefarious work, fell the same night pierced by a knife, God thus awarding him what he deserved for his wickedness'.

Despite these irregularities, however—which could be and indeed mostly were, as soon as the manuals gained official recognition, ironed out—the influence of the penitentials on the society through which they were gradually disseminated was a civilizing one. In the first place, since their purpose was not so much to punish the offender as to restore him to harmonious relations with God and his fellow men, they presented an example to a barbaric age—and this at a time when there was a move amongst the barbarian leaders to codify their various tribal laws—of a force working towards the suppression of violence and the establishing of law and order. Secondly, by their insistence on the obligation of every Christian to do penance for his sins, they helped to draw attention to the obligatory nature of the secular law. Thirdly, by advocating as a rule restitution rather than retribution they helped to promote the idea that there might be a satisfactory alternative to revenge and reprisals. And fourthly, by adapting to their own requirements local legal practice with regard to 'composition'—so that, just as vengeance, according to Celtic law, might be computed in return for a money payment to the injured party, so might penance be redeemed by a payment to the Church—they helped to encourage the development of this progressive trend in the secular law.

As might have been expected of the monkish authors of the penitentials, when they looked, as they did in the case of composition, to the secular law for guidance, they usually picked on those elements in it most conducive to the maintenance of order. But this was not all. For, wherever the Church took over rules from barbarian or Roman law, it tended to have a mitigating and softening effect on them—as, for instance, happened when the Church incorporated the age-old punishment of exile into its system of punishments, and by adding a new dimension to it, transformed it.

To both the Roman and the barbarian, the prospect of exile, whether perpetual or for a given number of years only, had been a bleak and cheerless one: and so it was too for those first Christians to be sentenced to it by a Church which—apart from the purely spiritual sanction of excommunication—could impose no more severe penalty, since, until the setting up of the Inquisition in the thirteenth century to fight heresy, it was thought inappropriate for God's representative on earth to condemn a man to lose that life which God, in His Infinite Wisdom, had given him. But, as the Church came to endorse the popular belief that the Martyrs' sufferings had endowed them with a special power to intercede with God for the remission of sins: and, as, by extension, that power came to be attributed also to fragments of the Martyrs' bodies or of their clothing and to those places in which, for their Faith, they had suffered martyrdom, so did the nature of an ecclesiastical sentence of exile become altered.* Slowly, the period of absence from home, family and friends assumed the character of a pilgrimage and what had hitherto been an essentially negative punishment, what had amounted indeed to an admission of failure (in that the lawbreaker was merely removed to another territory, there very probably to continue his anti-social activities) became instead a process of regeneration, whereby the sinner hoped that through the performance of his pilgrimage and through the good offices of the Martyrs his sins might be forgiven him and he would be restored to his proper relationship with both God and society.

Neither the date at which the spiritual value of a pilgrimage was offically recognised nor the various stages by which penal pilgrimage evolved are recorded. Of the former, we know that, at the turn of the fourth and fifth centuries, St Jerome was complaining of Jerusalem that 'there is such a throng of pilgrims of both sexes that all temptation, which you might in some degree avoid elsewhere, is here collected together';[9] of the latter that, although several sixth-century Irish penitentials enjoin periods of wandering far from home as penance for the more serious sins, it does not seem to have been until the ninth century that many Bishops or confessors imposed sentences which required sinners to make pilgrimages to specific shrines. But, from the middle years of the tenth century onwards, it is clear that pilgrimages, whether voluntarily undertaken or imposed as a punishment, were becoming increasingly

---

* Although by no means all the Martyrs' 'relics' can have been genuine—of the pieces of the 'One True Cross' exhibited in the churches of Western Europe in the High Middle Ages it has been suggested that a decent-sized copse might have been reconstructed—the income that a religious establishment could derive from the possession of a famous relic was so considerable that not only less exalted clerics but even a Bishop and a Saint, in his zeal to acquire an especially venerated piece of bone for his own church, could behave in the most unedifying manner. Thus, in 1199, while enjoying the hospitality of the monks of Fécamp Abbey, Bishop Hugh of Lincoln, later to be canonised, upon being invited to worship a bone, supposed to have been a part of St Mary Magdalene, promptly borrowed a knife from his chaplain and tried to cut away the wrapping. The owners of the relic looked on in horror. The wrapping refused to give. Exasperated, the future Saint applied his teeth to the package, at last succeeding thereby in biting off two tiny fragments of bone, which he handed to his chaplain for safe-keeping: and, when the monks he had so despoiled of their treasure accused him of behaving more like a dog than a Christian, evaded them with the neat, if not altogether Christian, rejoinder that had they not all but a little while before partaken of the Host and had they not 'passed Him on into our inward parts?'

5 *A pilgrim setting off on his travels.*

common. There was even a growing number of people who made
their living out of pilgrims. For, despite the official view of the
pilgrim as the *peregrinus Christi* or *pauper Christi*, the exile or poor
man of Christ, pilgrimage was good business. Sea captains ran a
profitable line in ferrying the less truly 'poor men of Christ' across
from Italy to the Holy Land, so sparing them the hazards of the long
overland journey.* And although poor pilgrims sometimes proved

* Such sea passages were not without hazards of their own: in the thirteenth century
Cardinal Jacques de Vitry was told (MS.Lat.17,509, fol.130 Bibliothèque Nationale,
trs. G. G. Coulton, *A Medieval Garner* Extract No.95, p.198) 'how certain abominable traitors, having received payment to furnish the pilgrims with victuals even to
the port [of their destination] have stocked their ships with but little meat, and
then, after a few days' journey, have starved their pilgrims to death and cast them
ashore on an island, or [most cruel of all] have sold them as manservants or
maidservants to the Saracens'. And he had 'known' as well 'certain sailors bound
for the city of Acre who had hired a ship from a man on condition that, if it perished
on the sea, they should be bound to pay naught. When therefore they were within
a short distance of the haven, without the knowledge of those pilgrims and
merchants who were on board, they pierced the hold and entered into a boat while
the ship was sinking. All the passengers were drowned: and the sailors, having
laden their boats with the money and goods of the pilgrims, put on feigned faces of
sadness when they drew near unto the haven. Therefore, having drowned the
pilgrims and carried away their wealth, they paid not the hire of the ship, saying
they were not bound thereunto unless the vessel should come safe and sound to
haven'.

an embarrassment to the keepers of the many hostels that sprang up along the main routes and in the Holy Places themselves, once again the richer ones were prepared to pay well for their comfort. Side industries also flourished. The *Guide du Pélerin de Saint-Jacques* describes how at Santiago de Compostella the stall-holders on the north side of the basilica offered the passer-by wine-skins, slippers, deerskin bags, purses, leather laces, belts, all sorts of medicinal herbs and 'a great deal else besides' while in the Rue de France, which led up to the basilica, were to be found the money-changers, the hostel-keepers and other merchants, amongst them the vendors of the cockle-shells which were supposed originally to signify that the person who sported one had made the pilgrimage to Santiago.

After reading this contemporary account of twelfth-century Compostella, there is little need of Chaucer's more famous satirical tale of the jolly band who set out from the Tabard Inn, Southwark, in the fifteenth century, on a pilgrimage to Canterbury, to explain why Erasmus, at the end of our period, was denouncing pilgrimages as tourist excursions. But if an ecclesiastical reformer like Erasmus may have objected to the spirit in which a lady like Chaucer's Wife of Bath had set out on her numerous jaunts — to Rome, Boulogne, Santiago and Cologne, as well as on three trips to Jerusalem — more objectionable still were some of the uses which others, neither as well provided for nor as innocently inclined to travel as the good Wife of Bath, made of pilgrimage. The widowed Knight de la Tour Landry might perhaps have been overdoing his instructions to his daughters when he warned them to avoid pilgrimages as they would the plague. But how dubious was the type of person to be met with on, for instance, a sea voyage from England to the Holy Land in the late twelfth century we learn from a statute of Richard I, which enacts: that if a pilgrim kill another, he shall be bound to the body of his victim and flung into the sea; that if a pilgrim attack another with a knife or so as to draw blood, his hand shall be cut off; that if a pilgrim strike another with the palm of his hand or so that no blood be drawn, then 'he shall be plunged in the sea three times.'[10] And of the large number of people who assumed the outward appearance of a pilgrim for their own nefarious purposes we get a disturbing notion, not only from the frequent complaints about beggars who had picked up a cockle-shell from a beach or in some other way pretended to be on a pilgrimage, but also from the amount of legislation against the great mass of outlaws, criminals and, from the fourteenth century onwards, vagrant peasants looking for a new job who were, the authorities said, to be found masquerading as pilgrims on all the highways and byways of Christendom.*

Between a voluntary pilgrim, whether genuine or fraudulent, and the person ordered to go on a pilgrimage there were two important practical differences. In the first place, a compulsory pilgrimage was supervised: the penitent, who was required to take an oath before the authorities swearing to purge himself properly, was then given a safe-conduct, which contained the details of his crime and was to be shown to the various religious authorities to whom he was ordered to present himself along his route and at his destination, where he must again report before proceeding to the shrine to make his offering and beg for pardon. And secondly the person who was sentenced to make a pilgrimage was frequently ordered to wear some distinguishing article, by which all those who saw him might recognise his crime; thus, for capital crimes, some penitents were required to go on pilgrimage wearing chains about their necks, arms and waists, while heretics were sometimes sent off dressed in a black garment, with a white cross on the front and on the back. In certain cases, moreover, the pilgrim might be directed to stay for a while in the Holy Place and there do manual labour; in others, he might even be sentenced to 'perpetual pilgrimage' and forbidden ever to return home.

Once again, the type of pilgrimage imposed as a punishment would depend both on the nature and gravity of the offence and on the rank and reputation of the offender; as would, likewise, the decision as to whether or not the offender might be allowed to buy his way out of making the pilgrimage—or indeed any other form of penance. For we have already noted how the penitentials had tended to imitate the secular law's rules about composition, so that the ancient severities enjoined as earthly punishment might increasingly often be commuted in return for a money payment or, in less serious cases, for the saying of so many masses or prayers; and from this gradual infusion of the principles of composition into the administration of penance there evolved the practice of granting 'indulgences'. These were documents or sometimes tokens, by which the authorities signified—after absolution had been granted and not before—that the penitent had, in one or other acceptable fashion, earned the remission of whatever temporal punishment may have remained due to him for his sin.

* In 1388, for instance, a statute of Richard II (12 R II, cap.7) decreed that all persons claiming to be pilgrims who could not produce letters of passage stamped with a special seal were, unless infirm or otherwise manifestly incapable of work, to be arrested.

Originally, therefore, an indulgence, which might be obtained
either from a Bishop or from the Pope, referred to a specific sin or
sins and allowed the remission only of that earthly part of the
punishment due to it or to them. But in the last decade of the
eleventh century, by which time the reformed Papacy was making
determined efforts to try to limit the powers of Bishops in all matters
relating to the dispensing of indulgences and the granting of
pardons, Pope Urban II was moved to declare that a special kind of
papal indulgence might affect the fate of the Christian in the here-

6 *The Torments of Hell, the relentless consequence of unrepented sins.*

after, as well as in this life. At Clermont, in 1095, Urban announced the first ever 'plenary' indulgence. To any Christian, who would confess his sins and embark upon the Holy War against the Infidel, the Pope promised the remission of all punishment due to him for his sins, not only in this world, but also in the state of Purgatory (officially promulgated by Pope Gregory the Great, who died in 604) into which the Christian soul was held to pass at the moment of death, there by its sufferings to become purged of its sins and so at last, it was hoped, be admitted—provided always the gift of Divine Grace was forthcoming—to Life Everlasting in the Kingdom of Heaven.

By the middle years of the thirteenth century indulgences already represented a major source of ecclesiastical revenue, and so corrupt was their administration that Berthold of Ratisbon claimed that the 'pardoners' or officers licensed by the Popes to dispense indulgences were one of the obstacles which stood in the way of right relations between man and God. 'Fie! penny-preacher, murderer of all the world,' he fulminates against the pardoner, in one of his sermons: 'How many a soul dost thou cast with thy filthy lucre from God's own sunlight to the bottom of hell, where there is no hope more for them! Thou promisest so much indulgence for a single halfpenny or a single penny, that many thousand people trust thee and dream falsely that they have done penance for all their sins with that penny or that halfpenny, as thou babblest to them. So they will do no right penance, and go straight hence to hell where there is no more hope for them . . . Thou murderer of right penitence, thou hast murdered right penitence in our midst, which is one of the seven holy things of the highest that God hath. It hath been so murdered now by penny-preachers that there are few among us who will still do penance for their sins; for they count upon thy false promises. For this penny-preacher preacheth to them so long and in such manifold words of our Lord's passion that men take him for a true messenger of God: for he weepeth in his preaching and useth all manner of deceit whereby he may coax pennies from his hearers, and their souls into the bargain.'[11]

Nor was the office made any more respectable by the fact that a large number of pardoners—who might, so Chaucer reckoned, make more money in one short day than the parson drew in a month or more[12]—were fakes. In general, indeed, the lives of many of these pardoners seem to have been spent in undoing the Christian work of the ordinary clergy: an impression which is confirmed by the frequency of the papal attempts at controlling their activities and in particular by a Bull of Urban V which, in 1396, described how pardoners had been in the habit of going on those feast days when the offertories were due to the clergy, into the churchyards and there preaching so volubly as to make the performance of Mass in the churches impossible and so diverting the offertories due to the priests to themselves.*

But although the Papacy may have shown itself anxious to try to check the irresponsible or illegal sale of indulgences, it is interesting that the Popes themselves were not above suspicion in these matters. The Kings both of France and of England appear to have been sceptical, for example, when Clement VI, 'desiring to procure the salvation of the souls of men', as the chronicler Jean de Venette puts it, 'decided to reduce to fifty years the interval between the plenary indulgences which are granted in the holy city of Rome every hundred years after the Lord's Incarnation. [The first such jubilee offer of a plenary indulgence had been made by Pope Boniface VIII in 1300.] For the life of man is perishable and transitory and the wickedness of men abounds in the world, woe is me! and increaseth. Therefore in the year 1350 he granted plenary indulgence to all who, truly penitent, would journey to visit the places sacred to the apostles Peter and Paul and the other saints in the city of Rome'.†[13] Although 'great numbers of both sexes went on this pilgrimage throughout the year', Philip VI of France, at least until Lent was over, and Edward III of England, for the whole duration of the offer, forbad any of their subjects to take advantage of this opportunity to facilitate their subsequent admission to the Kingdom of Heaven.

Whether, in fact, as Jean de Venette believed, Pope Clement VI had the salvation of Christian souls uppermost in his mind when he advanced the date of the second jubilee offer of a plenary indulgence, or whether, as some others would seem to have supposed, his main purpose was to boost the papal revenues, we have no means of telling. But what is clear is that, while most Christians continued to profess reverence for the Pope as their spiritual leader, both the papal court and the representatives whom it sent out on commission to prosecute its business were by this time so generally discredited that even the threat of excommunication by the Pope himself had lost a good deal of its former terror. For, even though, as early as the middle years of the eleventh century, Pater Damiani

* The office of pardoner was officially abolished by the Council of Trent in 1562, on the grounds that 'no further hope can be entertained of amending' their ways.

† While St Peter's position in God's household was that of gatekeeper, St Paul held the important post of seneschal and, as such, served the dishes of Divine Wisdom to those who sought to partake of the feast.

had complained at the immoderate use which the clergy had been making of these anathemas—by the 'lesser' form of which the excommunicate was excluded from receiving the sacraments and from Christian burial, and by the 'greater' form of which he or she was further debarred from any sort of intercourse with fellow Christians—we have seen how later on in the same century, in 1088, a papal decree of excommunication had still been sufficiently potent to bring the Emperor Henry IV crawling on his knees to Pope Gregory VII at Canossa. But despite the grandeur and malignance with which these anathemas might be pronounced ('Let him be damned in his going out and his coming in,' Clement VI cursed the Emperor Louis of Bavaria in 1346. 'The Lord strike him with madness and blindness. . . . May the wrath of the Omnipotent burn itself into him in the present and future World')[14] the trouble with excommunication was that the Church had no material sanctions by which to enforce these essentially spiritual censures, whose more alarming effects might well not be felt until the excommunicate had presented himself before St Peter at the gates of Heaven. The more indiscriminately the anathemas were pronounced, especially in a world that was coming increasingly to believe in a personal relationship between the individual and God and his Saints, the more obvious did this weakness become.

While, therefore, the lack of material sanctions by which the Church could enforce its most terrifying sentences led to such sentences becoming increasingly ineffectual; and while the rapacity of the Papacy served to bring its justice into such disrepute that increasing recourse was had to the secular courts; there were yet some offences which, by seeming to challenge the fundamental premises upon which the whole structure of medieval society was thought to depend, called down upon those who committed them the full force of both sets of laws acting together. Where this happened, as it did most signally and with most unfortunate long-term results, in the case of wrong-believers or heretics—who presumed to question the official Christian doctrine of those whom God had appointed to expound it—the authorities were prepared to forget their rivalries and co-operate in such a way that the secular arm might provide the material sanctions with which ecclesiastical justice was so ill-equipped.

The various heresies and the means by which the authorities sought to suppress them will be discussed in a later chapter, as too will the way in which the inquisitorial form of trial came eventually to be incorporated into the secular law of those countries, like France, where the theocratic or descending, rather than the feudal or contractual, theory of authority and law predominated; but we must at this point remark that, as from the twelfth century onwards, more and more severe measures were introduced to deal with the growing numbers of heretics, the Church, for its part, neither forbad the use of torture to extract 'free confessions' from suspected heretics nor shrank any longer, once the heretic had made such a confession, from imposing the death penalty (this to be implemented by the secular authorities). And so, here again, with the setting up in 1230 of the Holy Office, and as a result of the unholy zeal which some officers of the Inquisition subsequently displayed in their determination to eradicate any trace of wrong belief, both the organized Church, in general, and the Papacy under whose control the Inquisition was established, in particular, were to give their Christian flock cause rather to fear and even loathe than to love or respect them. Indeed, to some Christians it seemed that by countenancing such ferocious measures, the religious authorities were embracing the ways of the Devil and hence forfeiting any claim to their spiritual allegiance: and so, gradually, as violence begat more violence, was the spiritual standing of the religious authorities still further eroded.

But whatever the atrocities perpetrated in the name of right belief and of God in the later Middle Ages (and, although Protestant writers with their own special axes to grind may have been inclined to exaggerate, these were many and horrible) and however often abused the machinery of ecclesiastical government and justice, it is, as always, important to bear in mind the medieval propensity for lingering, obsessively and sometimes almost lovingly, on what was wrong with this impermanent world here below. 'For', as Jean de Venette had said, 'the life of man is perishable and transitory and the wickedness of man abounds in the world, woe is me! and increaseth'—a view of mankind and of human life that is reflected in the great majority of medieval documents that have come down to us. Accounts of miscarriages or abuses of ecclesiastical justice are inevitably, therefore, numerous—but no more so than contemporary complaints against the various secular law courts. And there can in fact be no doubt that in its basic approach to the question of punishment, by which it sought to purge rather than to wreak vengeance on the offender, the Church took a very much more humanitarian line than the secular authorities, on the development of whose systems of justice it thus exerted a mitigating and a generally civilizing influence.

3

Crime and Punishment

EDIEVAL SECULAR LAW was a mixture of Roman law and Germanic barbarian law, a mixture everywhere inter-woven with Christian doctrine and dogma but one in which the relative proportion of barbarian to Roman law varied from region to region and from one time to another. As a general rule in the Italian peninsula and in those other countries whose territories had, before the collapse of Rome, been long-settled and administratively integrated provinces of the Empire, Roman law tended to predominate; in lands which, like Britain had been far-flung imperial outposts and in those parts of Western Europe that had never bowed to the Roman yoke at all, barbarian law.

By the time of the barbarian invasions—and already for some centuries, indeed, before Romulus Augustulus, last titular Emperor of the West, was deposed and expelled from Ravenna by the German soldier Odoacer, acclaimed King of Italy by his army, in A.D. 476—both the jurisprudential theory of Roman law and the means by which that law was applied and enforced had been so much reviewed, revised and amended as to have produced a judicial system so sophisticated that the world had not previously seen its like. Throughout the Empire there were magistrates and a hierarchy of officials appointed to keep law and order. And, even though the task of synthesising the law, begun in the fifth-century Code of the Emperor Theodosius II (d.450), was not to be resumed until the following century when the Emperor Justinian's Code completed this mammoth undertaking, yet still there were throughout the Empire, as there had been before the birth of Christ, men well-versed in the intricate mass of official legislation, who knew how to prosecute and defend cases in front of the judges.

With such a body of official legislation, as with men specially trained to administer it, the barbarian in the forests was unacquainted. To the barbarian, law was tribal custom, as it had been handed down from one illiterate generation to another in the collective consciousness of the tribe. And, since the barbarian community was a military one in which right was most commonly associated with might, the prerogative of administering this tribal custom was assumed, naturally enough, by the chieftains, whose position of authority over their fellow tribesmen depended upon their being, and upon their showing themselves to be, the mightiest men among them. Thus, in barbarian society, the civil and the military functions, which the Emperor Constantine (d.337) had finally succeeded in separating from one another in the Roman world, coincided. For the tribal chieftain—although he might, when campaigning, consult a council of warriors or, when dispensing justice, a council of wise men or elders—was both commander-in-chief of the tribe's military resources and its supreme judge: a situation from which there evolved, as private ownership of land gradually replaced communal tribal ownership, the Germanic principle that territorial property ownership carried with it the right to administer justice to the inhabitants of that property; and as a result of which, after the disintegration of Charlemagne's Empire, when Western Europe split up into a multiplicity of feudal units, the local warlords had little difficulty in establishing their right to sit in judgement upon their feudal underlings in all matters that were not claimed as the exclusive concern either of the Church or of a feudal superior.

Amongst the barbarians, where an appeal to justice amounted to little more than an appeal to brute force, the mightier the chieftain (provided always that he chose to apply the law and not to impose his own will) the greater the likelihood of obtaining justice from him. But the possession of the right to dispense justice did not necessarily stifle self-interest; nor, necessarily, did it promote in its possessor any interest in behaving justly. If the barbarian acted in defiance of some tribal taboo—if, for instance, he ran away from the enemy in battle or defiled his mother—then the whole tribe might be concerned to see that the sentence of death or exile be carried out, that the tribe should be free from contagion; but where an offence was committed by one member of the tribe against the life or property of another, there was no such popular animus against the offender. Damage to life, limb and property were all of them personal or, at most, family matters: matters of concern to and therefore canvassed by only the injured and offending parties, either or both of which opposing sides might, if there seemed to be a chance of judgement being given in its favour, appeal to the chieftain to decide their dispute. But should the chieftain be known to be predisposed in favour of the rival faction or if, on the other hand, he was thought to be too weak to enforce his decision, there could be little point, clearly, in submitting a cause to his judgement. The preferred solution, in such unpromising circumstances, was a direct appeal to the final arbiter: both chieftain and his justice were ignored, and the party that considered itself injured sought to establish its rights and exact retribution by armed force.

The impulse to self-help was thus strong, while the only remedy known to the barbarians for an affront or an injury was vengeance: vengeance often violently exacted, and vengeance often out of all proportion to the original mischief that was thought to have demanded it. Eyes called for more eyes, teeth for more teeth and blood for more blood. But, although it does not seem to have occurred to the military minds of the barbarians that an act of violence—a murder, say, or the burning down of a neighbour's shack—might be seen as a crime against the society whose peace it disrupted, it did, in due course, become apparent to them that the fighting strength of a tribe, upon which it must depend both for conquest and survival, was sorely diminished by the long-drawn-out private wars and blood feuds in which generation after generation of warriors felt themselves honour-bound to exterminate one another. And so the barbarians gradually came to accept that in the interests of the tribe, if not actually of a more peaceful existence, honour might perhaps be as well satisfied, where a relative had been killed, by a compensatory payment as by retaliation in kind and the further shedding of blood. At first, before money began to circulate in the barbarian world, the compensation would be made over in cattle or other livestock; but, by the time of the barbarian descent upon the Roman Empire, most Germanic tribes had their own fixed scale of payments, according to which, the more exalted the rank of the person killed, the larger would be his 'wergeld' or the amount of money stipulated as being due to his family.

Such then, in brief, was the law and the attitude to the law which the barbarians brought with them out of the North: a law and an attitude both of them very different from those that the new Kings of Europe were to meet with amongst their Roman subjects when, the looting and the pillaging finally over, they had to turn their minds to the internal organisation and government of their newly-won kingdoms. But although the barbarian rulers may have been quick to adapt what they had not destroyed of the Roman admini-strative system to suit the circumstances of their own rule—and although even in the fifth century the Kings of Burgundy and of Visigothic Spain were following Theodosius II's example and ordering that the laws of their kingdoms be written down—it was still not for some time yet that Roman and barbarian law were to have any more than an indirect effect on one another. For, in the initial period of their settlement, it was the barbarians' usual policy to keep conquerors and conquered apart: and, hence, their general practice to allow their different populations to decide matters between themselves according to their own law—so that in Burgundy, for instance, the judges whom the barbarian Kings now began to appoint were instructed to use King Gundobard's *Lex Romana Burgundiorum* in cases involving Romans, while in 'trans-national' disputes, as in disputes between two of the conquering race, Burgundian tribal law was to be applied. And so it happened that in any one kingdom there might be at least two and perhaps more secular legal systems existing side by side; a situation about which Archbishop Agobard of Lyon was to exclaim in the middle years of the ninth century that if there were five people in a room together it would be as likely as not that each of them would base his argument upon a different set of laws.

The earliest recorded legislation aimed at uniting Roman and tribal law into a single system is thought to have been that made by the seventh-century Kings of Spain, who, in the *Liber Judicorum* or *Fuero Juzgo*, now began to encourage those mixed marriages between former Roman subjects and Visigoths which previous kings had forbidden. The first Title to Book XII of the third edition of the *Fuero* (A.D. 693) is interesting, particularly, in that it instructs the judges that mercy should be shown most especially to the poor and, more generally, as an indication of the important part played by Christianity in transforming the barbarian attitude to law and to justice. 'It is meet for us,' the Title declares, 'who decree that severity which is necessary for the guilt of men, to add remedies pleasing to God, for unfortunates. We therefore exhort all judges . . . we solemnly warn them, shrewdly to proceed in all cases for the purpose of investigating the truth of anything, and to examine the contentions in all matters apart from their acceptance by the people, at the same time tempering the rigour of the law some-what when the lives of persons are at stake, particularly of those by poverty depressed'.[1]

While the palliative influence of Christianity here speaks for itself, it was in fact the Church, too, which was chiefly responsible for introducing the barbarians to those aspects of Roman law which did most to affect their views on society, on the rights and duties, respectively, of the governors and the governed, on crime and disorder and on the role of the law. For, not unnaturally, the Church's own vision of law, justice and order—as well as its system of ecclesiastical justice—owed much to the law of the Empire in which it had itself grown up; so that Christianity acted in effect as a filter, gradually transmitting to its converts that part of Roman law which the Church had, with such emendations or changes of emphasis as were necessary to make it consistent with the teachings of the Bible and the Church Fathers, incorporated into its own Scheme. To much of medieval Europe, in this way, the Church brought the first indirect knowledge of Roman law; and even in those southern countries, like Visigothic Spain, where the barbarians had themselves come into direct contact with the Roman Codes, it was nonetheless through the eyes of their new religion and with the help of their new Christian advisers that the barbarian rulers came to understand the deeper implications of Roman law both for themselves, as Christian Kings, and for their tribesmen, whom the Church now encouraged them to think of rather as their subjects.

But, between Roman law itself and Roman law as it had been modified by the Church, there was one most significant difference: for the consent of the citizen, which the Romans had posited as the theoretical basis for the authority of the State and hence for the duty of the citizen to obey its law, the Church had substituted Faith in God and the duty of the Christian to obey those whom the Divine Will had put in authority over him. And so it was with the Christian subject's membership of the Church serving instead of the consent of the governed as the basis for the authority of the governor, that the Christian Kings learned of their God-given duty, as divinely appointed heads of State, to maintain order, as the Roman State had done, by the provision of justice; and of their corresponding and equally Roman right, where the good order of their kingdom was disturbed, to take for themselves, as a fine, at least some part of the compensation payment, which had hitherto been due in toto to the injured party. 'For the meaning of the crown in this', as Don Ramon Muntaner was to comment on the coronation of King Alphonso IV of Aragon in 1328 (some quarter of a millennium after the reforming Popes had set themselves to try to divest kingship of the semi-priestly qualities which earlier generations of churchmen had most inconveniently ascribed to it) 'that the crown is round, and as in a round thing there is no beginning nor end, it signifies

Our Lord, the True, Almighty God, Who has no beginning and will
have no end; and because it signifies God Almighty it has been
placed on the King's head, and not in the middle of his body, nor at
his feet, but on his head, where the understanding is; and therefore
he should remember God Almighty and be resolved to gain, with
this crown he has taken, the crown of Heavenly glory, which is an
everlasting Kingdom. And the sceptre signifies justice, which he
should practice in all things; as the sceptre is long and strong, and
like a rod which beats and punishes, so does justice punish, to
prevent the wicked from doing evil and to improve the condition of
the good. And the orb signifies that, as he holds it in his hand, so

7 Portrait of the Emperor Otto III, showing the symbols of majesty.

should he hold his dominions in his hand and power and, as God has entrusted them to him, he should defend and rule and govern them with truth and justice and mercy, and should not consent that any man, either for himself or for another, should do them any injury.'[2]

To persuade the barbarian rulers of their important position in the Divine Scheme was one thing, however, and to reconcile the tribesman with his new role as dutiful subject quite another. In the general turmoil of the early Middle Ages, it was no easy task for either the Church or its new allies, the Christian Kings, to prevent the independent-spirited warrior from taking the law into his own hands and visiting his own justice on his enemies as and how he saw fit to do so. Indeed, the atavistic conviction that a personal injury should in fact be personally avenged would die hard: as late as 1231, for instance, a French code granted by the Abbey of St Bertin to the town of Arques was to stipulate that a man convicted of intentional homicide must be handed over to the relatives of the victim to be slain by each member of the family 'in turn'.[3] And yet, continued recourse to self-help and the barbarian tradition of personal justice notwithstanding, as first one and then another of the Christian kingdoms came to be ruled for a while by relatively strong Kings, so did those Kings try to impress upon their subjects, by whittling away, or even abolishing, the ancient rights of the relatives to compensation, that the State, and not the individual, was responsible for punishing the law breaker. So, for example, in France, in 596, did the Merovingian King, Childebert, and his council decree that, 'since it is just that he who knows how to kill should learn to die',[4] the old system of money payments should in cases of rape and homicide be replaced by the death penalty. But more usual, in the earlier stages of the process especially, than total exclusion of the family's rights, was the division of the compensatory payment between the injured party and the State. And so again in France, in the eighth century and the ninth—by which time King Childebert's law would seem to have fallen into abeyance—did a series of Carolingian capitularies give the proportions according to which the traditional compensation was to be split between the victim and the State, both of whom were now deemed to suffer through the commission of the various breaches of the peace with which the capitularies dealt.

While increased royal power enabled the more powerful monarchs to impose laws compelling acceptance of the State's right to compensation when they were broken, the growth of royal justice in its turn helped, of course, to emphasise the obligatory nature of the law. But it was, nevertheless, due as much—if not, indeed, more—to the efforts of the Church as to the physical authority of the Kings that the idea of the sovereignty of the law gradually took root, as it did, in the medieval consciousness. For not only did the Church boost royal authority by proclaiming, in the words of St John Chrysostom, that 'it is the divine wisdom and not merely fortuity that has ordained that there should be rulership, that some should order and others should obey';[5] and not only did it advise on what laws should be introduced and how, and assist in the drafting of legislation as well as in the actual administration of the law: but, slowly, as it laboured to educate the general mass of its adherents to a fuller understanding of their religion, so, by imperceptible stages, did it succeed in firing the medieval imagination with the Christian vision of an eternal and unchanging Divine Law, of which human law was held to be the reflection and from which, therefore—even though the Divine Law was known perfectly only to God—all human law that did not contravene His eternal commandments was held to derive its ultimate sanction.* Thus, to the right and duty of the State to punish the law-breaker for having violated the supposed interests of society was added the Christian horror of the law-breaker as someone who had sinned against the Divine Law of God: a horror that would all too often lead, in the later Middle Ages, as one group of partisans after another accused its opponents of having insulted the Divine Majesty, to fanaticism; but one that, in the earlier medieval period, played a crucial part in stimulating both the sentiment of justice and belief in the Rule of Law.

By the time Christian Europe was seriously threatened, in the eighth and ninth centuries, by pagan invasion from without, the belief in a divinely ordained Rule of Law had become firmly established in the European Christian mind. And it is a measure of the joint achievement here of the Church and the secular rulers of the first centuries of the Middle Ages that, even when centralized government gave way to the arbitrary rule of local warlords—as it did, for instance, in the Carolingian Empire, after the death of Charlemagne's grandson, Louis the Pious, in 843—this belief was not shaken. Rather, in fact, the reverse. The worse civil disorder and the general lawlessness became, the more brightly, by contrast,

---

* Although, necessarily, in a tainted world, the Divine Law could be known perfectly only to God himself, some part of it might, however, be revealed to men through inspired study of the Scriptures; and part of it again through seeking out those principles which had by long usage become established in the customary law of the various nations and thus provided—except, of course, where they were discordant with God's Law—a universal body of 'natural law'.

did the vision of a world ideally ordered in accordance with God's Law seem to shine; and when, at length, the development of feudalism restored some semblance of stability to Christian Europe, the new feudal social structure came to be seen as the divinely-designed means of promoting an Ideal Order, in which the forces of evil at work in the universe would be vanquished, and harmonious relations between man and God assured, by the obedience of each and every member of the feudal hierarchy to the law.*

Conformity at every level then, and in all matters, became essential for the salvation of the soul: to achieve the purpose of his earthly life the Christian was obliged not only to submit to the decisions of the Church courts and of royal justice but also to abide by the customary law of the region in which he lived or was staying, the conventions governing his relations with those both above and beneath him on the feudal ladder and the ever-increasing number of rules and regulations that applied to people working in whatever occupation his might happen to be. But although the actual administration of justice had tended, after the collapse of the old order, to pass more and more into the hands of the district bully-boy, the supremacy, in the secular field, of royal justice was never challenged. The King or the Emperor, by virtue of his theoretical position at the apex of the feudal pyramid, remained the fountain of secular justice, the guardian of order and law, from whom all lands and, hence, all rights of secular jurisdiction were finally held. And no sooner had the infidel invader been either beaten back or assimilated into Christian Europe than the feudal monarchs set about turning the theoretical supremacy of royal justice, to which from all lower courts there was a right of appeal, into reality. Where the Church had helped their predecessors with the ground-work, there the feudal Kings continued to build; and when the Church

---

* Just as every object, inanimate as well as animate, would have its allotted place in the Divine Hierarchy, as it was perfected by St Thomas Aquinas in the thirteenth century, so did all things come, in the later Middle Ages, to have their own legal status or 'ordo', as a result of which they might be made to answer for their actions in court. Thus, sometimes, were swords or cooking pots which fell from their shelves or hooks, causing damage, brought to trial while, in 1478, some cockchafer grubs which had wrought havoc in the fields were tried before a court at Basel, where, four years earlier, the mayor had sentenced a cock to be burned alive for having so far forgotten its proper function as to lay an egg; and so too, at Laôn, was a pig who 'had strangled and mutilated a young child in its cradle, son of Jean Lenfant, cowherd, condemned by the common hangman to be hanged by the neck until he be dead, upon a wooden gibbet . . .' (Berriat-Saint-Prix, *Mémoires de la Société des Antiquaires de France* tom. VIII, 1829 pp. 403ff. trs. G. G. Coulton, *A Medieval Garner*, Extract 313, pp 678–679.)

began to show unmistakable signs, in the eleventh century, of regretting the strength of the foundations it had so carefully assisted in laying, it was already too late for it to do any lasting damage to the notion that royal justice received its ultimate, divine sanction directly from God—and not, as the reforming Popes now insisted, through the gift of God's representative, the Church.

It is ironic that in its struggle against the secular rulers, and most particularly against the Emperors, the ecclesiastical party should have encouraged recourse to the original Roman law Codes as a source of legal maxims that could be used to support the Church's claim to an over-riding authority, upon which all secular authority must necessarily be dependent. For the men who had compiled the Codes were not theologians but lawyers trained in a tradition to which the supreme authority of the State had long been funda-mental; and, however much the actual provisions of later Roman legislation might have been affected by the official adoption, in the early fourth century, of Christianity as the one and only State religion of the Empire, the Codes in fact proved just as useful a weapon in the hands of the growing number of lawyers in the royal or Imperial employ as they did to the advocates of the Church's cause.

Whatever temporary or even permanent advantage appeals to Roman law may have gained for either side, in a controversy that was to be won in the end, as we have seen, by the secular powers, the revival of Roman law studies was of still greater importance to the development of European law, in that it provided medieval lawyers and judges with an example of a systematically organised body of law. Since the first barbarian attempts at setting up some form of judicial machinery, the people charged with its administra-tion had been faced with the often impossible task of ascertaining what exactly the customary law on any given point might be. But, from the eleventh century onwards, as future secular lawyers and judges as well as Canon lawyers pored over Theodosius's and Justinian's Codes, so did they discover in them basic legal princi-ples against which they could measure the confused jumble of customary law.

For a century or more before the founding of the first Universi-ties, many of which would have faculties of law, the Roman law schools at Ravenna, Bologna and Pavia were drawing students from all over Europe. But, despite the international nature of civil law studies, the tradition of customary law was in many countries too strong to allow much either of the actual content of Roman law or of its procedural rules to be absorbed into the secular legal system. Most directly affected by the revived study of Roman law were, therefore, Italy, Spain and Southern France, where a good deal of Roman law had already found its way into the barbarian law. Thus in Provence, in the eleventh and twelfth centuries, Justinian's law was used as the highest authority to settle all disputed points of law while, in the Norman Kingdom of Sicily, the Assizes of King Roger were actually based on Justinian's Code.

Elsewhere—in Northern France, in the Low Countries, in Scandinavia, Germany and the British Isles—although its influence was less directly felt, the impact of Roman law on the later development of medieval law was, nevertheless, still considerable. In the first place, just as juridical study taught Canon lawyers and secular lawyers alike how the whole corpus of Canon or secular law might gradually be sorted out and rearranged, so did a knowledge of Roman legal procedure help the various secular authorities to introduce a more efficient judicial procedure of their own. In the second place, the Church, with its reformed Canon law and with its initial success, at least, in pushing its grandiose claims continued to act as a filter. And, lastly, there were certain topics upon which barbarian law was as good as silent. Most notable amongst these was trade, in which more and more people were beginning to engage: for, as the expansion of trade led to increasingly complicated relations between buyers and sellers, so, naturally, did the merchants look to the only model available to them, the Roman, for a law of contract and of obligation and of tort by which to try to regulate their commercial activities.

In areas, therefore, such as commerce, where barbarian law was lacking, as well as through the study of civil law and, indirectly, through the agency of the Church, some part, at least, of Roman law became incorporated into the legal systems of every Christian European country. To Germany, where a bewildering profusion of overlapping customary law jurisdictions prevailed, it was in fact introduced as the final official authority (although in its developed Italian form and not by direct reference to the Codes) with the setting up of the Imperial Court of Justice, the Reichskammergericht, by the Emperor Maximilian I in 1495. But even where customary law was most firmly established—even in England, for example, where the jurists Glanville, Fleta, Britton and Bracton all insisted that the basis of the Common law was to be found in precedent or, in other words in the decisions of the courts, as summarised in the *Year Books* and the law reports—Roman law still played its part both in helping to promote the growth of more effective justice and in moulding the actual laws.

Neither the growth of more elaborate, professionally-staffed judicial systems, however, nor the development of organised and more readily accessible written bodies of law — nor even the general subscription to a belief in an ideal Rule of Law — could ensure that the law would necessarily be obeyed. In many cases, the people who administered the law were so patently corrupt that to have submitted to their authority would have been obvious folly; in others, individuals or, sometimes, large groups of people, claimed that this or that law had no binding force because, in their opinion, it contravened the Eternal Law of God: but, whatever excuse may or may not have been put forward, in the vast majority of cases, then as today, laws were broken either through genuine ignorance of them or because the lawbreaker, although well aware of the law, simply preferred to disregard it.

Enforcing the law is one of the besetting problems of the twentieth century; and so it was too in the Middle Ages. In the absence of anything resembling an organised police force, and despite the increasing number of different officials who were appointed, especially in the later Middle Ages, to see that accused criminals were brought to trial, it was still the local community, even at the end of the medieval period, which was chiefly responsible for accusing and for apprehending the criminal. For in the same way that the barbarian expected compensation when a member of his family was killed, so was he expected to pay up when a relative of his who had killed someone was unable to pay the wergeld demanded of him; and as the barbarians abandoned their nomadic way of life, so was this family responsibility gradually transformed into a territorial community responsibility. In some countries the original grouping was done numerically. In Anglo-Saxon England, for instance, the population was divided into 'tithings' of ten men, while it would seem reasonable to assume that the larger English groupings, known as 'hundreds', were composed, originally at least, of a hundred men. Under the Anglo-Saxon Kings, the members of the tithing and the hundred would stand surety for one another, as well as paying and receiving the fines due for breaches of the peace committed within its territorial boundaries. But during the early eleventh-century Danish occupation of England, when the occupying forces were in constant danger of assassination at the hands of the subject race, the Danes made use of the existing system to pronounce any freeman who could not name his hundred or tithing an outlaw.

Throughout Christian Europe, although local details of course varied, the general pattern was the same: to insist that the individual must be able to prove membership of some specific community came to be seen everywhere as the soundest way of preventing people from straying far from where they themselves and their activities would be well known; and to hold the individual members of a community collectively responsible for any crime of which they failed to produce the perpetrator was reckoned as the best way not only of ensuring that a close watch would be kept on all strangers but also of encouraging the community, even when the suspected criminal was one of their own number, to hand the supposed culprit over to the appropriate authorities. In some places, this authority would be a feudal lord, to whom the King had granted, over and above his automatic feudal right to deal with minor infractions of the law that occurred within his fiefs, a further right of jurisdiction over more serious criminal offences; in the towns, it might be the governing body of the community, which had been granted or had purchased similar rights from the crown: but usually for the graver crimes, and always for certain categories of crimes, such as treason, which were traditionally reserved to the King, it would be the royal judicial officers, sitting either in courts that were held regularly in what had come to be recognised as centres of royal justice or on peripatetic commissions.

Next, if and when a suspected criminal was brought before any sort of tribunal, the law had to provide some means of ascertaining whether or not the accused person was guilty. Here again medieval procedure differed from one time to another as well as from place to place but, broadly speaking, it may be said that, whereas Roman law tended to put the burden of proof on to the accuser, who had to produce witnesses to testify to the veracity of his assertions, barbarian law was inclined to rely rather on a series of negative proofs by which the accused sought to establish his innocence.

In the opening period of the Middle Ages, the most widely used barbarian method of proof was compurgation, a process whereby the parties involved either swore on oath, several times and in several places, that what they claimed was true, or, more commonly, found a requisite number of 'compurgators' to swear with them, not as to their factual knowledge of the case, but that by participating in the oath they endorsed it. So, in the sixth century, did Bishop Gregory of Tours clear himself of having uttered reproachful words (which, in fact, he knew to be true) against the Merovingian Queen, Fredegunda, by taking oaths on three different altars, after he had celebrated Mass on them, and so did Fredegunda, herself, when she was openly accused of adultery, succeed in establishing the disputed legitimacy of her son by persuading three hundred noblemen to support her oath that the child had actually sprung from the loins of her dead husband. As in these two instances, the number of separate oaths or of compurgators generally depended both on the gravity of the crime and on the status of the principal parties involved (in Anglo-Saxon England the oath of one thegn was worth that of seven villeins), while there was also, as a rule, a marked bias in favour of the accuser. Thus, in Anglo-Saxon England, again, where the accuser could, in certain cases, substantiate his claim by swearing to it on oath in four churches, the defendant, if he wished to rebut the charge, was required to swear oaths of negation in twelve churches.

It might be thought that the change from oaths sworn in the name of one or other of the pagan divinities—or even, as the Norse warrior in the *Volundarkvida* swore, 'by board of ship, by rim of shield, by shoulder of steed, by edge of sword'—to oaths sworn before Christian priests, and often on holy relics, in the name of the One True and Almighty Christian God, would have put a stop to the frequent and quite shameless abuse of such a practice. But this does not seem to have happened. Amongst Christian barbarians, as amongst their pagan ancestors, the various inducements to perjury would appear to have remained as pressing as ever; and it was, in fact, due largely to this all too obvious flaw in the method that, by the ninth century, compurgation had already been superseded in many areas by the increasingly popular alternative of submitting the case to 'the judgement of God' by means of the ordeal. This means of proof, in principle long-since known to the majority of Aryan peoples, including the Greeks, was now refashioned by the early medieval authorities into a number of elaborately formalised rituals, in the administration of which, as with compurgation, the Church was once again called upon to play a central (and, incidentally, highly profitable) role.

Most frequently used of these appeals to the divine judgement was the ordeal of boiling water, which was especially to be recommended, according to Archbishop Hincmar of Rheims, since the water was representative of the Old Testament flood, in which only the virtuous few had escaped destruction, while the element of fire pointed to the general conflagration of the Last Judgement, in which every Christian knew that all subsequent distinctions between the righteous and the wicked must finally be made. The three days before the ordeal, the accused person was commanded to spend fasting and in prayer. On the day itself, when, after the celebration of a mass at which the officiating priest adjured 'this body and blood of Our Lord Jesus Christ', as the accused partook of it, 'to be to thee this day a manifestation', the various utensils were solemnly blessed, the fire lit, and the exorcised water brought to the boil. Then, in the case of the 'single' ordeal, for minor offences, the person seeking to clear himself was either required simply to plunge his hand into the water up to his wrist and withdraw it again or he might be made to retrieve a stone or a ring from an appropriately measured depth; but, where the seriousness of the crime called for the 'triple' ordeal, the whole forearm had to be thrust into the water, whether there was something to be picked up from the bottom of the cauldron or not, right up to the elbow. After immersion, the hand or arm was bound up in a cloth, and sealed with the signet of the judge, so that, in theory at least, the wound could not be tampered with during the three days which must elapse before the bandage was removed and the accused's guilt or innocence decided by whether or not he still showed visible signs of having been scalded.

Older, probably, than the ordeal by boiling water was the ordeal by fire, which had its roots in the belief, subscribed to by many primitive peoples, that, if the gods so desired it, human beings could, like Shadrach, Meshack and Abednego, withstand the normal physiological effects of fire. The preliminaries to the ordeal by fire—as, indeed, to all the ordeals—were much the same as for the ordeal by boiling water: namely, fasting, prayer, the taking of the sacraments and the exorcism or blessing of all the paraphernalia involved. Similarly, too, the member or members that had been exposed to the fire were bound up and sealed to await inspection three days later. In certain cases, the accused was blindfolded and made to hazard a walk over red-hot ploughshares, six, nine or twelve of them, laid out before him on the ground; in others, without a blindfold, he (or very often she, this being considered an excellent way of testing a lady's chastity) was actually made to press the naked foot against each ploughshare; but the most usual form of trial by fire compelled the subject to hold in his hand or to carry for a specified distance, usually nine feet, a lump of red-hot iron, the weight of which was fixed by law in proportion to the magnitude of the alleged crime. In England, for the 'simple' ordeal, the iron weighed one pound while for the 'triple' ordeal, which the Laws of Henry I prescribed for plotting against the King's life, false-coining, secret murder, robbery, arson and felonies in general, it weighed three pounds.[6]

The third of the best-favoured methods of trial by ordeal, the ordeal by cold water, was based on the belief that the pure element of water, being divinely influenced, must necessarily reject the body of anyone guilty of a crime or of sin; and so differed from the ordeals by fire and by hot water in that it would seem to have needed a miracle to convict the accused rather than to exculpate him. When this type of ordeal was employed, upon completion of the familiar religious rigmarole, the accused was bound hand and foot and lowered into the water on the end of a rope, in which there would have been a knot made at anything between 'a long hair's breadth' to half a yard from where it was fastened around 'the middle' of the body. If the accused, as he sank, pulled the knot down with him so that it broke the surface of the water, he was cleared; but if the accused, and the knot with him, floated, there could be no question but that he was guilty.

In order to emphasise the divine character of the judgement to be obtained by it, the ordeal was, wherever possible, held in or just outside a church, in which, as a rule, the different vessels and implements used in the ritual would also be kept. But although the Church derived an important part of its revenue from the admini-stration of the various forms of ordeal—including the more unusual ordeals, among them that of the consecrated bread or cheese, which the accused was commanded to swallow—it was, in fact, the Papacy which took the lead in engineering their desuetude. As early as 1070 Pope Alexander II forbad the use of the ordeal in the case of ecclesiastics since they were, he claimed, a popular inven-tion, quite devoid of any sort of canonical authority; and a century and a half later the Fourth Lateran Council (1215) struck what proved to be the final blow to the system by forbidding any priest to perform the religious ceremonies which were, ultimately, the essential ingredient upon which all such trials were based.

But, long before this papal ban on ecclesiastical participation, many people had become sceptical as to the efficacy of trial by ordeal. In England, in 1166, the Assize of Clarendon decreed that persons accused of murder, robbery or any other felony should immediately be submitted to the water ordeal—but with these significant provisos: if the accused had at any point confessed to the crime or was found in possession of stolen property he was not to be allowed this privilege, while if 'common report' held him guilty, even where he passed the ordeal, he was to be given eight days in which to leave the kingdom, on pain of being declared an outlaw. If it is, perhaps, hard to believe, as Albertus Magnus suggests,[7] that a concoction of radish juice, white of egg, lime, mallow and psillus seeds could enable a man to grasp hold of a red-hot weight without sustaining any injury, it is very much easier to credit the numerous contemporary assertions that some kind of collusion had taken place, or even that money or other valuables had changed hands, between the accuser or the accused and the officiating clerics. Indeed, so low had the reputation of ordeal sunk by 1215 that the Papacy met with little difficulty in having its ban locally enforced: in England—where Professor Maitland, on examining the extant records for the years 1201–1219 (*Pleas of the Crown*, 1.75), discovered only one case in which the accused was not cleared by the ordeals of water and the hot iron—it was officially abolished, 'seeing that the judgement of fire and water is

8 Preliminary to the trial by battle, the plaintiff and the defendant in a law suit take their final oath before the judge.

forbidden by the church of Rome', only four years later, in 1218; in
Southern Italy it was abolished by the Neapolitan Code of the
Emperor Frederick II in 1231; and in Germany, although the practice lingered on longer than elsewhere, the Council of Wurzburg
repeated the papal decree in 1298.

Akin to trial by ordeal, in that it too represented an appeal to
divine justice, and yet distinct enough from it to survive the papal
legislation of 1215, was the judicial duel, or trial by battle. An early
favourite with the Irish Celts, the Slavs and the pagan Norsemen—
the last of whom, if they coveted a piece of land, might challenge its
present owner to single combat, thereby inviting the gods to settle
the question of future ownership—the earliest Christian version of
this form of trial was introduced into Gaul, and thence gradually to
the whole of Western Europe, by the Burgundians. To a warlike
age, whose popular religion was both militant and deeply concerned with considerations of 'justice', the idea that the divine
judgement would make itself manifest through the sword had an
obvious appeal; nor was there any possibility, as the Emperors
Charlemagne and Otto II (d.983) both pointed out, of such a
method of proof being so abused as was the increasingly discredited system of compurgation. But, despite this undoubted
advantage, there were occasions when the advocates of trial by
battle were hard put to it to explain why God should have seemed,
to all appearances, to desert the more innocent party in favour of
the more guilty. Thus, in the year 1100, for example, when threats
of excommunication persuaded a certain merchant to denounce a
monk named Anselm for having sold to him, on oath of secrecy,
some sacred vessels which he had stolen from the church at Laôn,
the consequent duel between the two men was won by the monk,
who was duly pronounced innocent; but when, later, Anselm, on
being convicted, by the water ordeal this time, of a similar offence,
confessed also to the first theft, the court was left to explain,
somewhat lamely, that the result of the duel had in fact been as God
had willed it since the merchant had been punished by it for having
broken his oath.

A judicial duel might be fought either on horseback or on foot,
and with a variety of different weapons. In some cases the precise
type of battle would be dictated by local custom, the nature of the
crime, or the social standing of the parties; in others, the choice of
weapons would be left to one or other of the protagonists, according again to local rulings on the matter. At Winchester, in 1456,
when one Jamys Fyscher, 'a fisher and tailor of craft', accused a
convicted thief, Thomas Whytehorne, who had turned King's

evidence in return for his life and an allowance of 1½d a day, of falsely accusing him as one of his erstwhile accomplices, it was, so Mayor Gregory of London reports, the judge, Mayster Myhelle Skylling, who ordered that both men should be clothed in white, and that they should hold in one hand three-foot staves of ashwood and in the other an iron horn, shaped like 'a rammyshorne' and as sharp at the smaller end as it could be made. In most countries, it was only when the accused criminal or his appellant was too poor to arm himself that the judge was instructed to equip him at the State's expense; but in England, in all criminal cases, the expenses incurred in the administration of judicial duels—and of the ordeals, too— were paid for by the State, so that we must suppose that the ashwood staves and the more curious 'rammyshornes' would have been supplied free of charge to Fyscher and Whytehorne by the court.

For an indication of the enormous difference between an eighteenth- or nineteenth-century duel of honour, with all its elegant trappings, and a medieval judicial duel, we can do no better than follow the dispute between Fyscher and Whytehorne through to its ghastly conclusion. For these two combatants, there was no Bois de Boulogne at dawn, no tender farewell supper, nor in fact any food at all, the evening before: the fight was to take place, as 'that most pityfullest judge of all this land in sitting upon life and death' directed, on the 'most sorry and wretched green that might be found about the town', after both men had fasted, 'having neither meat nor drink'. Indeed, says Mayor Gregory, 'it is too shameful to rehearse all the conditions of this foul conflict; and if they need any drink they must take their own piss'.

As usual, the battle itself drew a large crowd of eager spectators, who, as generally happened in such cases, were as rabid in their loathing of the 'approver' for having turned King's evidence as they were fervent in their support of 'that true man, Jamys Fyscher'; so fervent indeed that they tried to prevail upon the judge to string Whytehorne up before the contest even began. Their appeal was dismissed. When the approver came 'armed out of the East side' and the defendant 'out of the Southwest side in his apparel' to kneel down and pray to God and all the world for forgiveness, they all of them prayed together with and for the defendant. This touching scene exasperated Whytehorne, who called out mockingly to know why Fyscher was making such a long show of his false belief? At which Fyscher jumped up off his knees and, swearing that his quarrel was as sincere as his belief, lunged at Whytehorne, unfortunately breaking 'his weapon' in the process. Whytehorne, true to the crowd's low opinion of him, fought dishonourably on, gaining the advantage, until the officials succeeded in disarming him and thereby rendered the fight, as it was supposed to be, equal again. From now on, with brief intervals for the contestants to regain their breath, it was to be unarmed combat, 'and then they bit with their teeth, that the leather of clothing and flesh was all to rent in many places of their bodies. And then the false appealer cast that meek innocent down to the ground and bit him by the member, that the poor innocent cried out'. But, by luck rather than strength, 'that innocent recovered up on his knees and took that false appealer by the nose with his teeth and put his thumb in his eye' — which proved so horribly painful that the approver cried mercy and Mayster Myhelle Skylling ordered the fight to be stopped so that the two men could tell their tales for the last time and the approver finally admit to having wrongly accused Fyscher, as well as twenty-eight other men besides him, and beseech mercy and forgiveness of God. 'And then he was confessed and hanged, of whose soul God have mercy. Amen', while the defendant, Fyscher, who might legally have been executed for having slain the King's approver, was in fact 'pardoned his life, limb and goods and went home', where he became a hermit and, not altogether unexpectedly, 'with short time died'.[8]

The right to contest or to prove a point by demanding a duel was not limited to the right of the accused so to challenge the accuser, and vice-versa. A witness, too, might be challenged. In England, in the thirteenth century, a party to a dispute might even challenge his own witness while, in France, witnesses were so often challenged, in the hope, should they be defeated in battle, of excluding their evidence, that it had by the end of the same century become common practice to disallow the testimony of a witness who could not legally be compelled to back up his assertions by force of arms.

Of such categories of people, who were either banned or exempted from engaging in trial by battle, there was a considerable and, as the Middle Ages advanced, a steadily increasing number. In 1140, Pope Innocent II forbad the judicial duel to all ecclesiastics while, as a general rule, minors, women and the physically in-capacitated were similarly debarred from either offering or accepting a challenge of battle.* In England, where a bodily defect

---

* The ban on the personal participation of women in judicial duels against men was not, however, universal. In 1228, at Berne, a woman entered the lists and soundly thrashed her masculine opponent. But such contests were usually governed by special rules. In some parts of Germany, for instance, the law laid down that the man was to be armed with three clubs and, with one hand tied behind his back, placed up to his navel in a three-foot-wide hole in the ground while the woman,

in the accuser deprived the defendant of his right to challenge him to a duel, the thirteenth-century jurist Bracton was of the opinion that, whereas the loss of the relatively ineffectual molar teeth did not qualify a person for exemption, the absence of the incisors (which were to play so crucial a part in the fight between Fyscher and Whytehorne) most certainly did.[9] And so too, for less humanitarian reasons, though not surprisingly in a society that considered a crime committed by a servant against his master or by a wife against her husband as treasonable, did the serf come to be denied the right of challenging the freeman, the leper the non-leper, and the bastard any person who had been born in holy wedlock.

But where a party to a criminal action was forbidden to give battle on grounds of impropriety or physical infirmity—as opposed to being banned from offering the challenge because of his social inferiority or a contagious disease—he or she was, as a general rule, permitted to appoint a champion to fight in his or her stead. Originally, it seems probable that the champion would have been a member of the accused's family, or else his freedman or a man in some other way dependent on him; but, with time, there emerged a class of free-lance champions, who sold their services to whoever was prepared to pay for them. In 1017, the Emperor Henry II, at Merseberg, and again at Magdeburg, used hired champions to decide which of the robbers awaiting trial in those towns was guilty by engaging them in single combat.

Since the loser of a judicial duel was always dishonoured and, quite often according to local custom, condemned automatically to death, it is not difficult to imagine the sort of desperado who would have been prepared to risk his neck in such an occupation. In England, prior to the Statute of Westminster of 1285, the champion could only be brought into the fight by the legal fiction of his first swearing an oath as a witness and then, as a witness, proceeding to the duel; with the result that, whereas the principal party might be punished by a fine or imprisonment, his champion, if he lost the battle, was liable to the traditional punishment of the perjuror, either hanging or the loss of a hand or a foot. Where, as sometimes happened, a religious foundation or a town maintained a permanent

who was free to dodge about the perimeter of the pit, was to be armed with three stones (weighing, variously, between one and five pounds) wrapped up in pieces of cloth. If the man touched the ground with either his hand or his arm, he forfeited a club; and if the woman struck him while he was disarmed she lost one of her stones. Should the woman be victorious, the man was executed; if the man won, the woman was buried alive. (See H. C. Lea, *Superstition and Force*, p. 153.)

9 *An elegant representation of the trial by battle.*

salaried champion, these men may have been a cut above the average; but by the thirteenth century, in France, the champion was considered to be on a par with prostitutes and the lowest type of criminal, while some thirteenth- and fourteenth-century German legal codes, not content with depriving them, like actors, jugglers and bastards, of legal privileges such as giving evidence or succeeding to property, actually went so far as to extend the application of these disabilities to include their children as well. Even in Italy, where the authorities on the whole took a more positive line, introducing regulations designed to minimise the chances of the system being abused rather than to penalise the champion simply for being a champion, it was still found necessary to insist that the champion must in no case be either ill-famed or convicted of any crime.*

Although, however, of all the various means of appealing to the

* In the thirteenth century, at Bologna, when champions were employed, a child put a card inside the clothes of each contestant, on one of which was written the name of the defendant and on the other the name of the plaintiff, so that no one should know, until after the battle had been decided, which champion represented which party.

supernatural for a judgement, trial by battle was to last the longest — in England it was not officially abolished by Statute until 1819 — there was, as early as the twelfth century, a growing move on the part of the secular authorities to limit, if not actually to prohibit, recourse to it. For, despite its continuing appeal to the man of arms, who saw in it the surest possible way of winning his case, to the increasing numbers of non-military men, as to the authorities, it seemed more and more to represent both a menace to the orderly administration of justice and an insult to God, on whose Holy Name it presumed to call for ratification of decisions that were, as often as not, manifestly unjust. As a first step, therefore, towards its restriction, it became usual for specific areas, most often cities or towns, to be granted local exemptions from trial by combat — as was London by Henry I and Nürnberg, in 1219, by the Emperor Frederick II. In 1260, an Ordonnance of St Louis forbad trial by combat in all the royal courts of France; and, although the practice seems to have been allowed in certain cases in Brittany until 1539, and in Normandy until 1583, it would appear that Charles VI's total ban of 1409 was on the whole successful in abolishing it — except under special licence from the King or the Parlement at Paris — in the courts even of the French barons, who had hitherto refused to be deprived of the financial advantages that accrued to them whenever trial by battle was prescribed by themselves or their representatives in their own courts.

Once again, then, it was the Church which took the initiative and the secular authorities who, in due course, followed suit. But the example here set by the Church was not merely a negative one, confined to bringing about the eventual suppression of trial by ordeal and by combat. It was also a positive one since, as we saw earlier, it was the Church which also showed the lead in trying to devise more satisfactory methods of procedure with which to replace the older forms of trial. When Alexander II forbad the use of ordeal for clerics in 1070, for instance, the Papacy sought to extend the application of a reformed system of compurgation — as a result of which, understandably, an even greater number of laymen than before either had their heads tonsured or volunteered to read a few words from the Scriptures, in the hope of convincing the courts of their clerical status and so evading the generally more rigorous process of the secular law. But, on closer acquaintance with Roman law, the Canon lawyers tended increasingly to abandon compurgation, particularly for more serious offences, in favour of an inquisitorial procedure, whereby the evidence was educed from the principal parties and the witnesses in a series of examinations, cross-examinations and, not infrequently, re-examinations. And thus, with the Canon law model, as well as their own civil law studies to help them, did Western European secular lawyers gradually succeed in developing forms of trial which, likewise, avoided appeals to the Divine Judgement by coming to rely rather on human judgements, and on human testimony that was no longer sworn to an oath by a whole host of friends or accomplices acting as compurgators but only by the actual person who was giving it.

In Southern Europe and in France, too, where the close co-operation of the Church and the Crown in the early thirteenth-century campaign against the Albigensian heretics had a profound effect on the subsequent development of royal justice, the introduction of such new methods of trial, although sometimes resisted, was relatively straightforward: the royal judicial officers or other competent authorities simply adapted the inquisitorial procedure to suit local circumstances and, as and when they could, substituted its use for that of the older forms of trial with which they at any rate, if not every sector of the community, had become so generally disenchanted. But in Northern Europe the process was more complicated. There the predominance of customary law not only precluded the adoption of an inquisitorial procedure based on the Roman system but required, moreover, that any new form of procedure must develop, or at least seem to develop, out of an older one. And where, therefore, outside Southern Europe and France, new methods of trial were evolved—as they had to be in order to fill the gap left by the abrogation of the ordeal—it was as a rule by a series of shifts of emphasis and, to us now, imperceptibly: so that, in England, for example, although we know that, after the Assize of Clarendon (1166), increasing use was made of the old practice of empanelling set numbers of local witnesses both to swear as to their knowledge of the facts of a case and to accuse suspected criminals before the courts, there is no record of the stages whereby 'juries' came to be used, as they are in all 'Common law' countries today, to decide cases.

If the Church may thus claim much of the credit for persuading later medieval lawyers to put more trust in purely human evidence, it must also share the blame, however, for having encouraged the secular arm to use torture to extract it. For, although, as we shall see presently, the barbarians had few scruples about inflicting tortures to heighten the sufferings involved in reprisals or punishment, the Spanish Visigothic Kings were alone among early medieval legislators in not following the Roman lawyers, who had restricted the use of torture to extort evidence or confessions, except in cases of treason, to slaves. And even though there is, in fact, no shortage of references in early medieval documents to torture being employed as it should not have been, and on persons other than slaves, yet still the tone in which such occurrences are reported is almost invariably disapproving. But once the papal ban on priests taking part in the administration of the ordeal had made that method of trial impracticable, it was not long before the secular authorities, especially in those countries where the ordeal came to be replaced by an inquisitorial system of trial, were to be found pointing to the example of the Holy Office as a means of justifying their own increasing reliance on torture in order both to obtain confessions and to elicit evidence from witnesses.

As early in the history of Western Europe as 358 A.D., the Christian Emperor Constantius II had decreed that, in cases of sorcery and magic, no dignity of birth or station could exempt a person from being subjected to the severest forms of torture: and, less than half a century later, that influential and authoritarian champion of orthodoxy, St Augustine, was to retract his previously expressed opinion and to recommend the use of torture in cases of suspected heresy. In *The City of God* (Book XIX, chapter 6), Augustine had denounced the use of torture as a means of assessing a person's guilt on the sound logical grounds that, should the accused individual 'be innocent, he will undergo for an uncertain crime a certain punishment, and that not for having committed a crime, but because it is unknown whether he committed it'; such a practice was therefore 'something . . . intolerable, something to be bewailed, and, if it were possible, washed away with floods of tears'. But the increasing popularity, particularly in Augustine's own North Africa, of the Donatist and Pelagian heresies, brought about a significant change of heart: since it was, in Augustine's view, even more important that the crime of heresy should be brought to light than that it should, necessarily, be heavily punished—in some cases, upon obtaining a conviction, the Church might after all display its clemency—he now quoted Christ's words 'Compel them to come in' (Luke, XIV, 23) to suggest that, although stretching, scorching or furrowing the flesh of possible heretics with iron claws might perhaps be going too far, they should at least be 'beaten with rods', if that would help to elicit a confession.

Whatever brutality St Augustine may in later life have sanctioned, though, *The City of God* was, after his *Confessions*, his most widely-known work: and from the time of Pope Gregory the Great onwards, the Church persisted in maintaining that confessions

10 *Various forms of torture current in Germany towards the end of the Middle Ages.*

dragged out of people under torture were invalid. But, despite this ecclesiastical prohibition, or more accurately in fact because of it, in the earlier part of the thirteenth century an ingenious process was devised, whereby it became possible to elude the obvious intentions of the ban while continuing to repeat it. According to this formula—which some claim as the brainchild of the Emperor Frederick II and others of King Alphonso 'the Wise' of Aragon, but which Pope Innocent IV, indisputably, made more respectable when, in 1252, he directed that torture was to be thus applied by the Inquisition in cases of suspected heresy—the accused person was tortured until he confessed and then, subsequently, invited to make a 'free' confession. If he refused, he was again tortured; and again, later, asked to make a free confession. At first, this procedure could only be repeated three times and, so far as the Inquisition was concerned, the infliction of the torture was to be carried out by laymen. But in 1256 came a papal Bull announcing that, in the interests of greater efficiency and to prevent the delays caused by having to employ secular torturers, the officers of the Inquisition and their assistants might grant one another dispensations for performing what were termed 'irregularities'; and with time many other of the earlier restrictions designed to regulate the way in which torture was to be applied were, likewise, either evaded or, quite simply, forgotten.*

Of the actual tortures employed by the Inquisition, those most usually resorted to were the rack, the pulley (also known as squassation), the 'iron boot' (into which wooden or metal wedges were hammered between the apparatus itself and the naked flesh of the leg) and the various forms of water torture, in which the victim was forced to swallow or to breathe in water, in such quantity or in such a way that he experienced the sensations of drowning, suffocation or both. But, in the Bull of 1252, Innocent IV had recommended that torture be applied to extract confessions from persons suspected of heresy *as it was applied in cases of robbery and theft*—or, in other words, as some secular authorities were already

---

* In 1498, so Johann Burchard reports (*At the Court of the Borgia*, ed. and trs. Geoffrey Parker, p. 160), Savanarola was 'tortured seven times before he pleaded mercy and *offered* to say and to commit to writing all the matters in which he had erred. And taken away from the torture chamber back to his cell, he was given paper and ink, and he wrote down all his crimes and faults'—amongst which were having made no confession since the age of twenty, giving communion with an unconsecrated host and using various tricks, including getting details of people's confessions from other friars, so as to pretend to have been granted divine revelations—'filling, it was said, eighty scrolls or more'. He was duly executed, along with two 'companions', on May 22 of the same year.

in the habit of using it. And as it was with the procedural formula by which the use of torture came to be admitted, so it was as a rule, too, with the tortures themselves: although the iron boot may possibly have been an ecclesiastical invention, the rack, the pulley and water tortures were all of them known in Western Europe long before Innocent IV authorized the Inquisitors to make use of them.

Broadly speaking, therefore, it would be fair to say that, while the Inquisitors may in later years have shown themselves as ingenious as anybody else in devising ever more excruciating methods of torture, a systematic use of tortures to extort confessions was first made in the secular courts of Southern Europe, where the Roman law schools flourished, in response to the papal ban, which was there most immediately effective, on priests administering the ordeal; and that, having been incorporated into the ecclesiastical scheme for the suppression of heresy, it gradually spread northwards, often with the Inquisition itself, until—by the end of the fourteenth century, in the case of France—it had become accepted practice wherever the authorities had adopted what has been referred to as an 'inquisitorial' form of trial. But this does not mean that elsewhere in Western Europe the use of torture for such purposes was unknown. In theory, it is true, both feudal and customary law frowned on the practice; but who can seriously argue that incarceration under 'peine forte et dure', for example, which was commonly used in England in the later Middle Ages to induce accused persons to plead before the courts, was in any way in keeping with the often cited Common law prohibition of testimony elicited by torture? Was it not torture to be locked in a cell, deprived of light, in the skimpiest of under-garments, with a weight on the chest, being given, on alternate days, three morsels of bread and three draughts of stagnant water, 'until you do. . . .'? Edward III certainly seems to have thought so: to Cecilia, widow of John Rygeway, of whose murder she was accused, he granted a pardon since she had 'after the manner of a miracle and contrary to human nature' survived forty days of such treatment, without even morsels of bread or draughts of stagnant water, in Nottingham gaol. [10]

By the end of the medieval period it was, in fact, only in the Scandinavian countries that instances of accused criminals being tortured to persuade them to avow either their own guilt or that of their accomplices was still found sufficiently remarkable to excite comment. But if the Norsemen can be congratulated on their exceptional resistance to this particularly unsavoury trend in later medieval justice, there was no Western European country at all which forbad the infliction of physical suffering as a punishment in itself or as a means of prolonging the agony of a capital sentence. Nor did even the Church forbid it. The tradition was everywhere too strong. The Old Testament—whose hero was given to wiping out whole tribes of those who displeased Him 'with fire and brimstone'—recommended, for the most serious crimes, death by stoning and, for many lesser offences, anything up to forty strokes of the lash. St Matthew, in his gospel, had written: 'The Son of man shall send forth his angels, and they shall gather out of His Kingdom all things that offend, and them which do iniquity; and shall cast them into a furnace of fire; there shall be wailing and gnashing of teeth.' At Rome, the law directed that the parricide, to give but one example, was to be put in a sack with serpents and thrown into a river. Amongst the barbarians it was the same: in avenging themselves on their personal enemies, the Germanic tribesmen did not hesitate to poke out eyes, chop off limbs or tear away scalps, while according to Tacitus it was customary for the tribe acting as a whole to condemn cowards, poor fighters and

11 A prolonged method of execution.

'notorious evil-doers' to be buried alive, with hurdles over their heads, in bogs.

With the idea of exacerbating vengeance by torture, then, everyone was familiar from the earliest years of the Middle Ages. But, for as long as barbarian justice remained a private affair, barbarian law on the whole confined itself to trying to discourage blood feuds—first, by settling how much should be paid in lieu of physical revenge, and secondly, by making efforts to see that this amount was actually paid. Since in the barbarian view, a crime affected only those people who were injured by it, there was, in effect, unity of punishment; and since, like the Romans, they considered a man of rank more valuable than an ordinary tribesman or citizen, they did little more, in the initial period following their conquest of Imperial territories, than introduce yet another distinction into their tables of compensatory payments—this new division being between the freeborn barbarians themselves and their formerly Roman subjects. Thus, in early Frankish law, while the life of the most illustriously born warrior, the Antrustian, was rated at six hundred gold pieces, the life of the provincial noble at three hundred and the life of the ordinary Frank at two hundred, the lives of the former Romans were reckoned as being worth only fifty or, at the most, one hundred. Similarly, under Lombard law, whereas a Lombard thief who avoided being captured in the act of stealing from another Lombard would have to give him nine times the value of the object stolen, for what he stole from a Roman, without being caught red-handed, he had to repay only twice the value.

But we have already seen how, under the influence mainly of the Church, the barbarian Kings' attitude to the law-breaker was gradually altered: with the result that they were increasingly inclined to move such crimes as could be said to disturb the peace of their kingdoms away from the purely private sector and to treat them instead as crimes damaging to the public order of the State. And, as their attitude to crime changed, so too, slowly, did their attitude to punishment. Not only did the earlier unity of punishment give way to a new plurality of punishments—so that, if a man committed murder, he might, quite apart from the ecclesiastical punishment of excommunication, be ordered to make two payments, the one compensatory, to the relatives of the murdered person, and the other, in the form of a fine, to the State—but punishment came to be seen also as a means of providing an example which might act as a deterrent to other would-be criminals. No longer, in such circumstances, were the authorities concerned simply to try to restrict blood feuds or even to compel restitution or the payment of compensation: people had to be taught that to break the law was to defy the State whose God-given right and duty it was to see that its laws were observed. And how better to terrify an unruly populace into accepting this fact than by inflicting upon those who broke the law the sort of corporal punishments suggested both by Mosaic and Roman law? Already, in the sixth century, as we saw earlier, the Frankish King Childebert had introduced legislation substituting the death penalty for money payments to the injured party in cases of homicide and rape; and by the time of Frederick Barbarossa (d.1190), in those parts of Northern Italy that were subject to the Emperor, the older Lombard law practice of requiring the criminal to make restitution had been almost completely superceded by a new system, equally applicable to everyone, of flogging, branding, blinding, amputation, outlawry or hanging.

So far as outlawry in particular was concerned, in later centuries it was to be used less as an actual punishment for crimes and more as a means either of constraining an accused person to appear in court or, where a court had found someone guilty, of coercing him into undergoing his sentence. In some cases, the declaration of outlawry might be made conditional upon the person's failure to present himself before the court, or to perform his sentence, or to abjure the realm within a certain number of days; but if, at the end of the specified period, he had not done as the court had ordered him, he, like any other outlaw, lost all his rights at law. On the one hand, this meant that his contracts were void, that his chattels became the property of the King, and that, if he held any lands, the King would enjoy their revenues for a year, before they reverted to the tenant-in-chief from whom ultimately the outlaw had held them; on the other hand, that it was the right, if not the duty, of anyone who had the opportunity of doing so, to kill him. In England, in the reign of Richard I, the price on an outlaw's head was the same as the reward offered for killing a wolf: five shillings.

But, despite the alternative uses to which outlawry might be put, the penalties inflicted by the secular authorities in Barbarossa's Northern Italy are generally representative of the sort of punishments that were imposed throughout Western Europe in the twelfth century—and upon which, indeed, Western European secular justice would continue to rely for some centuries afterwards. For although it was already common practice by then to allow most forms of punishment to be commuted in return for payment of a fine, there would always be large numbers of criminals unable to scrape together the money needed for the fine, as there would be also crimes deemed so awful that the remission of the prescribed punishment would be considered out of the question. In fact, from the twelfth century onwards, it was precisely this type of crime that seemed to be almost daily on the increase; and, as the authorities became, accordingly, more and more hysterically committed to their vision of an essentially feudal Ideal Order—to which the actual facts of life, of course, bore less and less resemblance—so did it appear to them to be of still greater importance that a resounding example should be made of those people who, in their eyes, were presuming to challenge the Divine Wisdom of God.

This idea that justice should be seen to be done was neither new, however, nor in any way confined to the authorities. The populace too liked to see criminals get their just deserts. Sometimes they watched the cathartic and edifying spectacle in silence; sometimes they wept for pity; and sometimes they crowded eagerly about the place of execution, urging the executioners on to do their grisly best. In the year 1204 or 1205, so Villehardouin tells us, the Byzantine ex-Emperor Murzuphlus, who had murdered the Emperor Isaac's son, Alexius, was arrested and brought before the new Latin Emperor Baudouin, at Constantinople. When Baudouin asked 'his people' what he should do with a man 'who had so treacherously murdered his lord' the crowd consulted amongst themselves until, at last 'it was agreed to inflict the following punishment: Towards the centre of Constantinople there stood a marble column, one of the highest and most finely carved that ever man's eye had seen. Murzuphlus was to be taken to the top of that column, and made to leap down in the sight of all the people, because *it was fitting that such a signal act of justice should be seen by everyone*. Murzuphlus was led to the column and taken to the top, while *all the people in the city flocked to the place to see that amazing sight*. Then he was cast down, and fell from such a great height that every bone in his body was broken as soon as he reached the ground'.[11] In the fifteenth century, the people of Mons paid a large sum of money for a convicted brigand in order that they might enjoy watching him being quartered while, in 1488, the citizens of Bruges were so pleasurably excited by the sight of various tortures being inflicted on some magistrates suspected of treason that the performance was extended, long after it had achieved its desired ends, for the sole purpose of their gratification.

Once the authorities were convinced that the spectacle of a criminal undergoing punishment must necessarily help to deter his

12 Executions in Bordeaux in 1377, with the burghers assembled for the spectacle.

fellow men from committing similar offences, it was inevitable that they should have cast about for ways of stepping up the horror-value of such cautionary exhibitions and so ramming their point home the more forcefully. In some cases, the refinements hit upon were purely repulsive: in parts of France and Germany criminals on whom sentence of death had been passed were tortured with red-hot pincers and plates before their execution; while, in different parts of Europe, people were variously boiled to death in enormous cauldrons, flayed to death, racked to death, pulled limb from limb by teams of horses or broken on the wheel. In other cases the particular form of suffering to be inflicted might be dictated by what contemporary opinion considered to be 'appropriate'.

With the concept of appropriate or fitting punishments, both barbarian and Roman law had long been familiar; but in the later Middle Ages it was to be developed into something of a fine art. Joinville, Louis IX's biographer, was full of admiration for his saintly subject who 'had so deep a love for our Lord and His Sweet Mother that he punished most severely all those who had been convicted of speaking of them irreverently or of using their names in some wicked oath. Thus I saw him order a goldsmith of Caesarea to be bound to a ladder, with pig's gut and other viscera about his neck, in such a quantity that they reached up to his nose'. He had 'also heard that, since I came back from oversea, he had the nose and lips of a citizen of Paris seared for a similar offence; but this I did not see for myself'.[12] In England, in the fourteenth century, Andrew Harcla, Earl of Carlisle, convicted of treason, had his entrails and bowels torn out as these were considered, perhaps oddly, to be 'whence came your traitorous thoughts'. Occasionally, as happened sometimes when heretics or witches were condemned to be burned to death, the authorities would announce that they were ordering the infliction of this or that particularly appropriate torture in order that the offender might be purged of his guilt and so reconciled to God; but on the whole, like Roman law's claim to believe that the object of punishment was the reform of the offender, such assertions of solicitude for the future well-being of the criminal were little more than empty phrases designed to justify the use of cruelty in the hopes of terrorising people into obeying the law.

Although the most elaborately contrived punishment shows were reserved, naturally enough, for crimes of the greatest magnitude, the principle that justice should be seen both to be done and to have been done applied to the punishments imposed for lesser offences as well as for the more serious crimes. The stocks,

13 *Four heretics are burned to death at Smithfield, London.*

pillories and ducking-stools, by means of which most minor misdemeanours were punished, were set up outside churches, on
village greens or in market places; and gallows were erected at
important cross-roads or other conspicuous places, where the
largest possible number of people might read the lesson implicit in
the grotesquely dangling corpses left to rot. For, even after sentence
of death had been carried out, the medieval authorities found ways
of putting the lifeless carcasses of their criminals to good use. To the
colossal gibbet outside Paris, at Montfaucon, the remains of
criminals previously beheaded, boiled or quartered were brought
from all over France to hang in wicker baskets beside the people
actually executed *in situ*. What was left of the body of Pierre des
Essarts, beheaded in 1413, was there pecked to shreds by hordes of
carrion crows before being returned, three years later, to his family
for burial.

Likewise calculated to serve as an admonition to others were the
punishments of branding with red-hot irons and amputations—
which had the additional advantage, in an age when identification

was everywhere a problem, of marking out the criminal as what he was. Here again, therefore, the limb or member to be cut off would often be dictated by what was thought to be appropriate to the crime: thus thieves might lose their covetous eyes or pilfering hands, and poachers the legs on which they had made their illicit rounds of the royal forests. But the connection was not always so clear. In the twelve days between Christmas 1124 and Epiphany 1125, for instance, the *Anglo-Saxon Chronicle* states that, on suspicion of alloying the coinage, 'all the moneyers who were in England' were, in accordance with orders sent from Normandy by King Henry I, 'deprived of their members, namely the right hand of each and their testicles below'.[13] Equally lacking in any immediately apparent logic were the Borough Customs of Portsmouth which directed that when a woman was convicted of theft 'her tetys shall be kyt of at Chalcross'.[14] Not infrequently, people were mutilated by accident; and might, like the Englishman John de Roghton, whose left ear was in the reign of Edward I removed by a horse's kick, obtain a certificate stating that the injury in question had not been sustained as punishment for any crime.

By the turn of the twelfth and thirteenth centuries, however, although branding was to remain a popular punishment in continental Europe, the use of mutilation was generally on the way out. In most countries it was the practice now to punish all felonies with death—usually by hanging but in Christian Spain as often as not by garroting—and the majority of minor misdemeanours by securing the convicted person to the pillory or in the stocks. But the royal thirst for money was meanwhile growing apace; and although in the last centuries of the Middle Ages an increasing number of crimes came to be classified as felonies, and so punishable by death, in fact the judges were more and more inclined to exact fines than to insist upon the physical penalties laid down by the law. Thus in Lincolnshire, for example, out of a total of 317 cases of homicide (114), robbery (89), vagrancy (65) and rape (45), which the Assize Rolls for the years 1201–2 record as having been dealt with by the justices, while 8 people were ordered to proceed to the ordeal, 9 pleaded ecclesiastical immunity and were handed over to the Church courts, 11 fled to sanctuary and 16 absconded and were outlawed, only 2 were actually hanged; the rest of the remaining 271 who were found guilty were fined, the sum of their fines here amounting to £527.12s.[15]

Also more frequently imposed as a punishment from the thirteenth century onwards was imprisonment, to which the Church had from an early period been in the habit of sentencing rebellious

14   *A man in the stocks.*

or disobedient clerics. In the monastic Rule of St Benedict (d.*c*547) Roman law's distaste for imprisonment seems to have prevailed: the only punishments there referred to are excommunication, corporal punishment, isolation from the other monks, exclusion from the daily services or other similarly humiliating restrictions. But the advantages to the Church (which could not, as we saw earlier, impose the death penalty) of a punishment which gave the offender time to reflect on his sins and repent, soon made themselves obvious; and by the tenth century, at any rate, the majority both of dioceses and monasteries had their own prisons—if not indeed two of them. Quite often the monastic prisons were situated near the infirmary, so that the sick in mind were side by side with the sick in body. Where there were two prisons, such penances for minor sins as were thought to require supervision would be enforced in one of them, while, in the other, the cleric who had committed a more serious offence would be condemned to languish for a given number of days, months or years, up to a maximum of the rest of his life.

So far as secular justice was concerned though, imprisonment was as a rule used before the thirteenth century for custodial purposes—or, more rarely, to coerce somebody into doing something—rather than as a punishment. In England, where punitive imprisonment is thought to have been in general use earlier than on the Continent, there is no specific record of imprisonment being recommended as a punishment until the last decade of the ninth century. Then, in c.890, came a law of King Alfred (I.S2,3) which ordained that, if a man failed to perform what he had pledged, he was to be imprisoned for forty days in a royal manor and there suffer punishments of the Bishop's devising. But even in England the real watershed did not come until the latter half of the thirteenth century when more and more statutes began to direct that, for what were on the whole either new offences arising out of the growth of mercantile and manufacturing activities or offences that interfered with the effective maintenance of public order, the convicted person was to be imprisoned. In some of these statutes, the length of the sentence was not mentioned; but, where a precise term was laid down, it was generally somewhere between forty days and three years, seldom longer.

A medieval prison might be anything from a makeshift village lock-up to a specially-built town gaol or the verminous and suppurating dungeon of some fortress. Gregory of Tours describes the sixth-century Frankish prisons (from which, he tells us, the relics of Saints had helped several good Christians to make miraculous escapes) as having wooden roofs weighted down with stones, and barred and bolted doors, behind which the prisoners sat in chains, with their feet clamped into stocks. As a general rule, however, in the Middle Ages it was the poor and the socially shunned prisoners who were liable to suffer the most terrible privations. In England, prisoners of war, hostages and approvers were maintained in prison at the expense of the State or the lord of the franchise prison. But most medieval prisoners were expected to pay their own way; which often meant not only that they must find money to get enough to eat but that they might be required to pay admission, release and other 'fees' to the gaoler. Occasionally governments intervened to try to regulate or even to abolish such fees; but since medieval gaolers were for the most part unpaid—in Siena, in the days of San Bernardino (d.1444), the head keeper of the city prison paid the Commune 300 soldi a year for his job—it was only natural that attempts at controlling the management of prisons should have been very commonly ignored. Thus, despite well-intentioned resolutions passed by the relevant authorities—

like that of the London City Council which in 1356 declared that the keeper of Newgate gaol should be of good character and must swear not to behave extortionately—there was still no end of complaints against the greed and inhumanity of gaolers. In 1348, for instance, the gaoler of Sarum was accused of keeping prisoners so long in the stocks that their feet rotted off, while of the nine inmates of Northampton Castle prison who died between August 1, 1322 and November 26, 1323, coroners' juries found that one had died of a wound he had received from an iron fork while resisting arrest, that one had died of 'natural causes', and the other seven of various combinations of hunger, cold, thirst, privation and the flux.[16]

As was usual, then, with medieval justice, a prison sentence meant one thing to those who were rich or influential and quite another to those who were not. Although the gaolers were held responsible for escapes, a large enough bribe might even persuade them to release people: so that in 1348, for example, we find a writ commanding that the keeper of London's Marshalsea gaol be arrested to answer charges of having helped prisoners to escape from his own custody. But, for those who had no hope of covering the cost of the fine the King would demand from the gaoler should they escape, there were stocks, chains, fetters, manacles, rings and collars to ensure that the gaoler should not be so embarrassed; and to live on, for those who could not pay for extra food, there were the by no means regular donations of the charitable. Sometimes selected prisoners were allowed to ask for alms at the prison gates or even, on certain days, to go about the town begging. Or sometimes priests or friars might preach sermons, exhorting their audiences to give generously to those suffering in gaol—as did San Bernardino when, during a drought in Siena, the authorities infuriated him by cutting off the water supply to the city prison, though not to the brothel next door.[17] But in the later Middle Ages the most substantial contributions to the welfare of poor prisoners came from the wills of people who, like the Englishmen John of Gaunt, Richard Whittington and Cardinal Beaufort, left sums of money for their relief.

Whether imprisonment was imposed as the sole punishment or whether it was accompanied by a fine, it was in either case common practice in the later medieval period to allow people to buy their way out of actually being gaoled. Indeed, in England it seems that many statutes recommended prison sentences simply in order to make the people condemned to them pay to have their sentences remitted. Where this happened, the courts did not so much offer the convicted person a choice of sentence as suggest to him that,

15 *Two criminals are publicly whipped through the streets to prison in 1370.*

were he to produce an acceptable financial inducement, the King might authorise his release. But, although the deal was thus in theory struck between the King and the subject who had disobeyed him, the particular sum to be paid was usually decided by an independent panel of local people of good character, who would have some rough idea of the guilty party's material circumstances. Only in times of exceptional public disorder or in the case of delinquent officials was the amount of the amercement fixed by the King or his justices. In effect, therefore, there was little difference between the payment of these 'fines' and the purchase of the pardons which later medieval monarchs were generally prepared to grant in return for sums of money, which were usually assessed, like the fines, in relation to the means of the offender. For just as the medieval King was considered to be God's appointed guardian of the law, so was he accredited with the exclusive right to show the divine quality of mercy to those who fell foul of it. If the King chose, for whatever reason that might come into his head, to pardon someone, there was in principle nobody who could quarrel with him. Thus Roger of Hoveden tells us, for example, how in 1189, Henry II's widow, Eleanor of Aquitaine, celebrated her release from the series of strongholds in which her late husband had kept her by making a progress through England, issuing pardons in the name of her son, the new King, Richard I—'inasmuch as, in her own person, she had learnt by experience that confinement is distasteful to mankind, and that it is a most delightful refreshment to the spirits to be liberated therefrom'—to all persons convicted of, or outlawed for, forest offences and to all those detained by royal justice or at the King's will. People detained for offences against the Common law were, meanwhile, to be released on sureties and the only prisoners specifically excluded from this blanket pardon were 'those evildoers who, for their evidence, had been pardoned life and limb, [who] were to abjure the territory of their lord, Richard, and depart therefrom, while the evildoers who, without any pardon of life and limb, had accused others of their own free will, were to be detained in prison until their cases should have received due consideration'.[18]

If some monarchs may have been moved to pardon people for purely personal considerations, however, and others by a desire to venerate the memory of Christ's suffering on the Cross, there can still be no doubt that the vast majority of medieval pardons were in fact purchased, either with money, or less often, with the promise of some other benefit to the King. In some cases, especially when campaigns were about to be fought on foreign territory, a King might offer charters of pardon to anyone who would guarantee to serve for a certain period at his own expense in the army. Or, in others, he might offer pardons for a given list of offences to anyone who paid a set sum. But, although the royal officials were occasionally directed to make enquiries as to the reputation of a person seeking a pardon, or to take sureties for his future good behaviour, there is little evidence to suggest that the authorities were greatly interested in whether the recipient of a pardon might have been innocent of the crime of which the courts had convicted him. Far more important, in their eyes, was the profit to be made out of granting pardons: so that on the whole, in the later Middle Ages, the buying of a pardon became a straightforward financial transaction; and once again, therefore, an important means of evading the full ferocity of the law was generally available to all but the impecunious, the friendless and those people who, whether as a group or individually, excited the particular enmity either of the King himself or of his judicial representatives.

4

Bandits, Freebooters and Outlaws

I N AN ERA as turbulent as the early Middle Ages, it is not surprising that the ecclesiastical authors of contemporary histories
should have been inclined to pronounce anyone who had protected or in some way benefited the religious foundations dear to
the chronicler to be a paragon of virtue, and anyone who had
opposed the chronicler's interests to be the most monstrous of
criminals. But, in the absence of any court records dating from the
earlier medieval period, the works of these authors are the only
source of first-hand information about the kind of men and women
who committed those offences which the laws of the early Middle
Ages were designed to prevent; and, predisposed as some
chroniclers undoubtedly were to glorify the deeds of local strong-
men whom royal judges would instantly have condemned as
criminals, it is nonetheless clear, from their accounts of life in the
first five or six centuries of the Middle Ages, that the most serious
obstacle to the maintenance of law and order was the tendency of
both rich and poor to used armed violence to serve their own
purposes.

Not that such behaviour was in any way new, or peculiar to the
Middle Ages. Already, in the Roman world, during the century and
more of chaos into which the Empire had been plunged by the
barbarians' rape of its territories, the authorities had been unable to
stop a growing number of disaffected or desperate people—of
those dispossessed by the incessant wars, of accused or convicted
criminals, of deserters from the Imperial standard and runaway
slaves—from resorting to pillage and armed robbery. But in the
sequel to the barbarian conquest of the Western Empire, after the

lands and the booty taken from the Romans had been divided amongst the victorious tribesmen, it was inevitable that the situation should deteriorate still further. For the survival of the new barbarian kingdoms would always depend, ultimately, on the strength of their armies; and the only way in which the impecunious monarchs of the early Middle Ages could hope to provide themselves, whenever the need arose, with competent fighting forces, was by appealing to those same bellicose instincts in their subjects, which they were, in all other circumstances, increasingly anxious to restrain.

On the one hand, therefore, it became the barbarian Kings' practice to require every freeborn landholder of military age (in the case of the Frank, in the sixth century, if he was fifteen or over) to serve, without pay, and armed and equipped at his own expense, for a certain number of days of each year in the army: while on the other hand, when his annual period of military service came to an end, the man who had been obliged to risk his life thus, for the prospect only of such booty as he might be lucky enough to take from his sovereign's declared enemies, was expected to return to his estates or his smallholding, and there live out the rest of the years as a peace-loving and a law-abiding fellow-subject and neighbour. But, although in time it became customary to allow a proportion of such people as could produce a stipulated sum of money to make a cash contribution towards the war-effort, instead of appearing in person on the battlefield, it was not nearly so simple a matter for the Kings to persuade the more belligerent of their subjects that they must, in the intervals between royal campaigns, contrive to live in some other way than by looting and rapine.

If early medieval methods of raising and disbanding armies may thus have done little to promote the cause of an orderly and a well-regulated society, the suppression of illegal violence was not made any easier either by the barbarian system of outlawry. As we have seen, to outlaw or to banish a criminal seldom achieved anything more than the removal of the malefactor from one theatre of action to another. And yet, in the early Middle Ages especially, it was not uncommon for persons convicted even of murder to be punished in this way. In the year 590, for instance, Bishop Gregory of Tours reports that when Count Macco of Poitiers succeeded in apprehending 'the sons of Waddo', who had been 'ranging the territory of Poitiers, where they had committed all manner of crimes, including many murders and robberies' (and who had specialised in waylaying and killing merchants to steal their goods), the two brothers were eventually induced, by torture, to reveal the hiding-place of a large portion of their stolen treasure: but, although the elder of these two murderers was executed, a sentence of banishment was deemed severe enough sentence for the younger of them.[1]

Of the subsequent history of the banished son of Waddo nothing is known. But of the sort of opportunities open to a person in his position some idea is offered by Bishop Gregory's account of a 'notorious riot' which had reached its climax, in the same neighbourhood, in the earlier part of the same year.

In the case of this particular, but by no means singular, 'scandal', the trouble had first come to a head in the early weeks of 589, when two inmates of the Convent of the Holy Cross at Poitiers, Princess Clotild, 'who boasted herself the daughter of King Charibert', and her cousin, Princess Basina, a daughter of King Chilperic, decided that they could no longer endure the lack of proper deference shown them by their Abbess, Leubovera—who treated them, said Princess Clotild, 'as though we were not kings' daughters but the offsprings of low serving-women'. By the end of February 589, Clotild had prevailed upon some forty or more of her sister nuns to vow not to return to their convent until Leubovera had been expelled from it; and this sworn band of confederates she led away to lay their list of grievances against the Abbess before the authorities. First, the ladies complained to Bishop Gregory, whose suggestion that they refer the matter to their own Bishop, Maroveus of Poitiers, they rejected on the grounds that 'it was through his deceit that they had first been driven to forsake the monastery'. Next they went to King Guntrum, from whom his kinswoman Clotild extracted the promise of a specially appointed commission, to be sent to Poitiers to investigate the alleged misdemeanours of Leubovera. But, when this commission proved slow in arriving, those of the nuns who had returned to Poiters 'put themselves in safety in the Church of the holy Hilary', and there 'prepared themselves for resistance, gathering about them a gang of thieves, slayers of men, adulterers, and criminals of all kinds . . .'

The leader of this band was said to have been one 'Childeric the Saxon', a man who Gregory later describes as having been 'guilty of manifold crimes, murder, riot and many other evil deeds'.[2] But of whether or not Childeric had originally been banished from Saxony no mention is made: very possibly he himself may have preferred, like many other persons of dubious reputation, to leave his homeland before the law could catch up with him. Be that as it may, though, by the time a delegation headed by four Bishops arrived in

Poitiers to settle the dispute, the rebellious nuns and their supporters were using the Church of the Blessed Hilary as a headquarters from which to wage open warfare on Leubovera; and,
when the ecclesiastical party came there to excommunicate the
nuns for their failure to obey an order to return to their convent, 'the
gang of ruffians . . . rose up against them and handled them so
roughly within the very walls of the church that the bishops fell to
the ground and could hardly rise while the deacons and other
clerics came forth covered with blood, and with their heads
broken'.

This, of course, was sacrilege; but, no sooner had the Church
dignitaries and their retinues beat a helter-skelter retreat from the
town, than Clotild persuaded the gang to seize all the monastery's
lands—in the process of which they thrashed any custodian who
offered resistance, and threatened, should they succeed in breaking
into the main building, to fling the besieged Abbess down from its
walls. For the time being, however, the monastery held out; and
despite renewed sentences of excommunication (on this occasion
pronounced more prudently, from a safe distance), and the strongly
expressed disapproval of both King Guntrum and his nephew, King
Childebert, it was only the severity of the ensuing winter that finally
compelled some of the beleaguering nuns to retire to other convents
or to the homes of relatives. As for Clotild, Basina and the
remainder of the ladies, the moment the weather began to improve,
they set about recruiting a still larger 'band of murderers, evil-
doers, adulterers, fugitives from justice, and men guilty of every
crime'—and these, on the eighth day before Easter 590, the
Princess Clotild 'ordered to break by night into the monastery, and
drag the abbess out by force'.

From now on matters move rapidly from bad to worse: the
Abbess, kept awake by 'gouty humours', hears ominous sounds
and has herself carried into the oratory containing the relics of the
Holy Cross, before which she prostrates herself; the bravos smash
their way into the monastery; Leubovera is discovered on the floor
of the oratory; one of the invaders, who has 'come to do the vile
deed of cleaving the abbess with the sword', is stabbed, instead, by
another thug; in the general confusion, Justina, the Provost (and
Bishop Gregory's niece), is taken for the Abbess; her veil is torn off,
her hair unfastened, and she is bundled away to be put into
custody; but, as day begins to break, the mistake is revealed; Justina
is ordered back to the nunnery; her captors also return; this time
they seize the right person; the wretched Leubovera is placed under
armed guard in Basina's lodging near the Church of St Hilary; and

Canto xxviij. doue tracta della qlita della noñ volgre
doue uide punire coloro che comisero schandalo et
seminatori discesma et doglialtre male opere fuxon
pricipy radici et cagioni come nello ito cap si ote.

Hi poria mai pur conparole sciolte
dicer delsangue et delle piaghe ap
chioza uidi pernarmi piu uolte

Ogni lingua percerto uerria meno
perlo nostro sermone et perlamente
channo atanto comprender poco seno

Selsadunasse ancor tutta lagente
chegia insu lafortunata terra

the following night, by the light of a great beacon set ablaze in an empty pitch cask, the monastery is ransacked.

On being informed of these outrages, Bishop Maroveus demands Leubovera's immediate release—or he himself will come, with the assembled townsmen, to set the Abbess free; but Clotild's only response to this threat is to select 'assassins', who are instructed, should any attempt at rescue be made, to put the Abbess to the sword; and when, some days later, a royal official named Flavianus manages to snatch Leubovera away from under the noses of her appointed murderers, a still more ferocious outbreak of violence ensues. At the convent itself, men are cut down and killed 'at the tomb of the Holy Radegund' and 'before the very Shrine of the Cross'. Then Basina makes her peace with her old Abbess—and more fighting promptly breaks out between the hoodlums who favour Basina and those who continue to support Princess Clotild. Then, Basina and Leubovera fall out again, then are reconciled again . . . until, at last, the tumult is put down, on royal orders, by the armed intervention of the local judge and administrator, Count Macco, whose men succeed in routing those of Clotild's supporters who do not flee to the forests 'by beating some with staves, by running others through with spears, and cutting down those who resisted most stubbornly with the sword'.[3]

Even if allowance is made for bias on Gregory's part—since he was, after all, uncle to Leubovera's loyal Provost, Justina, as well as having been personally involved in the affair—this whole episode still provides a typical example of the way in which all too many people, in the early Middle Ages, chose to settle their differences. And typical also is the fact that, although the two Princesses who had first started the rebellion were subsequently condemned by an ecclesiastical court and, once again, 'suspended from communion', it was only a matter of months before a council of high-ranking churchmen had been prevailed upon by the ladies' relative, King Childebert, to restore them to full membership of the Church. Indeed, the only unusual thing about 'the notorious riot of the nuns at Poitiers' is the efficiency with which Count Macco and his men put a stop to it: for while it was not uncommon, for persons of rank and title especially, to be granted a pardon for the most appalling of crimes, it was by no means always certain that the local representatives of royal authority would perform their appointed duties. In

16 A page from Dante's Inferno. *Dante and Virgil observe the Sowers of Discord, who had used armed violence to serve their own earthly ends, being continually split apart in Hell by a black demon with a sword.*

some cases, their failure to do so might be explained in terms of their relative weakness as compared with the strength in arms of the law-breakers; but not infrequently the royal officials' derelictions of duty were wilful—the result, not of impotence in the face of insuperable odds but, quite simply, of the officials' preferring their private interests to those of the Crown.

Small wonder, in such circumstances, that the chroniclers should have failed at times to distinguish between what the secular authorities of their day would have considered the illegal use of armed force, and its legitimate use. And small wonder either, in a world where few kingdoms were free for long from the menace of attack from without, that contemporary histories should tend to devote more space to the activities of Kings and important warlords than they do to the individual careers of the kind of people whom Princess Clotild set upon the Abbess Leubovera. Yet, despite the dearth of detailed case histories, there is no reason to suppose that the chroniclers' frequent allusions to the prevalence of criminal violence are exaggerations. For in an age when the bulk of the population depended for its livelihood on a system of agriculture, whose fruits were as meagre, by modern standards, as they were liable to seizure by predatory fellow-countrymen or enemy armies, it was not unusual for whole districts to be threatened with starvation; and in an age, generally, of weak royal government, what was there to deter starving people from emulating the example of the many royal officials and (with the growth, in response to the threat of foreign invasion, of feudalism) the many feudal lords, who did not hesitate to take whatever they wanted from whomsoever, and from wheresoever, they pleased? The answer, as a rule, was very little: because even in those areas whose feudal overlords did in fact try to ensure that crimes committed within their jurisdictions were punished, it was seldom difficult for the suspected criminal to evade arrest. Sometimes he might succeed in doing so merely by fleeing to another fief; or, alternatively, he might think it wiser to take refuge in the virtual sanctuary of the vast tracts of woodland or forest, into which few non-criminals dared venture for fear of the multitudes of bandits and robbers who infested them.

In the mid-eleventh century, according to William of Malmesbury (who wrote his *Chronicle* a hundred years later), 'the public roads and highways throughout all Italy were thronged with robbers to such a degree, that no pilgrim could pass in safety unless strongly guarded. Swarms of thieves beset every path, nor could the traveller devise any means of escaping them'. Indeed so great was the terror inspired by these thieves and robbers whose 'rage was equally bent against the poor and the rich', that 'the journey to Rome was discontinued by every nation,' says William, 'as each had much rather contribute his money to the Church in his own country, than feed a set of plunderers with the produce of his labours.'⁴ But whatever this passage might seem to imply to the contrary, the situation in Italy was in fact not so very much worse than elsewhere. For as long as Western Christendom had been threatened with invasion by Moslems, Magyars or Vikings, its rulers had been more concerned to protect their frontiers against the potential invader than they were to control the widespread lawlessness which the threat of pagan invasion did so much to encourage; and thus it was not until the danger of such invasion had been averted, that the rulers of the Christian West were able to give their more serious attention to internal security.

However, although a series of mid- to late-tenth-century victories over the forces of paganism may have allowed subsequent Christian Kings more time in which to concentrate on trying to make royal government more effective, the elimination of the threat of Infidel invasion also left large numbers of their subjects, all of whose particular talents or aptitudes had been of value in repelling the Infidel, with a great deal of time on their hands. Foremost among such subjects were the feudal magnates, some of whom had become richer, and others more powerful in terms of armed services due to them, than the King or the Emperor to whom they swore fealty; then, below the mightiest of the warlords in the feudal hierarchy, but by nature just as belligerent, there were the lesser nobles, to whom in their turn the knights and the lower ranks of fighting men owed both fealty and armed service; and not to be forgotten either was the miscellaneous rabble of cooks, grooms and foragers, of horse-dealers, pimps and other camp-followers who had become accustomed to earning what living they could by catering for the wants, needs or lusts of the military. That reduced demand for these people's various services should have led many of them to turn what advantages or skills they possessed to illegal purposes was no more than inevitable. And, to make matters worse, a steady growth in the population was creating a shortage of land.

When, at Clermont, in 1095, Pope Urban II proposed a crusade, His Holiness's chief concern was to help the Byzantine Emperor expel the Seldjuk Turks from Asia Minor. In return for this assistance, His Holiness hoped the Greek Church might at last be persuaded to recognise Roman supremacy. But Pope Urban II was also a Frenchman, a Frenchman who was horrified at the way in

17 A highway robbery.

which large areas of France in particular were being devastated, not
by external enemies, but by the rougher and more aggressive
elements in the native population. Since the Council of Clermont
had been convoked to discuss, among other things, how better to
secure the observance of those truces, known as *Truga Dei*, during
which the Church declared that all fighting was forbidden by God,
there were more laymen present than was usual at an ecclesiastical
gathering; and to those, on Tuesday, November 27, from a platform
specially erected in a field outside the east gate of the town, the
Pope made his appeal. Rich and poor alike, he said, should stop
fighting against one another. The martially inclined should go
instead, under God's leadership, to the aid of their fellow Christians in the East. Anyone who fought in the war against God's
enemies would earn the remission of all temporal penalties due for
his sins; anyone who was killed fighting for Him would thereby
gain absolution.

Of the nobly-led detachments of crusaders who set off in the
summer of the following year, most made the journey across
Europe, and into Asia, in a reasonably orderly manner. But not so
the disorganized hordes of people, who, their imaginations fired by
the preaching of popularly acclaimed 'prophetae', like Peter the
Hermit, did not hesitate to exchange their few possessions for
weapons and travelling gear in their eagerness to embark at once on
an adventure which held out the promise of rewards both material
and spiritual. In recent years much of Northern France and Western

Germany had been ravaged, not only by a particularly virulent form of plague, but by a succession of droughts, floods and famines. Before winter was out, many victims of these calamities had joined forces with a motley assortment of monks who had absconded from their monasteries, and of bandits, outlaws and other violent criminals, all of whom were keen to try their luck in a new quarter: and, by early spring 1096, they were already beginning to move south-eastwards, in bands large and small. Some of them, while still on German soil, butchered as many Jews as they could lay their hands on and looted their property. Others, who disregarded the Hungarian King's request that they refrain from pillaging while passing through his country, were set upon and routed by King Coloman's soldiers. Others again, upon reaching the suburbs of Constantinople, broke into the houses of the Greeks, and stole the lead from the church roofs; and, when the Emperor Alexius tried to put a stop to this vandalism by shipping them across the Bosphorus into Asia, were reported to have taken to torturing and massacring Christian Greeks—and, it was alleged, to roasting Christian babies on spits—before most of them were in their turn massacred, more than twenty thousand of them, at Civetot, by the Turks.

Appalled as all good Christians must of course have been to hear of the disaster that befell that so-called 'People's Crusade' at Civetot, it must nevertheless have been a relief to the rulers of the countries from which they had set out to know that the twenty thousand people who had been slaughtered would not be returning. And good riddance also, from the authorities' point of view, to the many adventurers, who, after driving the Infidel out of the Holy Land, stayed on and made their homes there. But, although the recapture of Jerusalem may have been an achievement more glorious than anything Pope Urban had dared hope for at Clermont, what the First Crusade altogether failed to do was to bring peace to the West. Undeterred by what Urban had had to say about the shedding of Christian blood, Kings, Dukes, Counts, Holy Roman Emperors and many even of Urban's successors continued, as did the more bellicose of their subjects, to make war on one another; and as meanwhile both the machinery and methods of warfare were becoming more sophisticated, so gradually did the practice of reinforcing feudal levies by hiring professional soldiers from other countries begin to gain ground.

Service abroad as a mercenary had long been a career especially favoured by landless younger sons, as well as by fugitives from the law of their own country and exiles. In the ninth century King Alfred had engaged sailors from Frisia to man the Anglo-Saxon fleet, and mercenaries known as 'lithsmen' to fight for him on land. But, until trade began to revive again in Western Europe, any extensive use of mercenaries had on the whole been precluded by the general lack of funds out of which to pay their wages: so that it is not until the late eleventh and early twelfth century, by which time the growth of commerce was stimulating the circulation of more money, that the chronicles begin to reverberate with shrill complaints about the atrocities perpetrated by bands of mercenaries.

To those who employed them, the advantages to be gained by hiring foreign mercenaries were threefold. In the first place, as foreigners, they were unlikely to have any local ties or allegiances which might prompt them to do otherwise than their employer commanded them. Secondly, they were as a rule better trained in the latest techniques of fighting than the general run of people who could be expected to assemble in response to a feudal call to arms. And thirdly, there was less risk of their defecting in the middle of a campaign than there was with, say, the farmer or the merchant, who might still be called into the field for so many days of every year by his feudal overlord. But, coincidental with these undoubted advantages, there were two very grave dangers attached to the hiring of professional soldiers from abroad. The first of these was that the foreigners might not confine their operations to doing what was strictly necessary to achieve the purpose for which they had been called in; and then again there was the danger that, upon the termination of their contract, the hirelings might refuse either to cease their military activities, or to move on to look for new employment elsewhere.

For the initial two years of a reign lasting from 1135–1154, King Stephen of England was well enough supplied with treasure to be able to pay Flemish and Breton mercenaries to keep his more rebellious subjects in order. But when his stores of treasure began to run out, and as more and more people became involved in the Civil War into which England was drawn by the rival claim of Stephen's cousin Matilda to the English crown, the whole country was thrown into such pandemonium that Stephen's reign is often referred to as 'The Anarchy'. Of 'the knights from the castles', William of Malmesbury reports in 1140, 'that they carried off both herds and flocks, sparing neither churches nor graveyards. Under-tenants, peasants, any who were thought wealthy, they kidnapped and compelled to promise anything by the severity of their tortures. After pillaging the dwellings of the wretched countrymen to the very straw they bound the owners and imprisoned them, and did not let them go until they had spent for their ransom all they possessed or could in any way obtain. Many breathed forth their dear lives actually during the tortures by which they were being forced to ransom themselves, lamenting their sufferings to God, which was all they could do . . . .' Given this lead by the Anglo-Normans, it was hardly to be expected that mercenaries whose wages were long overdue would sheathe their swords and sail away back to the continent. 'Under King Henry,' says William ruefully, 'many foreigners, displaced by trouble in their native land, sailed to England and lived in undisturbed peace under his wings: under Stephen many from Flanders and Brittany, who were wont to live by plunder, flew to England in the hope of great booty.'[5]

But by no means all professional soldiers went abroad in search of employment. On the whole, those trained fighting men who could find ways of earning a living in their own country stayed there. Not a few of them divided their time, when the King or their feudal overlord had no need of their services, between banditry and hiring themselves out to anybody who was willing to pay them. Such a man was Thomas de Courcy, who, 'it appears', says Guibert of Nogent, an early twelfth-century French chronicler, 'attained power to ruin hosts of people by preying from early youth on the poor, and pilgrims to Jerusalem'. In spite or perhaps because of his reputation for cruelty — in order to terrify his prisoners into parting with enormous ransoms, it was said, he attached weights to their feet and then, stringing them up by their thumbs 'or even their private parts', had them 'beaten madly with cudgels'—it was de Courcy whom the citizens of Laôn decided to hire as their champion when the King of France sent a force to punish them for responding to the withdrawal of the town's right as a commune by murdering, not only their Bishop, but several members of the local nobility. The citizens were soon to regret their choice: for it was not long before their intended protector had been persuaded, probably by an offer of better terms from the King's men, to change sides. Having burned to death a 'great assemblage of both sexes and all ages' in the church to which t'iese people had fled from him, de Courcy gave instructions that some other citizens, whom he had taken prisoner, should be taken away and incarcerated; and when it seemed to him that these captives could have been hustling along rather faster than they were, he ordered 'the bones under their necks, called the collar bones, to be pierced, and had cords inserted through the holes in five or six of them, and so made them travel in terrible torture'.[6] With hired champions, whether or not they were foreigners, there was always the risk that they might turn into the scourge of the very people who had called them in to protect them.

Of the foreign soldiers employed by the Kings of France in the eleventh, twelfth and thirteenth centuries, the majority came either from Flanders and Brabant, or from Northern Spain. Some of these wore a light chain hauberk known as a 'brigandine', a word which, in shortened form, very quickly acquired a new meaning: while so closely did the Northern Marches, and those parts of Spain nearest to the Southern borders of France, become associated with mercenaries, that when, in 1179, Pope Alexander III sought to include freebooting soldiers in a ban against unrepented Paterine, Cathar or Publican heretics being given Christian burial, he expressed himself thus: 'And as regards the Brabanters, Arragonese, Navarrese, Biscayans and Coterells,* who exercise such enormous cruelties against Christians, as not to pay any respect to either church or monasteries, or to spare widows or orphans, young or old, or any age or sex, but who, after the manner of pagans, lay waste and ravage in every direction, we do similarly enact'.[7]

Having, so he hoped, dealt with the mercenaries themselves, Pope Alexander attempted to strike at the root of the problem by ordering the excommunication of all 'those who shall hire, or retain, or encourage them'. But few people took any notice. The following year King Philip Augustus of France recruited a new troop of Brabançons to harry the lands of the rebel Count of Sancerre and several other vassals who were giving him trouble; and, when they had performed this task to his satisfaction, sent them off into Aquitaine, to assist Henry II of England's eldest son, also named Henry, to make war on his father. On their way to Limoges, the Brabançons stopped off, in late February 1183, at the small town of Noaillé, whose inhabitants shut the gates against them, but then, most imprudently, began to jeer at them and to taunt them, from what they fondly imagined to be the safety of the ramparts. Infuriated by the townsmen's insults, the Brabançons broke through their defences and, once inside the town, embarked upon an orgy of massacring, burning and looting which reached its crowning moment when the invaders discovered that the townsmen had very helpfully put all their most valuable possessions in the church.

* In the opinion of the people of Toulouse, says Roger of Hoveden, from whose history the text of this decree is taken, the word Coterell owed its origin to a large knife known as a *coterel*; but others, however, claimed that it derived from the Latin *cotarius*, meaning a cottager, from whom the Coterells were in the habit of extorting protection money.

18   Thirteenth-century soldiers in pitched battle.

Well-pleased with their luck, the Brabançons stuffed the assembled wealth of Noaillé into their kitbags and proceeded to Limoges, where both the younger Henry and the citizens gave them a warm welcome, and everything passed off smoothly until it became apparent that the rebel son of the English King had no money with which to pay the mercenaries. Perhaps, the younger Henry suggested, the monks of the Abbey of St Martial might like to help out? Well, perhaps yes, they might be able to make some contribution, the Abbot conceded, playing for time. But, when the money did not seem to be forthcoming, the Brabançons grew impatient: within the space of a few days, and to the outrage of the local population, the monks were driven out of St Martial, Grammont and the Abbaye de la Couronne, and the three monasteries pillaged.

That something must be done to stop the depredations of these bands of mercenaries-turned-brigand was by now becoming clear not only to churchmen and to the rich townsmen and nobles, whose property they threatened to despoil, but also to more humble people. In late November 1182, Pierre, Bishop of Le Puy, received a visit from a carpenter named Durand, 'who looked stupid and when spoken to seemed even stupider'.[8] With him the carpenter had brought an image of the Virgin Mary holding the infant Christ, which bore the inscription 'Lamb of God who takes upon himself the sins of the world, give us peace'. This picture, Durand informed the Bishop, had fallen from Heaven; and, what was more, the Blessed Virgin had herself appeared to him in a vision and told him that he must gather together a band of brave and virtuous men whose sworn purpose it would be to stamp out bandits and brigands. The Bishop was unimpressed. And said so. But scoff though Bishop Pierre might, by Christmas Durand had already collected a hundred followers. By Easter 1183, the number had risen to five thousand; and now it was decided that another Durand, Durand du Jardin, a Canon of Le Puy, should draw up the rules of an association which became known, from the distinctive white capuchon which its members were enjoined to wear, as the Capuchonnés. The aim of the Capuchonnés was to eradicate all brigands, and so to re-establish peace. To the front panel of his capuchon every member of the association was to attach a pewter medal, on which were a representation of the Virgin and a copy of the text inscribed on the parchment which their patroness had dropped out of Heaven. All Capuchonnés were to lead a regular and an honest life; they were not to gamble or to frequent taverns; nor were they to utter indecent oaths, wear long clothes or carry daggers. From Le Puy, the movement spread swiftly into the surrounding areas of Berri, Languedoc, Gascony, Provence and Auvergne, attracting into its ranks knights, Bishops and Abbots, in addition to a very much larger number of labourers and artisans: and in July 1183 it was a group of Capuchonnés from Auvergne, Limousin and Berri who fell upon the Brabançons who had sacked the three monasteries in the neighbourhood of Limoges, and, at Dun-le-roi, overcame and butchered them 'like wild animals mastered by a powerful hand'.[9]

So far, and for a little longer, all went well. A few weeks later three thousand more freebooters were massacred in Auvergne by a group of Capuchonnés led by Count Robert IV. But then some members of the association began to use their strength in arms for purposes quite different to those which the founders of the movement had intended. Tiring of tracking down well-armed and often ferocious brigands, these people now turned their attention to attacking the clergy and rich nobles. And once again the wheel went full circle: before even the year that had witnessed the victory of the Capuchonnés at Dun-le-roi was over, the authorities had found it necessary in several parts of Central and Southern France to call upon either professional soldiers, or such local forces as they hoped would prove reliable, to suppress bands of Capuchonnés who had taken to brigandage.

As so often happened in the Middle Ages, a summons to arms, even when made in the name of the Virgin Mary and for the express purpose of eliminating brigandage, had proved irresistible to many brigands—some of whom were probably seasoned operators from the outset, others, at the moment of joining the Capuchonnés, only potential freebooters or bandits. But the infiltration of criminals into bodies ostensibly committed to their pursuit and punishment was not confined to such ruffians throwing in their lot with ill-organized and ill-disciplined popular movements, like that of the Capuchonnés. Quite apart from corrupt judges, corrupt sheriffs, corrupt forest wardens, and the whole host of officials against whom complaints of venal and unjust practices were so often made, there were also some royal officials who led, as it were, a double life: who might, on the one hand, be members even of a royal household—and yet, on the other, did not shrink from aiding and abetting, or even taking part in, highway robberies and other crimes of violence more generally associated with outlaws and the most vicious sorts of malefactor.

One of the fullest accounts of a medieval highway robbery, and most particularly of the subsequent investigations into it, is that given by Matthew Paris in his *Chronica Majora* of an ambush that

took place on the London-Southampton road at a narrow defile in
the forest near Alton in Hampshire.[10] According to the chronicler's
report, when King Henry III and his court were at Winchester,
shortly before the beginning of Lent 1248, there came to him two
merchants from Brabant who complained that they had been
attacked in the Alton pass and robbed of 200 marks by a collection of
'robbers and freebooters', some of whose faces they recognised as
belonging to members of his court; if necessary, they were prepared
to prove these charges by engaging in single combat with those
whom they accused; and, unless their money was restored to them,
they would do their best to see that the property of English
merchants in Brabant was taken away from them. So King Henry
summoned the bailiffs and freemen of the district of Southampton
and 'with a scowling look said to them: "What is this I hear of you?
The complaint of despoiled people has reached me. . . ."' There
was, he said, no county or district throughout the whole extent of
England so infamous as this, or polluted by so many crimes; even
when he was present in the city or its suburbs, or in neighbouring
places, robberies and murders were committed. Nor was that
enough; even his own wines were exposed to robbery and pillage,
being carried off in stolen carts by these malefactors, who laughed
and got drunk on them. How, the King demanded of his audience,
were 'such proceedings [to] be any longer tolerated?' A jury of
twelve men must be chosen from the city of Winchester and the
county of Southampton, and sworn to give the names of any people
whom they knew to be thieves.

When the twelve men had been duly sworn in but declined to
name any suspects, the King became furious. Indeed it was only
with difficulty that he was dissuaded from having them all 'put in
the lowest dungeon' of Winchester Castle. A new jury, however,
which had no doubt heard of the fate so narrowly avoided by its
predecessor, was more compliant: amongst the people accused
were 'some of the citizens and many of the inhabitants of the
district, who were formerly considered good and liege men, who
abounded in rich possessions, and some of whom the King had
deputed, as guardians and bailiffs, to protect that part of the
country, and to apprehend or drive away robbers . . . and some
even who were superintendents of the King's household, and
crossbowmen in his service . . .'. Of those indicted some sought
sanctuary in churches, and others succeeded in escaping from the
district altogether; while of those who were actually arrested and
proven guilty, says Matthew Paris, many were fined, thirty hanged
and another thirty sent back to prison to await execution. On their

way to the gallows, the condemned criminals who had been members of the King's household asked their escort to 'tell the lord our king he is our death and the chief cause of it, by having so long withheld the pay which was due to us when we were in need; we were therefore obliged to turn thieves and freebooters, or to sell our horses, arms, or clothes, which we could not possibly do without'. But although apparently the King 'was touched with shame and grief' to receive such a message, 'and gave vent to his sorrow in protracted sighs', there were in fact no reprieves, nor even pardons after death, for the erstwhile functionaries of the royal household.

Despite the severity of the sentences meted out to those actively involved in the robbery of 1248, the forest round Alton continued to be a favourite haunt of brigands. In February 1260 a gang of robbers attacked the King's baggage in the same pass while, after Henry III's victory over the rebel Simon de Montfort at Evesham in 1265, it was in the Alton forest that Adam de Gurdun, one of the many supporters of de Montfort who preferred outlawry to the stern terms of the pardon offered by the 'Dictum' of 1266, made his base. From the depths of the forest, de Gurdun terrorised large areas of Berkshire, Wiltshire and Hampshire, until he and his gang were finally brought to bay by a considerable force of soldiers under the leadership of the future King Edward I, who himself took on de Gurdun in single combat and defeated him.

If in 1266 it may have been the unsatisfactory terms of the proposed pardon that prompted large numbers of de Montfort's supporters to remain outside the law, there were other good reasons too why people might choose to be outlawed. For although, in the thirteenth century, an outlaw could still be killed with impunity by anybody, the likelihood of this happening was often very much slighter than that of a person accused of a crime being found guilty by a court of law. In the case of 'ill-famed' persons or 'notorious evil-doers', and also of strangers to an area in which a trial for armed robbery took place, it was well known than an accused person was usually convicted; while, even in those cases where an innocent person was accused of some crime by his sworn enemy, there was always the danger that the adversary might have gone to the further trouble of bribing the judges, or of bringing influence to bear on witnesses or a jury. In these or any other unpropitious circumstances, there was obviously little to be gained by submitting to the due process of the law; indeed, guilty or innocent, the more serious the crime of which a person uneasy about the verdict was accused, the better advised was he or she to settle for outlawry or, having first taken sanctuary, confess the crime and swear 'to abjure the realm'.*

It is generally agreed today that if Robin Hood ever in fact existed, the most probable time for him and his merry men to have been active in Sherwood Forest would have been at some point between de Montfort's rebellion in 1265 and the Peasants' Revolt in 1381. But whether or not Robin may have been an historical personage, both the Robin Hood ballads and metrical romances such as the mid-fourteenth-century *Tale of Gamelyn* are of value to us here for the insights they provide into popular attitudes to violence, and to justice and the law. In the *Tale of Gamelyn*, the eponymous hero is the third son of a man of property, now deceased, and the victim of a wicked elder brother, who, as Gamelyn's guardian during his minority, has betrayed the trust placed in him by mismanaging his young brother's estates, to his own considerable advantage. When at last Gamelyn comes of age and, during a feast at which there are several rich churchmen among the guests, complains about his brother's dishonesty, the brother laughs at him and gives orders that he be tied to a post. But all the 'good' servants are on Gamelyn's side: and now decide to rebel against the tyranny of the hated brother. As soon as Gamelyn has been cut loose from his post, he and the 'good' servants and his loyal bondmen all fall upon the brother and his guests, and give them a brutal thrashing. Indeed, so great is the amount of blood spilt that when the Sheriff and his men arrive to investigate the disturbance, there is nothing for it but to flee to the woods — where Gamelyn and his followers soon meet up with a band of outlaws, and, in time, after he himself has been outlawed, Gamelyn takes the place of the old king of the outlaws, who has been pardoned by the King and so leaves the forest to return to the estates which have been given back to him.

Under Gamelyn's leadership, the outlaws make a speciality of preying upon rich churchmen. But although life in the forest is pleasant enough, when Gamelyn hears that his eldest brother is mistreating the peasants he decides that it is his duty to emerge

---

* Complaints made in 1315–16 to King Edward II about abuses and neglect of proper procedure with regard to sanctuary and abjuration resulted in a statute (9 EII), which declared that: 'When a robber, murderer or other evil-doer shall fly into any church upon his confession of felony, the coroner shall cause the abjuration to be made thus: Let the felon be brought to the church door, and there be assigned to him a port, near or far off, and a time appointed to him to go out of the realm, so that in going towards the port he carry a cross in his hand, and that he go not out of the king's highway, neither on the right hand, nor on the left, but that he keep it always until he shall be gone out of the land; and that he shall not return without special grace of our lord the king.'

from the security of the forest and to represent the poor people who have been wronged by his brother at the impending shire court.* Knowing that, as outlaws, his followers might quite lawfully be killed on sight, he nobly insists on their staying behind in the woods, while he goes alone to the court. But what Gamelyn does not know is that his brother has recently been appointed Sheriff. When he presents himself before the court, he is promptly arrested and bound by his brother's minions—and all seems lost until, suddenly, the day is saved by the Sheriff's and Gamelyn's middle brother, Sir Ote, who offers to go surety for Gamelyn's appearance at the next assize.

In the interval which elapses before his trial, Gamelyn goes back to the forest, and to plundering, while 'that false knight his brother' sets about the business of packing the jury against him. And, sure enough, at the assize, although there is no sign of Gamelyn, the court duly finds him guilty of all the crimes for which he has been indicted. Poor Sir Ote: it looks as if he will be hanged in place of the condemned man for whom he, like a true brother, has gone bail. But at this moment Gamelyn and his men break into the court, and the tables are turned. A new jury composed of outlaws sits in judgement upon the Sheriff, the justice and the jury which found Gamelyn guilty, who are all of them condemned as criminals and hanged; after which, Gamelyn and his followers go to their lord the King, who, not content with pardoning them, one and all, and restoring their lands to them, actually goes so far as to make Sir Ote Sheriff in his wicked brother's stead and Gamelyn Chief Justice of the Forest.[11]

Neither in the *Tale of Gamelyn,* nor in the better-known Robin Hood ballads, is there anything to suggest a horror of violence: in the *Tale of Gamelyn,* the hero and his supporters take an active delight in breaking their enemies' bones, while the attitude of the ballads to bloodshed is on the whole one of indifference. Together with the general acceptance of violence as being in the natural order of things, likewise common to both the *Tale of Gamelyn* and the ballads, is the underlying assumption that everything that is wrong with the world is due, not to any inadequacy in the system, but to the wickedness of those people who are appointed or elected to run

---

* An early fourteenth-century Outlaw's Song explains why its singer prefers the freedom of living in the forest to the uncertainties of the world outside in which the law is supposed to rule: 'For this reason,' the song goes, 'I will remain in the forest, in its delightful shade; for there is no falseness and no evil law in the wood of Belregard, where the jay flies and the nightingale sings unceasing.' (*Anglo-Norman Political Songs*, ed. I.S.T. Aspin, p. 69.)

it. Typical of so many disaffected individuals or groups in the
Middle Ages, neither Robin nor Gamelyn envisages any funda-
mental changes: on the contrary, all they ask is that the King (who is
always quick to recognize their virtues, is ever ready to pardon their
misdeeds), be freed from the influence of his evil counsellors and
officials; that corrupt Sheriffs or justices, and corrupted juries, be
replaced by good men like Sir Ote, Gamelyn and Gamelyn's fellow
outlaws.

If in the real world of the later Middle Ages there may have been
many officials just as corrupt, in their own ways, as Robin's sworn
enemy, the infamous Sheriff of Nottingham, it is on the other hand
doubtful whether there were many flesh and blood outlaws who
stole from the rich and gave to the needy. For although Robin was of
yeoman stock, and Gamelyn the son of a knight, both were in fact
the idealised champions of the poor and otherwise oppressed
people, who, while suffering the greatest hardships, were least able
to do anything about setting things to rights. Coming from a social
background somewhat superior to that of the people whose dissatisfaction and yearnings they express, Robin and Gamelyn are
folk heroes who deal with corrupt officials, with overfed ecclesiastics—who were especially unpopular with humbler people
because they were so often exacting and tyrannical landlords—and
with the undeserving rich, in a way that the dispossessed peasant,
say, or the villein who had been reduced to penury by his lord
insisting upon his buying his freedom, could only ever dream of
doing.

Two areas in which fact and fiction do seem to have corre-
sponded, however, are in Sherwood Forest and in the tendency for
leaders of outlaw bands to be of more or less 'gentle' birth. Unlike
the leaders of the Peasants' Revolt in 1381, or of Jack Cade's
similarly political uprising in 1450, very few of the chiefs of criminal
gangs who are known to have been active in fourteenth- and
fifteenth-century England were born peasants; while, as early as
1276, John de Lascelles, the then steward of Sherwood, had met
with an adventure which might have come straight out of a later
Robin Hood story. Having arrested, in Sherwood Forest, two
poachers armed with bows and arrows, de Lascelles took them to a
house in Bledworth and there ordered his servants to watch over
them, until he had time to take them into Nottingham and hand
them over to the Sheriff. But during the night the steward's
servants were overwhelmed by a gang of twenty men, variously
armed with swords and bows and arrows, who broke into the
house where the prisoners were being kept, beat up the guards,

released the prisoners, and then went on to de Lascelles' own house to smash the windows and shout abuse at him.

As for Robin Hood's 'merry men', so obviously for any gang of outlaws who had made their homes in the forest, the easiest way to obtain food was to kill the deer and other game, much of which, in England since the Norman Conquest, and in France since Carolingian days, was reserved to the Crown. Wherever what were known as 'Forest Laws' existed, they were particularly arbitrary and savage. In 1293, the English Parliament decreed that no proceedings were to be taken against foresters, parkers or warreners if they killed poachers who resisted arrest. Inevitably, such severity provoked much resentment, and, occasionally, acts of insolent defiance. On August 24, 1272, a band of poachers who had killed eight deer in the forest at Rockingham were reported to have cut off the head of a buck and impaled it on a stake with a spindle in its mouth to make it gape towards the sun 'in great contempt of the lord king and his foresters'.[12] In this case, it is still the King, or at any rate his foresters, who is the enemy. But, long before the end of the thirteenth century, the nobility had succeeded in browbeating the weaker of their monarchs (at the signing of Magna Carta the Barons had forced King John to make concessions regarding the Forest Laws) into allowing them a certain share of what had originally been an exclusively royal prerogative; and by the time of the Peasants' Revolt, in 1381, the complaint was no longer against the King or about the harshness of the Forest Laws, which could usually be evaded by paying a fine, but against the privilege, virtually exclusive, of the rich to hunt what many less well-off people so desperately needed to eat. Yet, despite what might today seem to be the obvious validity of Wat Tyler's and his colleagues' objection to this situation, nothing was done to change it. Very much the opposite: in 1390, in response to a petition complaining about common people who had been seen hunting with greyhounds in lords' and other important landowners' parks and warrens on religious festivals, when they should have been in church, Parliament passed an act limiting the right to hunt to the forty shilling freeholder for laymen, and to the cleric with an annual income of over £10; and a century and a half later King Henry VIII took a step backwards into the earlier Middle Ages by reintroducing (although only for a few years) the death penalty for poachers.

But while the poor and the hungry may have been driven to steal game, and even the odd farm animal, by their aching bellies, others seem to have made the theft of livestock a full-time criminal profession. In 1417 an order went out that Richard Stafford, a knight who was also known in those parts of Sussex and Surrey which he ravaged as 'Frere Tuk', should be brought before the King's Council for having broken into people's parks and warrens. Of the scale on which Frere Tuk had been operating, unfortunately, no indication is given. But, if the executors of the Earl of Lancaster are to be believed, it would seem that some criminals must have gone in for stealing animals in a very big way indeed: when they were asked to estimate the value of livestock stolen by raiders from his estates in the North Midlands during the two years 1327 and 1328, the figure the Earl's executors eventually came up with was an astonishing £5,200.

Apart from poaching and rustling, the crimes most popular with the leaders around whom gangs of criminals gathered in four-teenth- and fifteenth-century England were theft, robbery, extor-tion and kidnapping. As a rule, the motive for these crimes was, quite simply, material gain, and few criminals seem to have minded much whether their victims were corrupt officials or men of unimpeachable good character. But sometimes there might be an additional element of revenge, the result of some wrong or injury which the criminal reckoned the victim had done him. This would seem to have been the case, for instance, in 1332, when Sir Richard Wylughby, a King's justice (later to be accused 'by the clamour of the people' of having sold laws 'as if they were oxen or cattle', found guilty of having accepted bribes and fined for it),[13] was held to ransom for the enormous sum of 1,300 marks; for among Wylughby's kidnappers were several criminals on whom he had previously pronounced sentence.

The leader of the band of men who thus took their revenge on Sir Richard Wylughby was Eustace Folville, of the course of whose criminal career it is possible to gather some idea from the frequent references to him in the court records during the seven years between 1326 and 1333. One of seven brothers (only the eldest of whom seems to have avoided being accused of active involvement in crime), the sons of John de Folville, Lord of the Manor of Ashby-Folville in Leicestershire and Teigh in Rutland, Eustace makes his first appearance in the criminal records when he is alleged to have been present on January 19, 1326, with his brothers Robert and Walter, at the murder on the road from Melton Mowbray to Leicester of Roger Bellers, a Baron of the Exchequer, by Ralph de la Zouche of Lubbersthorpe. For this crime six men were indicted; but all of them evaded arrest, and in August were outlawed. Next month Eustace was said to have been involved in several robberies in Leicestershire. For these and other crimes, four Folville brothers were indicted; but early in 1327 they were included in a pardon granted in celebration of the formal beginning of Edward III's new reign. During the course of the following two years the records claim that Eustace was known to have committed at least three murders, a rape and three robberies. But again, in early 1329, Eustace and three of his brothers were granted a general pardon— in recognition, this time, of the service they had rendered the government by directing their energies against the rebellious Earl of Lancaster. Later that year the Folvilles were reported to have stolen goods worth £200 from some merchants of Leicester. In 1331 Eustace was himself attacked in his home, and two or more Folvilles were paid £20 by a canon of Sempringham and the cellarer of the Cistercian house at Haverholm to destroy a watermill belonging to someone against whom the two churchmen had a grudge. Then, on January 14, 1332, came the kidnapping of Sir Richard Wylughby, a crime for which the Folvilles joined forces with several members of another well-known Midland gang, the Coterels, with whom they were alleged to have shared out the ransom money at Markeaton Park, the property of a man who it is thought may have been the chief lay patron of both the Folvilles and the Coterels, Sir Robert Tuchet. Once again Eustace managed to avoid arrest; once again he was outlawed; and once again, in 1333, 'in return for the good services which he had rendered in the Scottish War'[14], he was pardoned. Thereafter, he is known to have served as a soldier in Scotland in 1337, in Flanders in 1338; at some point to have been knighted, in 1346 to have been involved in a robbery, and in 1347 to have died.

From the evidence it would seem that Eustace Folville's methods were straightforward: he and his followers either took what they wanted, or accosted their intended victims face to face and offered them the simple choice between their life and their goods. But some of Eustace Folville's contemporaries knew of more sophisticated ways of extorting money from people. In 1332, Roger le Sauvage, an associate of the Coterels, sent a letter by his 'official bearer', Henry de Wynkeburn, to William Amyas, the second richest man in the city of Nottingham and several times its mayor. Amyas was instructed that he must give £20 to the man who would come to him with the other half of an indented bill which had been delivered to him with the letter; if he failed to hand over the £20, all his property outside the city walls would be laid waste. Whether or not the former mayor complied with this order is not recorded, but still more peremptory in tone was a threatening letter received some four years later by one Richard de Snaweshill. If Richard did not instantly dismiss 'him who you maintain in the vicarage of Burton Agnes', he would receive 'such treatment at our hands as the Bishop of Exeter had at Cheap'—Bishop Stapleden had been murdered in 1326—and the missive was signed Lionel, 'The King of the Rout of Raveners', who gave his address as 'the Castle of the North Wind, in the Green Tower', and the date as 'the first year of our reign'.[15] While there are several instances of blackmailers who, like Lionel, seem to have derived additional satisfaction from couching their threats in the style of writs and other royal correspondence, there were also criminals who succeeded in obtaining money by serving false writs and warrants on people. Of Roger de Wennesly (who had at one point been employed to hunt down the Coterel gang, but later joined its ranks), it was alleged that when he was released on bail by a court presided over by William de Herle, the Chief Justice of the Common Pleas, he at once began forging 'pretended letters to arrest certain persons . . . by means of which he extorted money daily'.[16]

Quite apart from freelance activities such as these, there was meanwhile no shortage of patrons, lay or ecclesiastical, who were prepared to shelter, to assist or to pay criminals for a share of the booty or for illegal services rendered. Thus had the Canon of Sempringham and the cellarer of Haverholm hired the Folvilles to destroy their enemy's watermill; and thus was Sir Robert de Vere, the Constable of Rockingham Castle in Northamptonshire, (who, with the same Canon of Sempringham, was accused of having been an accessory to the kidnapping of Sir Richard Wylughby), said to have given orders that the people who delivered food to the Castle should leave it outside the gates, so as to prevent them from becoming familiar with the faces of the twenty or thirty armed men whom he was reported sometimes to have harboured there. In an age when belief in armed force as the best way of settling differences still led to the continual proliferation of feuds—and in a country, moreover, where the law relating to property ownership still encouraged forcible entry as one of the most effective methods of establishing title—it was inevitable that, even in times of comparative good order, many of those Englishmen who could afford to pay them should have employed people who were more proficient in the use of violence to do their dirty work for them, and so minimised the risk of themselves being indicted before a court. But the tendency both to commit and to commission acts of criminal violence was generally more pronounced when the King was away fighting for long periods in France or at times of national crisis, such as Mortimer and Isabella's rebellion during which the Folvilles and the Coterels were at their busiest, the years following the Black Death or Richard II's minority when unrest among the peasants and artisans was presenting more and more of a problem. In 1378, three years before the eruption of the workers' disaffection into the Peasants' Revolt, the preamble to a statute described how large numbers of people were forming themselves into armed bands and 'having no consideration to God, nor to the laws of the Holy Church, nor of the land, nor to right, nor justice, but refusing and setting apart all process of the law, do ride in great routs in diverse parts of England, and take possession and set them in divers manors, lands, and other possessions of their own authority, and hold the same long with such force, donning many manner apparel-ments of war; and in some places do ravish women and damsels, and bring them into strange countries, where please them; and in some places lying in wait with such routs do beat and maim, murder and slay the people, for to have their wives and their goods, and the same women and goods retain to their own use; and sometimes take the king's liege people in their houses, and bring and hold them as prisoners, and at the last put them to fine and ransom as it were in a land of war; and sometimes come before the justices in their sessions in such guise with great force, whereby the justices be afraid and not handy to do the law, and do many other riots and horrible offences, whereby the realm in parts is put in great trouble, to the great mischief and grievance of the people'.[17] And similarly, a century and a half later, the first Parliament to assemble after the long and ghastly Wars of the Roses was told how 'divers persons in grete nombre . . . have often tymes in late daies hunted, as well by night as by day, in divers forests, parkes and warrenes . . . by color wherof have ensued in tymes past grete and heinous rebellions, insurrections, rioutts, robberies, murdres and other inconveniences'.[18]

From the thirteenth century onwards, with the gradual loosening of the old feudal ties and allegiances, it had become increasingly common for persons of substance to guarantee their protection and support to lesser people, who might or who might not become members of their patron's household, who might or might not wear his 'livery'. And just as the Folvilles and Coterels had been alleged at one time to have been members of Sir Richard Tuchet and his brother's household, 'wearing their robes and living with them',[19] so were many other known criminals to be found making alliances, sometimes temporarily, sometimes on a more permanent basis, with the local gentry, the great magnates and, not infrequently, religious houses. It was to the havoc wrought by such arrangements that the Commons of England were pointing when in 1348, the year of the Black Death, they petitioned Edward III to introduce legislation whereby the nobility should be prevented from maintaining, whether 'privately' or 'openly', those robbers, thieves and other malefactors on foot and on horseback, 'who throughout all the shires of England, go and ride on the highway through all the land in divers places, committing larcenies and robberies'.[20] But no amount of legislation could stop many rich and influential medieval people 'maintaining' the sort of retainers of whom the Dominican friar, John Bromyard, was to write: 'No hounds were ever readier for the chase, no hungry falcon for the bird it has spied than are these to do whatsoever their great lords bid them, if he should want to beat or spoil or kill anyone.'[21]

A particularly hideous example of the lengths to which retainers might go in the service of their master is provided by the murder in 1445 of Nicholas Radford, a prominent lawyer and former justice of the peace, who was a friend of Lord Bonville, the sworn enemy of the Earl of Devon. On the night of October 23, 1445, the Earl of Devon's son, Sir Thomas Courtenay, rode into the yard of Radford's home at Upcot and gave orders that the outhouses be set alight. When Radford came to the door, he was told that neither himself nor his property should come to any further harm. Accepting this assurance, he allowed Courtenay and his men into the house—and immediately the men began to loot the house, while Courtenay insisted that Radford should supply him with food and drink. Courtenay had come, he informed Radford, to take him to his father. But how, Radford enquired, was he to ride there when all his horses had been taken? He would ride well enough, Courtenay said; after which, he took his leave and six of his men fell upon Radford with swords and daggers and killed him. Four days later, more men were despatched by the Courtenays to Upcot, in order to hold a mock Coroner's Inquest on Radford, at which they brought in a verdict of suicide, and to compel the deceased lawyer's servants to sing a lewd song as they carried what remained of his body to its grave. Not until late in the following year was Sir Thomas Courtenay, who had made no effort to conceal his responsibility for the murder, indicted by an Exeter jury; and even then, so great was the influence of the Courtenay family in Devon, and so ineffectual the administration of justice in that remote area, that the crime went unpunished.

Nevertheless, although a good deal of the blame for the prevalence of criminal violence in England in the later Middle Ages must be laid at the door of the nobility and gentry, who were so ready to offer employment and protection to evil-doers, a large share of the blame is also due to the later medieval Kings for their readiness, if not indeed their eagerness, to pardon outlawed or convicted criminals in return, either for money or for military or other armed services. In the course of only six years, as we have seen, Eustace Folville received no less than three pardons, two of them because he had fought against the King's enemies, for crimes that included murder, rape and armed robbery; while in 1335, in accordance with the quite frequently used expedient of setting criminals to catch criminals, Nicholas Coterel was made Queen Philippa's Bailiff for the High Peak district of Derbyshire. Of the likely outcome of such a policy, some idea may be had from the fact that, within two years of his appointment, Nicholas Coterel stood accused of interfering with the collection of a parliamentary subsidy at Bakewell, as well as 'having been guilty of many other oppressions by the pretext of his office'.[22] Similarly, when two outlawed associates of the Coterels, Sir William de Chetulton and Sir John de Legh, were pardoned, and then commissioned, together with James Stafford, a well-known gang leader, to capture two other robbers, it was a matter of months only before they were in Nottingham gaol accused of attempting to rape the widow of Sir John de Orresby. Like Eustace Folville, both Legh and Chetulton subsequently served their King in his Scottish wars: in 1336 they were instructed to recruit archers in Cheshire and lead them north into Berwickshire.

With pardons so easily obtainable, a declaration of outlawry began to lose much of its force.* Although popular fear of outlawry was still great enough in 1381 for Wat Tyler to demand that 'sentence of outlawry be not pronounced in any process of law',[23] there are several instances of outlawed felons, who, in the later fourteenth and the fifteenth century, did not bother, either to flee to the woods, or to buy pardons, even when this was on offer at very reasonable terms.

Violent, however, as life in later medieval England undoubtedly was, there were, in fact, many areas of Western Europe where law-abiding people lived in still worse fear for their possessions and

---

* By the mid-fourteenth century judicial opinion seems to have been agreed that only justices were allowed to put to death persons outlawed for felony. But not everybody knew this. In 1397, William Speke of Spadling and others were pardoned for having, as they thought quite lawfully, cut off the head of an outlawed felon.

their lives.* In the part of Germany sometimes known as West-phalia, for instance, the lawlessness was such that the local rulers of the semi-independent princedoms, cities and bishoprics into which the territories of the Holy Roman Empire were gradually splitting up, were persuaded to allow extraordinary powers to the Vehmic Tribunal, a system of courts about whose sinister proceedings in private (as opposed to those which were conducted in public) there has been much conjecture, but little is known. Thought by some to be descended from a secret tribunal set up by Charlemagne to ensure that the Saxons, who had been forcibly baptised Christians, should not revert to paganism, the Vehmgericht was not only a court but a Holy Order. To each of a series of tribunals, all of which were usually summoned to an annual Chapter-General at Dortmund or Arensberg by the Emperor or his Lieutenant, the ruler or rulers of the territory over which the particular tribunal was to have jurisdiction appointed a number of 'free counts', who, in their turn, nominated 'free judges'. The judges, whose appointment had to be approved by the rulers, were to be of pure bred German stock, of exemplary piety, and must not belong to any other religious Order; while their initiation was the occasion of a ceremony involving unsheathed swords, lengths of rope and the swearing of oaths whereby the judges pledged themselves, on pain of the direst penalties, never to betray the secrets of the Order, whose interests they would henceforth put above all else.

So far as their publicly performed duties were concerned, the most important job of the 'free judges' was to seek out and to punish robbers, bandits and raptorial nobles, who behaved as if they were beyond the reach of the law. If such a criminal was caught in the act, and there were three or more judges present, the trial and the infliction of the penalty might take place on the spot. Otherwise, the malefactor was summoned three times before the tribunal, and if, on the final occasion, he failed to appear, he was outlawed by a ferocious sentence, which, besides depriving him of all rights at law, abandoned his body to the beasts of the field, and his neck to the birds of the air. For all serious offences, the usual punishment was death by hanging—this to be carried out by the youngest of the judges who had tried the case. But effective as the

---

* According to Sir John Fortescue, who was Chief Justice in the troubled middle years of the fifteenth century, the English were especially to be admired for the large numbers of armed robberies they committed; French and Scots criminals lacked 'heart', and were, by comparison with their English counterparts, poor lily-livered creatures who only dared commit larcenies. Fortescue, *The Governance of England*, ed. C. Plummer, pp. 141–2.)

Vehmgericht may at first have proved as a means of combatting the widespread anarchy which was so greatly encouraged by the plethora, in later medieval Germany, of overlapping and conflicting jurisdictions, the Holy Vehm was, on account both of its preoccupation with secrecy and of the gifts with which the free judges were expected to reward the free counts who admitted them into the Order, more susceptible to corruption than almost any other court. From the mid-fifteenth century onwards, there was a strident crescendo of protest against the enormities perpetrated in the name of justice by members of the Vehm; a crescendo to which the electors of the Empire eventually responded in 1512, at the Diet of Trier, by deciding that the time had come to try to suppress the institution—a task which turned out to be more difficult than they had expected. Nevertheless, although members of the Vehm continued to pronounce judgement upon people until well into the latter half of the sixteenth century, the Vehmgericht had long since come to be regarded, by governors and governed alike, as more of a menace to the cause of justice and the maintenance of public order than a help.

Badly hit, too, by brigandage was France, which, from 1338 until 1452, provided the theatre of operations for the so-called 'Hundred Years War' between the Kings of France and of England, and their various combinations of allies.

It was during the first two or three decades of this war—into which most of the neighbours with whom the Kings of France shared a common frontier were, at one time or another, drawn—that professional soldiers finally came to outnumber feudally raised forces in the armies of both France and of England. For, while still insisting upon the principle that every free man owed military service to his sovereign, later medieval monarchs had become increasingly keen to extract money from the steadily growing number of their subjects who were obviously ill-suited to military life: and, with the proceeds, to hire trained professionals. Rather than call out the old form of feudal levy, therefore, later medieval rulers tended to make arrangements whereby the military commanders among their vassals bound themselves to serve for an agreed period in the royal army, at the head of an 'indentured retinue' of such and such a number of men. Then, with the money they had collected from those who had been excused military service, the rulers would contract with independent captains, who might be of native birth or of foreign, to supply them with mercenaries. And then again they might resort to the useful expedient of offering a free pardon to criminals who volunteered to support themselves for a specified

19 The execution of Aymerigot Marcel, a fourteenth-century French brigand.

time as soldiers in the service of their King; in which case, when the specified period expired, any criminals who had availed themselves of the offer would, as likely as not, be put on the pay-roll.

However, even after it had become customary for most soldiers to receive some sort of monetary payment, the nature of medieval warfare remained basically unchanged. Campaigns were not fought all out, with a view to exterminating the enemy: except where wars were embarked upon in the name of the One True God, against heretics, the main objective of the aggressor was still plunder.* To a prince or to the ruling body of a City State, this might mean the winning of new territories; to the nobles and military captains, it meant taking castles and fat ransoms from enemy nobles and captains; and, to the rank and file of most armies, it meant seizing virtually anything they could lay their hands on.

Officially, there were strict rules about the distribution of booty — just as there were most elaborate rules which were, in theory,

* In 1283, a band of Almugavars, or foot mercenaries, left behind by King Peter of Aragon to garrison the town of Perelada, were 'so maddened by the thought of the plunder which the rest of the army might be winning in skirmishes against the French', that they set fire to the town they were supposed to be protecting and took advantage of the resulting confusion to pillage it. (Don Ramon Muntaner, *Chronicle*, Chapter CXXV.)

supposed to govern every aspect of warfare. The English King and his commanders claimed one third each of all captured spoils, and left the rest to the soldiers; while Spanish Kings, it seems, were content with a fifth share of the loot. But who, in the excitement of plundering an enemy baggage train, or of taking over a town surrendered by the enemy, was going to stop and make an inventory? The Flemish-born chronicler Jean Froissart gives an account of how, in 1346, before the battle of Crécy, Sir Godfrey of Harcourt, the Marshal of England, persuaded King Edward III to desist from his declared intention of putting the whole population of the captured town of Caen to the sword, and to authorise him instead to issue a proclamation to the English army, which announced, 'in the King's name, that none should dare, on pain of the gallows, to start a fire, kill a man or rape a woman. This proclamation', the chronicler continues, 'reassured the townspeople and they allowed some of the English into their houses, without attempting to harm them. Some opened their chests and strong-boxes and gave up all they had, on condition that their lives were spared. But notwithstanding this and the orders of the King and the Marshal, there were many ugly cases of murder and pillage, of arson and robbery, for in an army such as the King of England was leading it was impossible that there should not be plenty of bad characters and criminals without conscience'.[24] So much for what was supposed to have been the peaceful occupation of Caen. At the battle of Crécy itself, it was apparently these same 'pillagers and irregulars, Welsh and Cornishmen armed with long knives, who went after the French . . . and when they found any in difficulty, whether they were counts, barons, knights or squires, they killed them without mercy. Because of this, many were slaughtered that evening', says Froissart, disgusted, 'regardless of their rank. It was a great misfortune and the King of England was afterwards very angry that none had been taken for ransom, for the number of dead lords was very great'.[25]

Amongst the troops, then, there seems to have prevailed an attitude very much less sophisticated than that subscribed to by the higher echelons of military society. And, for this, there was very good reason: because the only soldiers worth holding to ransom were of course the 'counts, barons, knights or squires', who on the whole expected to be held to ransom by people of similar quality. During the fighting that had led up to the surrender of Caen in 1346, Froissart tells how the Constable of France and the Count de Tancarville took refuge from the English army in a gate-tower, looking out of which at 'the truly horrible carnage which was taking place in the street . . . [they] began to fear that they might themselves be drawn into it and fall into the hands of archers who did not know who they were'. But to their enormous relief, in the midst of the massacre, the two French noblemen caught sight of Sir Thomas Holland, a one-eyed English knight, whom they recognised 'because they had campaigned together in Granada and Prussia and on other expeditions, in the way in which knights do meet each other'. As Sir Thomas came within earshot, they hailed him by name; and, having reminded him of their acquaintanceship, asked him to make them his prisoners. This Sir Thomas was 'delighted' to do, 'not only because he could save their lives but also because their capture meant an excellent day's work and a fine haul of valuable prisoners, enough to bring in a hundred thousand gold moutons'.[26]

Given such behaviour on the part of a Constable and a great nobleman, it is perhaps understandable that, as more and more of France was laid waste by one army after another, certain 'wicked men' should have begun to say 'that the nobility of France, knights and squires, were disgracing and betraying the realm, and that it would be a good thing if they were all destroyed'. In Beauvaisis this idea caught on like wild-fire: and the gentry of the region were soon being terrorised by bands of men who were said to have chosen as their king a man named Jack Goodman, who was the 'worst of the bad', and after whom they were called 'Jacks'. 'I could never bring myself,' declares Froissart, 'to write down the horrible and shameful things they did to the ladies. But, among other brutal excesses, they killed a knight, put him on a spit, and turned him at the fire and roasted him before the lady and her children. After about a dozen of them had violated the lady, they tried to force her and the children to eat the knight's flesh before putting them cruelly to death.' As more than sixty big houses and castles were razed to the ground, and those of their occupants who fell into the Jacks' hands were hacked to pieces, the nobility fled the district, many of them taking refuge in the town of Meaux in Brie. But the presence of 'at least three hundred noble ladies and their children' in one place only acted as a lure: from as far away as Paris, discontented villeins began to converge on the town, where 'the wicked people inside did not prevent them from entering', and nine thousand men, 'all filled with the most evil intentions', were in a short while thronging the streets around the market place, into which the nobles had barricaded themselves.

A bold plan, clearly, was needed—and was supplied by the Captal de Buch, who, returning from Prussia, with his cousin Gaston-Phoebus, Count of Foix, had been told how the Duke of

Orléans, a few other nobles and many noblewomen were in danger of being penned up and murdered in Meaux, and had therefore hastened over with his and the Count's joint force of forty lances* to see if they could be of assistance. Under the supervision of the Captal and the Count, the nobles and their men were drawn up, under their respective banners and pennons, in fighting order, to look as impressive as possible. Then, the gates of the market place were flung open, and 'the villeins, small and dark and very poorly armed', were suddenly confronted with a spectacle which made them turn tail 'in such panic that they fell over each other'. At which point, 'men-at-arms of every kind burst out of the gates and ran into the square to attack those evil men. They mowed them down in heaps and slaughtered them like cattle . . . In all, they exterminated more than seven thousand Jacks on that day'.[27]

Of the putting down of the Jacquerie at Meaux, Froissart was to hear first-hand accounts when he spent Christmas 1388 at Orthez, the seat of the Count of Foix, in South-Western France. For not only did Froissart then have several interviews with Count Gaston-Phoebus himself, but one of his fellow guests 'at the sign of the Moon' was a Gascon squire, known as the Bascot de Mauléon, who had fought under the Captal de Buch in Prussia and at Meaux. Having observed that this 'man of about fifty-five with the appearance of a bold and experienced soldier' had 'arrived with plenty of baggage and followers', the chronicler further noted that he 'had as many pack-horses with him as any great baron, and he and his people took their meals off silver plate'. Soon, by means of a cousin of the Bascot's with whom Froissart was on good terms, an introduction was effected; and one night, as the three men were 'sitting at the fire . . . after supper and waiting for midnight to come when the Count had his supper', the Bascot began to talk about his past.[28]

With alterations only as to details of time and of place, the 'Reminiscences of the Bascot de Mauléon, Freebooter' might have been recounted by any number of military captains, or 'routiers', who took advantage of the general confusion engendered by the Hundred Years War to hold the countryside to ransom. But, in one respect, the Bascot behaved better than many: his loyalty to the King of England was a matter of pride to him, and he never changed sides.

The first time the Bascot fought in battle was at Poitiers, under the

---

* Used in this sense, a 'lance' meant a unit made up of one mounted fighting man and his auxiliary soldiers and servants. Thus the Count and the Captal's force of 'forty lances' would probably have numbered about two hundred men.

Captal de Buch, where he had the good fortune to take a French knight and two squires his prisoners, and so earned himself three thousand francs. The next year he fought in Prussia with the Captal and the Count of Foix, and on the way back to Gascony was involved in the suppression of the Jacquerie. After that, since there was a truce between the Kings of France and England, the Count returned to Orthez, but the Captal and the Bascot put themselves on the payroll of the King of Navarre, who 'was making war on his own account against the Regent of France'. 'With others who were helping us' the Captal and the Bascot now took to raiding 'into the Kingdom of France and especially into Picardy', where 'we became masters of the farmlands and the rivers and we and our friends won a great deal of wealth'. Then, when Edward III resumed hostilities against France in the autumn of 1350, the Captal was summoned to join the King at Rheims, and with him went the Bascot. But in the following year came the Treaty of Brétigny, which stipulated, amongst other things, 'that all fighting-men and companions-in-arms must clear out of the forts and castles they held'. This was a serious blow to the 'poor companions'. So 'the leaders held a conference about where they should go and they said that, though the Kings had made peace, they had to live somehow'.

Although the Bascot does not mention the fact, according to Froissart's earlier account of the affair, it was a captain of freebooters named Regnault de Cervoles, also sometimes known as the Archpriest*, who hit on the bright idea of punishing Pope Innocent VI for the part he had played in negotiating the terms of the hated peace treaty by blackmailing the Papal Court, then resident at Avignon. In his earlier account Froissart says that 'after the Archpriest and his men had pillaged the whole region, the Pope and his college opened negotiations with him. He entered Avignon with most of his followers by friendly agreement, was received with as much respect as if he had been the King of France's son, and dined several times at the palace with the Pope and the cardinals. All his sins were remitted him and when he left he was given forty thousand crowns to distribute among his companions. The company left the district but still remained under the command of the Archpriest'.[29] But as told by the Bascot—who had been among 'the captains of all nationalities, English, Gascons, Spaniards, Navarrese, Germans, Scots and men from every country', who had made

* Regnault de Cervoles was not a clerk in Holy Orders; the soubriquet 'Archpriest' derived from the by-no-means unusual fact that he was by law entitled to the revenues from the curacy of Velinai in the Dordogne, on condition that he supplied and paid a cleric to do the curate's job in that parish.

20 *The sack of a town.*

their way to Avignon in 1360–1361—the story is a slightly different one. Whatever deal may or may not have been concluded with the Archpriest, in the Bascot's version, three-fifths of the mercenaries were finally persuaded by a payment of sixty thousand francs from the Pope and the cardinals to accept the Marquis of Montferrat's offer of work in Italy, where the Marquis was at war with Milan; while the remaining two-fifths—among them again the Bascot— stayed behind in France. There they continued to hold more than sixty forts from which, in the Bascot's own words, 'we held the whole country to ransom. They couldn't get rid of us, either by paying us good money or otherwise'. In a night attack, the companions took the important town of La Charité on the Loire, which they kept for a year and a half; while, in the district round Nevers, they held 'about twenty-seven towns and castles . . . and there was not a knight or squire or man of means who dared to venture out unless he had bought one of our safe-conducts'. Not 'even the Archpriest, who commanded in Nevers and was a loyal Frenchman at the time', (or, in other words, had been pardoned his past crimes and was now employed by the Crown), could do anything about it, 'except through knowing the companions—on account of which we did do something for him when he asked us to'. All of this, the Bascot suddenly informs Froissart, we were doing 'with the knowledge of the King of Navarre, and in his name'.

And so the story of the Bascot's life rolls on. At the Battle of Cocherel in 1364, between the King of Navarre's forces, led by the Captal de Buch, and the French, the Bascot was taken prisoner. As luck would have it though, he was captured by a cousin of his, a 'fellow called Bernard de Terride'. This Bernard arranged for a safe-conduct, under cover of which the Bascot was allowed to go back to the castle which he then held at Le Bec d'Allier, near La Charité, where he counted out the thousand francs' ransom money agreed upon, and gave it to one of his men to take to Paris. Later that same year, with Sir John Aimery, an English knight who was piqued at having been ambushed, while 'out marauding', by the Archpriest's men, and forced to pay a ransom of thirty thousand francs, the Bascot made a plan to try to capture the town of Sancerre, and with it the 'Sancerre boys', Jean, Louis and Robert. But, when the time came to put the plan into action, things went badly for the Bascot, worse still for Sir John. The Sancerre boys had got wind of the attack; an ambush was laid; and after 'a hard and nasty battle', during which Sir John received wounds that were to prove fatal ('for the man who was looking after him' in an inn, with strict instructions from his captor to see that he be kept alive to pay his ransom, 'through sheer viciousness and carelessness, let him bleed so much that he died'), all those of the 'English' party who had not been killed were taken prisoner and shut up in the Castle of Sancerre, pending negotiations for the surrender of La Charité and all the castles and garrisons round it. After this came a campaign in Brittany, where the Bascot picked up two thousand francs in ransom money, then another, in Spain, where 'we drove King Peter out' of Castile, and another, soon afterwards, which put King Peter back on his throne. 'Then war was started again between the King of France and the [Black] Prince. We were kept very busy because they fought us really hard and many English and Gascon captains were killed, though I stayed alive, thank God.'

Now, in 1388, the Bascot was in two minds about whether or not to sell his castle at Thurie to the King of France, who had given special powers to the Count of Armagnac and the Dauphin of Auvergne to purchase towns and fortresses from companions who were fighting for, or had fought for, the English. A few captains had already sold up and left the district. But then Thurie was so admirably situated. Since its capture it had brought the Bascot in, 'through plunder, protection-money and various strokes of luck which I've had, one hundred thousand francs'. The Bascot must tell his new friend how, at a moment when he had seemed to be threatened with poverty, he had sent men to spy out the lie of the land, and how, eventually, they had taken the town. 'Outside the place there is an excellent spring, to which the women from the town used to come every morning with their pitchers and buckets to draw water and carry it back on their heads. I determined to have the place and took fifty companions from Castelculier, and we rode a whole day through the woods and heathland. At about midnight I placed the men in ambush near the town and went on myself with five others dressed as women, with pitchers in our hands. We reached a meadow outside the town and hid ourselves in a hay-stack, for it was about midsummer and they had just cut the hay. When it was time for the gate to be opened and the women began coming out to the spring, all of us took our pitchers, filled them and started towards the town, covering our faces with kerchiefs. No one would have recognized us. The women we met on the way said: 'Holy Virgin, how early you've got up!' We disguised our voices and answered in their patois: 'Yes, haven't we?' and so we went past them and reached the gate. We found no one there to guard it except a cobbler who was setting up his lasts and rivets. One of us blew a horn to bring up the others who were waiting in ambush. The cobbler was paying no attention to us, but when he heard the

horn he asked us: 'Hi, girls, who was that blowing a horn?' One of us answered: 'It's a priest going out for a ride. I don't know if it's the vicar or the town chaplain.' 'Oh yes,' he said, 'it's Master Francis, the parish priest. He's very fond of going out in the morning after hares.' Immediately after this the rest of us arrived and we entered the town, where we found not a man ready to put hand to sword in its defence.'

It is not difficult to imagine the appreciative guffaws which the Bascot's tale must have elicited by the fireside, among the jugs of wine, at the sign of the Moon, in Orthez. But few enough towns or castles were taken, without bloodshed, by freebooters masquerading as ladies. And what about the people who had provided the hundred thousand francs' worth of 'plunder, protection-money and various strokes of luck', which the Bascot boasted of having raked in since his capture of Thurie? Among them, there would have been ecclesiastics, other captains and merchants, from whom it was usually possible to extort money or horses or manufactured goods. But there were few people from whom something could not be extracted; peasants might be made to part with livestock, grain or other foodstuffs, while the very poor might be good for horseshoes or iron nails. If nothing was forthcoming, or if protection-money was overdue, there were, as there always have been, ways of persuading people. Some of these were ingenious; almost all of them were brutal. In addition to mutilating, whipping and burning anybody who refused to hand over what he might well not possess, bands of marauding soldiers who terrorized France during the Hundred Years War were reported to have shut their victims in bread chests, to have tied them up 'like sausages', to have stuffed them into sacks and to have crushed their chests and stomachs under millstones, so that they spewed forth their entrails.

In 1359, the year after the Jacquerie, and the year before the Treaty of Brétigny, the chronicler Jean de Venette went back to the village of his birth, not far from Compiègne. He found it a charred ruin. 'Any vines that were left in the vineyards,' Jean records sadly, 'were not pruned or kept from rotting by the labours of men's hands. The fields were not sown or ploughed. There were no cattle or fowl in the fields. No cock crowed in the depth of the night to tell the hours. No hen called to her chicks. It was of no use for the kite to lie in wait for chickens in March of this year nor for children to hunt for eggs in secret places. No lambs or calves bleated after their

21 A medieval drinking party; the man on the right has evidently consumed too much.

mothers in this region . . . No wayfarers went along the roads, carrying their best cheese and dairy produce to market. Throughout the parishes and the villages, alas! went forth no mendicants to hear confessions and to preach in Lent but rather thieves and robbers to carry off openly whatever they could find.'[30]

To many of the people despoiled by freebooters, there was little choice left but to throw in their lot with the pillagers, who were sometimes no better off than themselves. A Letter of Remission granted to one Jean Petit, in the earlier part of the fourteenth century, speaks of the difficulties which faced an ordinary soldier when peace was declared. 'Since my youth,' Jean Petit, also known as 'Barjat', had pleaded with the King, 'I have served in your wars under various captains and men of arms. I have soldiered in different places against your enemies the English and other adversaries. Then peace was made: I got neither pay, nor wages, nor any other form of remuneration—or, at least, not much. As a result, I was forced to live in the fields, to live off your land and your subjects, to pillage, to steal and to hold to ransom . . .'[31] It is a familiar story; and one that can be told from two points of view. 'The country people are so assailed from all sides at once,' runs the text of another, later Letter of Remission, 'that they no longer know whom to trust or who to take for an honest Frenchman. Their life in these troubled times is nothing but one long agony. Hunted like wild beasts, they are ceaselessly on the watch and can only work surreptitiously to gather that little food which will save them from dying of hunger. At the slightest alarm, they run terrified to hide themselves with their women and children in caves and cellars, among the reeds in the marshes or among the thickest underbrush in the forest.'[32]

At the lower levels of military society, then, there were the men-at-arms, the archers and the crossbowmen, many of whose plights, when a truce was declared, were little different from those of the peasants who were desperately trying to scratch a living out of a devastated terrain. At the highest level, there were the nobles, who, when a truce was agreed upon, might look forward to returning—in the case of the English, across the Channel—to their estates. And in between there were the semi-professional and the professional knights and captains, many of whom had, like the soldiers they commanded, no homes to return to in peace-time, but who, because of their powers of leadership and their skill in commanding armed men, were generally better able to find lucrative, new, or alternative, employment. Some of these became leaders of robber bands and preyed, indiscriminately and quite openly, on anybody they considered worth preying on. Others, like the Bascot, did their best to throw a cloak of respectability over their nefarious activities by claiming that all their victims were, in some roundabout way, the enemies of a ruler or a government to whom they had always remained loyal. But others, a few others, do seem in fact to have striven to honour their contracts and to restrain their followers from harming anyone except in legitimate pursuit of what would have been held to be legitimate warfare.

One of the mercenary captains mentioned by both Froissart and the Bascot as having been present when the Papal Court at Avignon was threatened in 1361 is Sir John Hawkwood, an Englishman from Sible Hedingham in Essex, who, when he died at Florence, in March 1394, was to be given the most lavish state funeral. For, during his thirty years of service in Italy, this 'late brave soldier' had become one of the most respected of the condottieri, or professional generals, whose armies the rich mercantile cities of Italy were by now in the habit of hiring to fight their wars for them. Indeed so trusted was Hawkwood by the Signoria of Florence, with whom he had a permanent contract — in Italy these were known as 'condotti'; hence 'condottieri' — from the year 1381 until his death, that he was even allowed into the city at the head of his men to put down civil disturbances that broke out between different factions of citizens.

The earliest evidence of Hawkwood having moved from France to Italy is to be found in a renegotiated condotta, dating from January 1364, between the city of Pisa and the 'White Company', a mercenary band made up mostly of what, to the Italians at any rate, seemed to be Englishmen, and who now insisted that Hawkwood replace their German leader, Albert Sterz, and succeed him as their Captain General. In the spring of the same year, the White Company, together with other hired bands of German and Swiss mercenaries, was despatched by the Pisans against their archrival, Florence. Having pitched their camps at Fiesole, on May 1 the combined forces of the mercenary bands attacked a prosperous suburb of Florence situated near the Porto San Gallo, and then spent a further week pillaging the surrounding countryside. At the end of this week, the leaders of the mercenaries were approached by Florentine emissaries. How many florins, the emissaries wondered, would it take to persuade the gentlemen. . . ? Hawkwood alone among the captains refused to be seduced; Sterz was re-elected leader of the White Company, which went over to the side of Florence, and Hawkwood was left to return to Pisa with a force of only eight hundred men.

22 *Systematic pillaging.*

During the course of the years which elapsed before he finally
took up more or less permanent employment with Florence,
Hawkwood was to continue fighting for Pisa, to move to Milan,
where he served the Visconti family, and to sign at least two
separate condotti with the Papacy. All these masters he tried to
serve honourably: indeed, it was due to his scrupulousness in
honouring one of his contracts with the Papacy, that Hawkwood
and his men became involved in the most regrettable incident in his
career. For, although in 1377 the Papacy was very much in arrears
with the monies due to Hawkwood under his condotta, he nevertheless felt himself bound to answer a call from the Cardinal Legate
Robert of Geneva, who claimed that the townspeople of Cesena
had been giving trouble to his occupying force of Breton
mercenaries. On arriving in Cesena, Hawkwood learned that the
Cardinal Legate had in fact already disarmed the people, and this he
felt to be sufficient action to prevent any further disturbances. But
the Cardinal Legate was insistent: in the interests of proper 'justice',
the people should be punished; since Hawkwood was under
contract to the Papacy . . . or had he decided to forswear. . . ?
Reluctantly, the condottiere gave in, and his men joined the Bretons

in massacring the unarmed inhabitants of the town, which they spent three days in ransacking.

Scrupulous as Hawkwood may have sought to be in fulfilling his contracts, not even he could always control his troops. In 1377, for example, he was unable to dissuade his men from taking up winter quarters in territory friendly to Florence, by whom they were now employed, rather than pitch camp in an enemy-owned area, which had already been pillaged. Sure enough, it was a matter of weeks only before the Florentine government was complaining about the bands of his men who were plundering the countryside just as if it had belonged to the enemy. On the whole, however, so long as there was money coming in, and so long as there was work for his men to do (in winter there often was none), Hawkwood succeeded in seeing that discipline was kept, and that those people who he had undertaken to protect were in fact protected. But then Hawkwood's integrity was generally reckoned, even in his own lifetime, to have been something rather out of the ordinary.*

More typical of the sort of foreign captains who offered the services of a private army to any Italian who would pay them was Albert Sterz, who had been bribed in 1364 to go over, with the greater part of the White Company, to Florence; or men like Werner von Ürslingen, the Swabian leader of the so-called 'Great Company', which is first heard of in action under his command in 1342. In 1345, when the Company's condotti with Pisa expired, Werner demanded a redundancy fee before he would agree to move the men on—and when he did so, after the payment had been made, it was only to ravage the neighbourhood. After three years roaming about Italy, pillaging, raping, holding people to ransom, murdering and looting even monasteries, Werner hired the Company's services to King Louis the Great of Hungary, and moved south to the kingdom of Naples, whose Queen, Joanna I, Louis was bent on punishing for having—as he and a great many other peole suspected—connived in the murder of her consort, Louis's younger brother, Andrew, whom she was well known to have found a most inadequate husband.

By the time peace was made, in 1351, between King Louis and Queen Joanna, Werner had done so well out of the war that he

---

* His reputation for integrity notwithstanding, Hawkwood was, like many other public figures in his day, the recipient of an admonitory letter from that great dictator of such communications, the illiterate, and subsequently canonised, Catherine of Siena. In her missive to Sir John, Catherine begged him to stop shedding Christian blood, and to go on crusade: to stop serving the Devil's cause, and become instead a champion of Christ in the fight against the Turks.

resigned his command and retired to his native Swabia. But it was almost a year before Queen Joanna could muster the forces necessary to expel the Great Company from the fortress of Aversa, where the mercenaries had installed themselves under the leadership of Montréal d'Albarno, a Provençal whom the Italians called Fra Moriale because he was a former member of the Knights of St John, from which Order he had been expelled.

No less unprincipled than his predecessor, Moriale was a brilliant organizer and a rigid disciplinarian. Under his direction, the Great Company was said to number about nine thousand men, who moved about Italy with a portable gibbet on which members of the association who had broken its rules were hanged. A council of the ablest lieutenants met regularly under Moriale's presidency to discuss policy and decide whom next to threaten. Secretaries and accountants took care of the association's correspondence and supervised the sharing out of all loot. During a period of unemployment, in 1353, this independent army succeeded in blackmailing 16,000 florins out of Pisa and Siena, 25,000 out of Florence and 50,000 out of Rimini. In the following year, however, Moriale made a fatal mistake. Leaving his lieutenants in charge of the campaign which the Company had been hired by Padua, Ferrara and Mantua to conduct against Milan, he himself went to Rome to collect some money that was due to him. Having previously lent money to the demagogue Rienzi, who had recently been restored to power in Rome, Moriale seems to have thought that he could count on a friendly reception from him. But, in fact, on his arrival in Rome, Rienzi promptly had him arrested: the former Knight of St John was tried and beheaded, as a 'notorious brigand and murderer'; and, after his execution, the Great Company split up into a number of smaller and very much more disorderly bands, each led by its own captain.

While in the fourteenth century many condottieri had been foreigners, by the time of Hawkwood's death in 1394 it was more usual for them to be of Italian birth. Some, like Muzio Attendoli, nicknamed Sforza, and his son Francesco, were to rise from relatively humble origins to positions of eminence (Francesco Sforza married the heiress of the last Visconti ruler of Milan, and, when his father-in-law died, succeeded, after some trouble, in having himself recognised as the new Duke); others, like the humane and civilized Federigo da Montefeltro, Count of Montefeltro and Urbino, were nobles who took to professional soldiering to supplement inadequate incomes. Some, like Muzio Attendoli and Federigo da Montefeltro, were men cast in the mould of Hawk-

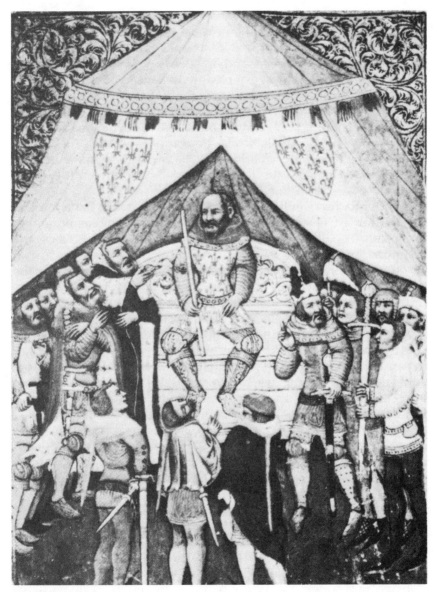

23 *A condottiere in his tent.*

wood; but there were plenty of others—like the thoroughly unscrupulous Cecchino Broglia, whom the Signoria of Florence thought of hiring as a replacement for Hawkwood—whose behaviour was more reminiscent of Werner von Ürslingen and Fra Moriale.

Prone as some even of the Italian-born condottieri were to turn brigand, there can be no doubt, however, that the practice of hiring these professional captains to fight against one another was on the whole beneficial to the peace and prosperity of what St Catherine of Siena had tried to encourage her fellow-Italians to think of as 'Italy'. For as long as the battles between the Kingdom of Naples, the Papacy and the Northern cities continued to be fought in this way, both the scale of the wars and the amount of destruction caused by them was relatively small; while, by comparison with the trail of devastation blazed by Charles VIII of France's army when he invaded Italy in 1494, the damage done by the fifteenth-century condottieri was almost negligible.

In order to discover how the King of France should have come to invade Italy in 1494 at the head of an army which was no longer interested in gaining mere tactical advantages or in holding the enemy to ransom, but one whose determination to win a conclusive, all-out victory left the Italians aghast, it is necessary to recross the Alps and trace the course of various changes which had taken place in the constitution of French armies during the middle and latter parts of the Hundred Years War. From a technical point of view, the most important contribution of the fourteenth century to warfare was the invention of gunpowder, which led to the development of very much heavier artillery: obviously, such artillery would require soldiers skilled in the use of weapons fired by gunpowder to operate them.* But, apart from employing more gunners, King Charles V (1364—80) had in fact gone a long way towards turning the French army into an integrated whole and bringing it more closely under direct royal control. While insisting that the captains make regular and proper returns to the pay corps, Charles V's great Ordonnance of 1374 also stressed the importance of the chain of command descending from the King himself, through his lieutenants (who were still usually Princes of the blood or great vassals), the Constable of France, the two Marshals and the Master of the Crossbowmen, to the captains and the officers of the pay corps in the base camp—and so on through their lieutenants and more junior officers. Having sought thus to standardise the grading of military personnel, the Ordonnance went on to deal with the numbers of men in each unit, and to give these a fixed order of battle. Each company, whether of men-at-arms, crossbowmen or archers, was to consist of a hundred men; while, from 1374 onwards, both men-at-arms and bowmen tended more and more to

* The other great military invention of the fourteenth century was the longbow, first used by the English to score a victory over the Scots at Halidon Hill in 1333.

be in the pay of the King (or of the town at whose expense they had been provided), rather than in that of the captains who led them.

Such then was the French army as reformed and reorganized by Charles V. But unfortunately Charles's successor, Charles VI, was neither as able nor as energetic as his father. During the long reign of this weak-headed and latterly insane monarch (1380–1422), the greater part of Charles V's work was undone; and, as large areas of France continued to be ravaged by both French and enemy armies, so did the fighting itself become increasingly bitter. When the people of Aquitaine complained to Henry V of England that one of his captains had set fire to fields of ripe corn for no better reason than to illuminate a path through the night for his men, the King is said to have retorted that war without fire was worth nothing, like sausages without mustard. Sentiments such as these are indicative of the steady move in the fifteenth century towards a new type of warfare in which scorched-earth tactics and the killing of as many as possible of the enemy came to be seen as the surest methods of achieving the new objective, a knock-out victory; while indicative of the sort of suffering that might be inflicted upon civilian populations, when soldiers trained in this school of war were made redundant, are the atrocities committed by the troops who were thrown out of work by the Treaty of Arras in 1435, and again, after hostilities had been resumed, by a subsequent truce agreed upon by France and England and Burgundy in 1444.

Like the first attempt, in 1439, of Charles VI's son, Charles VII, to reimplement the measures first introduced by Charles V's Ordonnance of 1374, his first effort at stamping out brigandage after the Treaty of Arras proved a failure. For although he did eventually succeed in persuading a large number of the brigands, whom their contemporaries referred to as Ecorcheurs (scorchers), to enter the service of German princes who were at war with one another, the brutality of the mercenaries was so indiscriminate, that within a short while the Germans had paid them 100,000 florins to return to France. Having profited from this lesson, however, when in 1444 Duke Frederick of Austria appealed for help in subduing the rebellious Swiss communes, the future Louis XI and his father agreed that he, the Dauphin, should himself lead the Ecorcheurs out of French territory—and so, it was hoped, tempt as many as possible of the freebooters into joining the force. This scheme worked: 30,000 Ecorcheurs assembled and, as they marched through Franche-Comté towards Switzerland, the looting began. Apart from pillage, arson, murder and rape, it was reported that the Ecorcheurs hung their victims up by the ankles, and smashed their

24   *The abduction of a respectable matron.*

left legs so as to induce them to ransom their right leg, or vice-versa.
Then, in August, the Ecorcheurs came face to face with the Swiss at
Basle: and routed them in an appalling blood-bath which came to be
known as the victory of Saint Jacques. Their mission accomplished,
the wily Dauphin now led the Ecorcheurs into Alsace and, as winter
was closing in, announced that there were reasons of State which
necessitated his leaving them there and returning directly to
France. The brigands prepared to install themselves for the winter.
The Count Palatine of the Rhine, the lords of Alsace and the Bishop
of Strasbourg all did their best to make them move on, wherever
they could wiping them out. To this the Ecorcheurs retaliated by
nailing people to the doors of their houses, or stripping them and

leaving them, tied to trees, exposed to winter winds, rain and snow. By early spring 1445, however, the Ecorcheurs were retreating in the direction of France. But such was the fear and loathing they inspired in the hearts of the population at large that, as they were passing through the narrow defile in the Vosges mountains known as the 'val de Liepvre', the local inhabitants rolled down stones, trees, rocks and anything else that came to hand on their heads—with the result that only 9,000 of the original 30,000 Ecorcheurs who had set out with the Dauphin found their way back to France.

As with his second plan for dealing with the Ecorcheurs, so with Charles VII's second attempt, in 1445, at reforming the army: both were in large measure successful. Of the Ecorcheurs who returned from Alsace, some were pensioned off and others absorbed into the army, as reconstituted by Charles VII, along lines similar to those laid down by Charles V's Ordonnance but with still greater emphasis on regularity and permanence. From 1445 onwards, the most effective elements in the French army were the professional gunners, the detachments of foreign mercenaries—men like the Swiss pikemen whom Charles VIII was to take with him into Italy— and the 10,000 regular, paid soldiers, who were organized into twenty 'compagnies d'ordonnance'. To this hard core there might be added, in time of war, not only feudal contingents and troops supplied by the towns, but also, after the year 1448, auxiliary detachments of 'francs-archers', who were recruited at the rate of one from every fifty households and derived their name from the fact that, besides receiving pay from the King when actually serving in the army, they were in peace-time exempted (or in other words 'free') from paying taxes.

In broad outline, therefore, the army at whose head Charles VIII invaded Italy in 1494 was already in existence some half a century earlier. But, Charles VII's reforms notwithstanding, there continued to be a strong connection between crime and the military. In 1455, for example, when the local headquarters of a criminal association known as the Coquille* was raided at Dijon, many of those arrested turned out to be soldiers who had been left at a loose end by the Anglo-French-Burgundian peace of 1453. And again, towards the end of the century, in his *Mémoires* of the reign of Louis XI (1461–83), Philippe de Commynes was to write of the way in which the 'troops . . . live off the country continuously without paying anything, committing other crimes and excesses as we all know. For they are not content just to live but in addition they beat and abuse

* See below pp. 174–6.

the poor people and force them to go to look elsewhere for bread, wine and victuals, and if any man has a beautiful wife or daughter he would be very wise to protect her carefully'.[33] In Commynes' opinion, it would have been easier 'to introduce better order' in 'our kingdom, which is more oppressed and persecuted in this respect than any other I know', if 'the soldiers were paid every two months at least', rather than at the end of the year. And, in citing infrequency, or worse still, lack of payment as the chief cause of antisocial behaviour on the part of the soldiery, Commynes was indubitably right; for it was not until the sixteenth century, and later, with the growth of more regularly paid, professional armies, which were kept under the direct control of strong national monarchies or city states, that Western Europe was to be free in peace-time from the 'crimes and excesses' of those people on whom its rulers relied to fight their battles for them.

5

Richman, Poorman, Beggarman, Thieves

ALTHOUGH MEDIEVAL METHODS of raising armies may have tended to encourage crimes of violence, there can be little doubt that in the Middle Ages, as in the sixteenth century when the Tudor chronicler Holinshed wrote his history, the majority of criminal acts took a form of theft, and that most thefts were committed because of poverty. In some cases the poverty may have been no more than relative; all too often it was abject.

In the tribal world of the German barbarians, the more vigorous members of the tribe might look after any number of weaker members whom they chose to adopt. But not where those weaker members were lepers or lunatics, or were monstrously deformed. According to the laws of both the Lombards and the Franks, people like these could have no place in a society whose ideal was the healthy warrior. Not that the healthy Frank or Lombard was afraid of contagion in the medical sense; his fear was rather a superstitious dread of those on whom the Gods had so obviously set the mark of their disapproval. Such a person was, worse than a useless mouth to feed, a possible threat to the tribe's continuing good relations with its Gods: he or she must be driven out.

But Jesus Christ had seen things differently. Had He not told of how the rich man, Dives, 'which was clothed in purple and fine linen, and fared sumptuously', on dying and being consigned to the torments of Hell, had lifted up his eyes and seen 'afar off' Abraham, and in his bosom Lazarus, the wretched beggar whose suppurating sores the dogs had been in the habit of licking as he sat at the rich man's gates hoping to be given a few crumbs from his table?[1] And had He not made a point of telling his audiences, over

25 A leper and a beggar are here refused charity by the Lord of the Manor.

and over again, that His mission was directed most especially towards the infirm and the poor, to whom it was the more fortunate man's duty to give alms?

By the fourth century of the Christian era, a series of Church Councils had laid down that the revenue which a Bishop received from his flock was to be divided into four parts. Of these quarters, one was to be retained by the Bishop, one was to be used to pay the clergy, one was to cover the costs of constructing and maintaining churches and ecclesiastical buildings and one was to be spent on relieving the suffering of the sick, the crippled and the otherwise needy. Frequently repeated in ecclesiastical texts of the following centuries, this so-called 'classical' division was incorporated by Gratian into his synthesis of Canon law, the *Decretum*, in which it was further stipulated that every Christian, as well as paying one tenth of his annual income to the Church in tithes, must devote some part of the remaining nine tenths to acts of personal charity. But in fact, well before the twelfth century when Gratian put together the *Decretum*, the administration of 'hospitality' had passed into the hands of the priests of the local parishes into which the dioceses had been divided. Since each parish was a separate economic unit, whose priest was responsible for the collection and disbursing of its revenues, most later commentators on the *Decretum* were agreed that the parish priest should follow the classical division—the only difference being that the priest to whom the tithes were now paid should retain one quarter for his own use, and pass on one quarter to his Bishop.

In 1215 the Fourth Lateran Council insisted that every church must offer that 'hospitality' which was 'due and customary': or, in other words, that parish priests must make provision both for the reception of pilgrims and wayfarers and for the relief of the local poor. In some parishes, the traveller or the person in need of succour might be put up in the priest's house; but in others there were by now 'hospitals', founded and maintained either out of the parish funds or, more frequently, by the bequest or endowment of a private person or persons.

Medieval hospitals were thus not hospitals in the modern sense of being places where people go to receive medical attention. They were almshouses, amongst whose inmates there might be found able-bodied wayfarers, as well as the old and the destitute, the disabled and, perhaps, the sick. In England at the time of the Fourth Lateran Council it has been estimated that there were about 170 hospitals. Some of these had room for no more than a handful of inmates, whereas foundations like St Peter's at York could accommodate as many as 200.

Although the mentally deranged were generally reckoned to be the responsibility of their families, it is nonetheless clear from the records of St Bartholomew's Hospital at Smithfield in London that mad people were often received there in the twelfth century, along with the dumb, the deaf, the blind, the crippled and the palsied. Also in London, the Hospital of St Mary's of Bethlehem (or The Bedlam—hence 'bedlam', meaning a madhouse or the inmate of a madhouse) seems to have specialised in offering a refuge to the mentally disordered long before it was officially recognized as a lunatic asylum in 1547. At the time of a visitation made in 1403, the Bedlam housed six men 'deprived of their reason' and three other sick men, while a mid-fifteenth-century list of London churches speaks of 'a chyrche of Owre Lady that ys namyde Bedlam. And yn that place ben founde many men that ben fallyn owte of hyr wytte. And fulle honestely they ben kept in that place; and sum ben restoryde unto hyr witte and helthe a-gayne. And sum ben a bydyng there yn for evyr, for they ben falle soo moche owte of hem selfe that hyt ys uncurerabylle unto man'.[2] Of how they 'ben kept in that place' some idea is given by a variety of articles mentioned in an inventory made in 1398 and quoted in the report of the 1403 visitation: 'Item cheynes de Iren, com vj lokkes. Item iiij peir manycles de Iren. ij peir stokky.'³

On the whole, however, the only medieval hospitals which were founded to accommodate persons afflicted with a specific sort of disease were the lazar-houses, or leper hospitals. In 1179 the Third Lateran Council declared that the prevailing attitude of the Christian community towards lepers had hitherto been one of unChristian selfishness; but since it was by then apparent that some forms of leprosy were catching—in the Middle Ages a 'leper', or 'lazar' was a person 'full of sores'; among the diseases from which he or she might have been suffering were tuberculosis, St Anthony's fire, scrofula, lupus and lepra—the Council's Canon *De Leprosis* went on to enact that leprous persons must not be allowed to live side by side with healthy people. Henceforward, both clergy and civil officials had a duty to report lepers, for whom a special service of separation was provided by the Church, and a special writ of exclusion (in England the writ *De Leproso Amovendo*) devised by the secular authorities. Once excluded by law, according to the English jurist Bracton, the leper lost all rights of bequeathing or inheriting property*; while at the performance of the ecclesiastical ceremony the leprous person was first comforted with assurances that he was sharing in the sufferings of the Christian Saviour, and then told never again to go into churches, bakehouses, markets or other public places, not to touch people, to have sexual intercourse with none other than his wife, always to wear the distinctive dark gown and cape of the leper and always to drink out of his own cup. 'Be thou dead to the world, but alive again unto God,' the priest would intone; and after the service was over the leper was allowed to choose between living in a lazar-house, or becoming a hermit or a wanderer. In 1256, the late Bishop of Norwich left £5 in his will to be given to lepers 'whether recluses or living together'.⁴ But despite bequests and other charitable gifts in their favour, and despite the papal exhortation of 1179 to behave in a more Christian manner towards them, lepers continued to be the objects of as much loathing as pity. When, for example, the Assizes of London ordained in 1276 that all leprous persons were to leave the city within fifteen days, they did so not only because their 'polluted breath spread the disease', but because the legislators were con-

---

* In the case of gently-born lepers, at any rate, who recovered from whichever form of 'leprosy' they had contracted, it seems that they were allowed to repossess the property which they had forfeited. In 1220 Nicholas de Malemeins contracted leprosy and was put in a leper house at Bidelington; but, when later his disease left him, he was allowed to take an oath of homage to his feudal overlord and enter his fief.

26 *A woman leper ringing her bell to warn others of her presence.*

vinced that lepers had been trying to pass on their affliction to others by leading a sinful life and going to bawdy houses 'that so, to their own wretched solace, they may have the more fellows in suffering'.[5] In France, during the reign of King Philip V (1316–1322) some lepers were accused of having maliciously poisoned wells— and, having been found guilty of so doing, were burned to death.

Partly from an atavistic horror of the deformed or the monstrous, and partly in order to reduce the risk of contagion, the first concern of medieval society with regard to lepers was thus to isolate them so far as was possible from contact with non-lepers.* Only after the leper's 'separation' could there be any question of trying to cure him. And even then attempts to do so were rare; for most people were generally agreed that, without the aid of a miracle (which might be worked by the administration of holy water or by the intercession of a Saint, or by a combination of both), leprosy was incurable.

Among the medical experts who contested this opinion, there were those who maintained that leprosy might be cured, at any rate temporarily, by 'the eating of a certain adder sod with leeks'.[6] But such a prescription is typical of the sort of remedies favoured by many Western European doctors, whose apparent ignorance of physiology or anatomy left their Jewish and Arab contemporaries quite dumbfounded. In his autobiography, the twelfth-century Arab writer Usama ibn Munqidh tells how 'the [Latin] ruler of Munaitira [Moinestre to the Latins] wrote to my uncle asking him to send a doctor to treat some of his followers who were ill. My uncle sent a Christian called Thabit. After only ten days he returned and

---

* In seeking to establish what degree of physical abnormality prevents a person from being 'free', with full rights before the law, the thirteenth-century English legal treatise known as *Fleta* decides (in Book I, Chapter 5), that whereas a 'monster' cannot be classified as free, it does not deprive a man of his free status 'if nature has added or diminished members in some small measure, though not extravagantly'. As an example of a permissible addition or diminution the treatise instances the man who is born either with six fingers on one hand or with four. Also 'free', in the opinion of *Fleta,* is the androgynous person, who, 'to be sure, is classed with male or female, according to the preponderance of the sexual organs'. But better evidence, probably, of the popular attitude towards so unfamiliar a phenomenon as an hermaphrodite is to be found in Matthew Paris's account of 'a new instance of degeneracy, appalling and theretofore unheard of, [which in 1246], in the see of Lincoln, struck horror into the hearts of all those who heard of it. A certain woman of noble descent, comely physique and free estate, who was married to a rich man and had borne children by him, made pregnant another woman of similarly satisfactory endowments, thus in a new and monstrous fashion "taking after her father." When she had begotten two sons of this woman, and had made her heavy with a third child, the mother, overcome with loathing for the strange and hideous act by which she had become pregnant, made a public declaration of both their guilt and compelled her companion in evil to make a full and open confession. She, for her part, shamelessly admitted her crime but most disgracefully sought to make light of her own blame, by charging her mother and asserting that she had been afflicted with the same vicious disposition'. Although, says Matthew, a gloss on a text from Genesis 'affirms that there are men who are "Men-Women", or alternatively "Men who mate with Men", doubtless meaning some sort of Hermaphrodite . . . Throughout the world the filthy and disgusting memory of such creatures is held in just abhorrence'. (Matthew Paris, *English History,* ed. J. H. Giles, Vol. II p. 166.)

27 *A leper praying before a priest, who protects himself from contamination by holding a handkerchief to his nose.*

we said 'You cured them quickly!' This was his story: They took me to see a knight who had an abcess on his leg, and a woman with consumption. I applied a poultice to the leg, and the abcess opened and began to heal. I prescribed a cleansing and refreshing diet for the woman. Then there appeared a Frankish doctor, who said: 'This man has no idea how to cure these people!' He turned to the knight and said: 'Which would you prefer, to live with one leg or to die with two?' When the knight replied that he would prefer to live with one leg, he sent for a strong man with a sharp axe. They arrived and I stood by to watch. The doctor supported the leg on a block of wood, and said to the man: 'Strike a mighty blow, and cut cleanly!' And there, before my eyes, the fellow struck the knight one blow, and then another, for the first had not done the job. The marrow spurted out of the leg, and the patient died instantaneously. Then the doctor examined the woman and said: 'She has a devil in her head who is in love with her. Cut her hair off!' This was done, and she went back to eating her usual Frankish food, garlic and

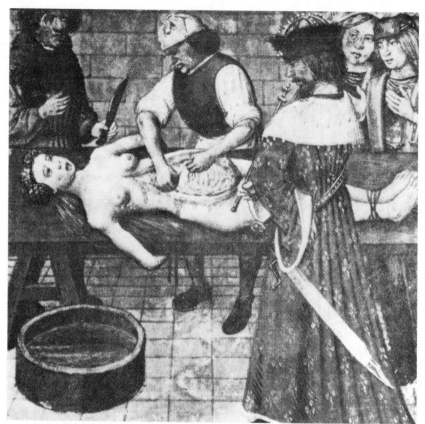

28 *A fifteenth-century surgeon performs a major operation.*

mustard, which made her illness worse. 'The devil has got into her brain,' pronounced the doctor. He took a razor and cut a cross on her head, and removed the brain so that the inside of the skull was laid bare. This he rubbed with salt; the woman died instantly. At this juncture I asked if they had any further need of me, and as they had none, I came away, having learnt things about medical methods that I never knew before.'[7]

In an age when the taking of medicines was usually accompanied by the incantation of a sacred formula—some of these addressed to Jesus, the Blessed Virgin or Christian Saints, but not a few of them invoking the Great Earth Mother and other pagan deities—it is perhaps not surprising that even the Court Doctor to King Edward II of England, who had studied at Oxford, should have been 'inspired', as he himself puts it, to prescribe some remedies which smack more of magic than of science. As a cure for diseases of the spleen, John of Gaddesden recommends in his *Rosa Anglica* 'the heads of seven fat bats'; while, for persons suffering from gall-stones, the royal doctor suggests massage with a tincture of crickets and 'those beetles which in summer are found in the dung of oxen'.[8] But for the general ignorance of scientific medicine there were in fact other reasons besides the popular association of healing with the miraculous or the magical. One of these was the lack of first-hand knowledge of the Greek writers, especially Hippocrates and Galen, on whose treatises medieval practitioners of medicine imagined their theories to be based; another was the ecclesiastical ban on dissection; and a third was the Church's refusal to allow clerics to take lessons in anatomy or to practise surgery, on the grounds that 'men vowed to religion should not touch those things which cannot be honourably mentioned in speech'.[9] Since all Universities were controlled by the Church, it was not until Pope Sixtus IV (1471–84) made dissection legal, so long as it was per-formed under ecclesiastical licence, that many physicians' ideas about how the human body functioned were anything more than conjecture. Almost certainly there would have been medieval doctors who would have subscribed, for instance, to the popular view that the stomach was a sort of cooking pot in which food was kept on the bubble by the heat of the liver. And although at some Italian Universities—such as Padua, Bologna and Salerno—the ban on dissection was never very strictly observed, at the University of Paris, on the other hand, it was not until 1634 that the faculty of medicine withdrew the embargo which it had placed on surgery in the opening years of the fourteenth century.

Since the attitude of the Church towards dissection meant that most surgical operations had to be performed by lay 'surgeon-barbers', the secular authorities were left with the task of safeguard-ing their subjects against being duped, or even physically injured by people who passed themselves off as pharmacists or doctors. The fourteenth-century writer Rutebeuf describes a typical pedlar of patent medicines, who announces that he is 'no poor common herbalist' but the specially licensed agent of Madame Trote of Salerno. 'My lady,' the herbalist informs his prospective clientele, 'sends us out into different lands and countries . . . to kill wild beasts in order to extract good ointments from them, to give medicine to those who are ill in body . . . And because she made me swear by the saints when I left her I will teach you the proper cure for worms, if you will listen. Will you listen?'[10] One herb in particular, which Madame Trote's agent has to offer, is so strong that if a piece of it no larger than the size of a pea were to be placed on the tongue of an ox, the animal would be certain to die; but if the herb is steeped in wine (preferably white wine but, failing wine of any colour, water will do) for three days, and the resulting beverage taken at breakfast time for thirteen consecutive mornings, 'you will be cured of your various maladies'.[11] Still more dangerous to the public at large than such purveyors of panaceas and ointments were the sort of medical practitioners whom a decree of Philip IV of France denounced as being 'ignorant of men's temperament, of the time and mode of administering, of the virtues of medicines, above all of laxatives in which lies danger of death'.[12] In 1421 an Ordinance of Henry V of England demanded that severe punishments be inflicted on all doctors not approved in their arts, 'that is to say, those of physic by the Universities, and the surgeons by the masters of that art'.[13]

Given not only the ignorance of some licensed practitioners of medicine, but the ubiquity of unauthorised quacks and fraudulent herbalists, it is understandable that a large number of the cures recorded by medieval chroniclers should be attributed to the miraculous intervention of God and the Saints, rather than to any form of medical treatment. In a petition for the canonization of 'Edmund, of happy memory, formerly Archbishop of Canterbury [d. 1240], whose body, that illustrious heap of earth', was in the Abbey church at Pontigny, the Abbot of that monastery and the Coventual Assembly of the Cistercian Order held there in 1244 are said to have claimed that 'in various and distant places on invoking his name . . . blind children are restored to sight, those lame from their birth recover the power of walking; the dropsical diminish in size; those deaf from birth recover hearing; the dumb from birth speak plainly; paralytic persons are restored to strength; those possessed by devils are freed from them' (the mentally deranged were often thought to be so possessed, and sometimes sustained severe injuries as pious Christians sought to beat the evil spirits out of their bodies); '. . . sufferers from quartan and other fevers escape death; some labouring under epilepsy, and various others afflicted with various and hidden severe diseases, some deprived of their limbs, and have become motionless as a log of wood; others who have become suddenly insane, others who are defiled by the disease of fistula, others polluted and disfigured by tumours, are, by the assistance of his merits, restored to their former health.' And so the list goes on: 'The flow of blood in women is stopped; one is cured of jaundice; the toothache of another is eased; foul spots die away from one, leaving no trace whatever; the ruptured, the hump-backed, those afflicted with gravel, and piles, and otherwise

29 *A cure attributed to the miraculous intervention of God; the sick man's ailment is symbolized by a demon.*

seriously afflicted, are cured; . . . and what is a wonderful circumstance too, brute animals also feel benefits through him . . .'[14]

Although in the case of Archbishop Edmund the monks' eagerness to have their 'illustrious heap of earth' canonized may perhaps have led them to exaggerate its powers (eventually, after delays occasioned by 'the whispers of slanders', Archbishop Edmund was made a Saint in 1246), it seems likely that some at least of the miracles reported by medieval chroniclers were in fact perfectly natural events. For so little did medieval people know about illness and death that skin colour, body temperature or lack of obvious breathing were often relied on as the criteria by which to judge whether or not a person was dead. King Louis XI of France was surprised to wake up one day to hear some of his courtiers lamenting his sad demise. Had he slept on longer, there might well have been those who would have put it about that he had been miraculously brought back from the dead.

Probably because of the advent of more virulent forms of plague, which killed off people already weakened by other diseases, it appears that from the middle years of the thirteenth century leprosy became less common, and that many lazar-houses therefore fell into disrepair or were converted to other uses. But whatever may have happened to the lazar-houses, although devout Christians continued to leave money for the endowment of hospitals (in England the number of hospitals had risen to more than 600 by the middle of the fourteenth century), there were, unfortunately, few safeguards whereby a testator could ensure that the purposes of his bequest would be honoured by those who were supposed to put them into effect. Of the Austin Canons, for instance, into whose hands the administration of many hospitals had by the thirteenth century fallen, Cardinal Jacques de Vitry says that 'under pretext of hospitality and dissembled piety, they are become beggars, extorting money by their importunities, with lies and deceits and every possible trick, feeding themselves and caring not for the poor'. Instead, 'through letters of indulgence, which they abuse for filthy lucre's sake, they get much filthy gain . . . And these filthy gains they spend in the most filthy fashion, in rioting and drunkenness, and other consequent deeds which they commit darkly in dark and secret places, and which, though they blush not to do, we are ashamed here to name. Meanwhile, keeping nothing of the institutions of the Rule save the outward habit, they receive almost all newcomers simoniacally . . . They turn these houses of hospitality and piety into dens of thieves, brothels of harlots and synagogues of Jews . . .'[15] More prosaically, Master Hugh, warden of the hospital of St John and St Thomas at Stamford, was in 1299 accused of defrauding the poor of their alms, of locking up the rooms in which strangers and the sick should have been accommodated and of neglecting the chapel. Other wardens rented out the rooms which they were supposed to offer gratis to the needy, while not a few collected the revenue due to their hospital without bothering either to visit it or to make arrangements for anyone to run it in their stead. So bad, apparently, was the state of affairs in the lazar-house at Kingston, that in 1315 the inmates tore down the building and left the area.

It was in an attempt to prevent such abuses in hospital administration that Pope Clement V in 1311 introduced the decretal *Quia Contingit*. While Bishops were required to make regular enquiries into the management of all hospitals in their dioceses, the wardens were made to swear on oath that they would run their establishments in the manner intended by their founders and that they would each year submit a copy of their hospital's accounts to the Bishop. Furthermore, as a means of trying to ensure that hospital revenues should be devoted to charitable purposes (and not to furnishing clerics with fat incomes), the decretal declared that wardenships of hospitals were not to be treated as benefices—a provision which meant that laymen as well as clerics might be appointed wardens of hospitals. But despite Clement V's insistence on strict episcopal supervision, during the course of the fourteenth century more and more hospitals succeeded in securing immunity from the Bishops' control; and, as they did so, the complaints about hospital administrators who used hospital funds and premises for their own benefit became louder and louder.

No less clamorous than the voices raised in protest against corrupt or deleterious hospital wardens were those which bewailed the sufferings of poor people in parishes whose priests were non-resident. In 1215 the Fourth Lateran Council sought to remedy the evils attendant upon such absenteeism by declaring that, wherever a priest did not live in his parish, he must appoint a resident vicar to perform his parish duties for him, and that the portion of the parish revenues which the priest must give his vicar should be fixed by the local Bishop. But from the large numbers of complaints about absentee priests and appropriated benefices (i.e. livings which were held by individuals or institutions who did not themselves discharge their duties towards their parishioners), it is clear that the decrees of the Fourth Lateran Council went largely unheeded. And so it was, for example, in England, that nearly two centuries later the government decided to intervene in an area which the secular authorities had on the whole hitherto been content to leave to the Church. 'Because divers damages and hindrances sometimes have happened,' a statute of 1391 reads, 'and daily do happen to the parishioners of divers places by the appropriation of benefices of the same places, it is agreed and assented . . . that the diocesan of the place upon appropriation of such churches shall ordain, according to the value of such churches, a convenient sum of money to be paid and distributed yearly . . . to the parishioners of the said churches, in aid of their living and sustenance for ever; and also that the vicar be well and sufficiently endowed.'[16]

Apart, however, from the Church's failure to prevent both clerics and laymen from abusing the Canon law—whose existing provisions with regard to the administration of charity the English Parliament was doing no more in 1391 than seeking to enforce—there was another consideration which was forcing the secular authorities to take a more active interest in the plight of the poor; and this was the alarming growth, during the course of the later thirteenth and the fourteenth centuries, in the number of men and women who were either thrown out of work or rendered unemployable by changes in economic and social conditions, or by the frequent pestilences which swept through Western Christendom in the later Middle Ages. In such insecure and restless times, many people had little choice but to become vagabonds; and, as they did so, so did the problem of relieving poverty become more and more closely bound up with that of suppressing the sort of vagrancy which was by now coming to be thought of as criminal. Thus, for instance, did the English Statute of Labourers enact in 1349, the year after the Black Death had caused widespread chaos in Europe and left millions dead in its wake, that nobody was to give alms to an able-bodied beggar. And so again did an Act of 1388 demand that, while beggars incapable of working should refrain from moving about the country, any able-bodied person who took to begging should be punished.

By ordering the punishment of able-bodied beggars, Richard II's government was not only striking a note that was to be taken up with a vengeance by some later English legislators (notable among them King Henry VIII whose parliament in 1550–1 enacted that able-bodied beggars were to be scourged from town to town with the lash), it was giving legal expression to a distinction which many earlier writers had tried to make between those who were to be deemed deserving of charity and those who were not. For although in the fourth century St John Chrysostom had been of the opinion that it was the Christian's duty to perform charitable offices indiscriminately, more representative probably of most medieval churchmen's view would have been that put forward by the later canonist, Rufinus, in his commentary on Gratian's *Decretum*, where he writes that 'if the man who asks is dishonest, and especially if he is able to seek his food by his own labour and neglects to do so, so that he chooses rather to beg or steal, without doubt nothing is to be given to him, but he is to be corrected . . . unless perchance he is close to perishing from want, for then, if we have anything we should give indifferently to all such'.[17] More outspoken on the subject of 'any man who is capable of body', and yet 'asks for his bread', is the character called False-Seeming in *The Romance of the Rose*. 'One would do better', says False-Seeming, 'to cripple him or punish him openly than to maintain him in such a malicious practice.'*[18]

Although medieval people may have sought thus to distinguish between the deserving poor and criminal beggars, it is nonetheless clear that, as the secular authorities introduced fiercer and fiercer laws aimed at dealing with vagabonds, the odds against this distinction being acted upon became progressively greater. Yet even if there may have been few mid-fifteenth-century Parisians who might have been moved, as Thomas of Celano tells us St Francis had been, to give their cloak and drawers to a scantily clad beggar, there would probably have been plenty of people in early thirteenth-century Assisi who would have enjoyed the sort of spectacle arranged by a Parisian impresario, who, in 1450, presented a pig as the prize for which four blind beggars were made to fight against one another with sticks. For what was beginning to change more and more rapidly in the later Middle Ages was not human nature, but the nature of life; and the force which had set this steadily accelerating cycle of change in motion was the revival, in the eleventh and twelfth centuries, of trade, and the growth of old and new towns.

* In offering a list of the categories of people who may be permitted to beg, False-Seeming claims to be following the thirteenth-century Paris teacher, William of St Amour (1202–72):

'If the man is such an animal that he has no knowledge of any trade and doesn't want to remain ignorant, he can take to begging until he knows how to perform some trade by which he may legitimately earn his living without begging.

'Or if he cannot work because of a sickness that he has, or because of old age or dotage, he may turn to begging.

'Or if by chance he has become accustomed by his upbringing to live very delicately, good men commonly should then have pity on him and, through friendship, allow him to beg for his bread rather than let him perish of hunger.

'Or if he has the knowledge, the wish, and the ability to work, and is ready to work well, but does not immediately find someone who may want to give him work at anything that he can do or is accustomed to do, then he may certainly obtain his needs by begging.

'Or if he has the wages of his labour, but cannot live on them adequately on this earth, then he may indeed set out to ask for his bread and from day to day go about everywhere, obtaining what he lacks.

'Or if he wants to undertake some knightly deed to defend the faith, either with alms, or by cultivation of his mind, or by some other suitable concern, and if he is weighed down by poverty, he may certainly, as I have said before, beg until he can work to obtain his needs . . .

'In all these and similar cases, if you find any further cases that are reasonable, in addition to those that I have given you here, the man who wants to live by beggary may do so, and in no other cases, if the man from St Amour does not lie.' (*The Romance of the Rose*, trs. Charles Dahlberg, Princeton 1971, pp. 200–201.)

30 A blind beggar being cheated of his drink by his boy.

In the earlier Middle Ages, when, brief spells of military service apart, most people's lives were essentially static, it was not only easier for the closely-knit rustic communities to take care of the poor but at the same time, as we have seen, dangerous (and, in the case of the serf, illegal) for people to venture far from their homes. But after the Infidel had been beaten back and travel became safer; once trade started to flourish again and Kings and feudal magnates began to grant varying degrees of independence to the expanding merchant communities (some of which, in parts of the Low Countries and in Northern Italy especially, became virtually autonomous communes, but others of whose town councils were given little more than the right to settle minor disputes between their own townsfolk)—as soon, in short, as the towns began to offer the more downtrodden or restless elements in society an alternative life to that of the beggar, the part-time bandit, part-time soldier or the outlaw, so did many people who had no experience of commerce or industry begin to flock into the new centres of commercial and industrial activity. For whereas it was difficult for the peasant to improve his lot in the Manor to which he was tied, there was always the chance in a town that even a runaway serf, who after a year and a day won his freedom, might die a rich man; while, less dramatically perhaps, any former peasant who became a member of one of the urban craft-guilds was likely to earn a better living from his new occupation than he would have done from tilling the soil.

Less hardship and greater profit, here then were the two dreams which drew men and women of all sorts and conditions to the towns, in pursuit of the commodity which might at last turn their dreams into reality—namely, money. But no sooner did money begin to circulate in larger quantities, than it seems to have struck a growing number of enterprising people that an excellent method of acquiring more of it would be to manufacture their own coin. As a

rule this was done by clipping the edges of genuine coins, which thus became underweight, and making new coins out of the clippings, which might or might not be mixed with a baser metal to form an alloy. In England, it was because he had been led to suspect that his own officials had been issuing base coin that Henry I gave the order that all the moneyers in the country should, in the twelve days following Christmas 1134, lose their right hand and their testicles. Since the uttering of false coin was in most countries held to be a treasonable offence, it was not unusual for blackmailers to accuse either royal officials or private citizens of debasing the coinage so as to make them pay a bribe to have the charges dropped.

Also generally rated as treason in England—and so debarring the person accused of such a crime from claiming benefit of clergy—was the counterfeiting of the King's seal. This might be done in one of two ways. While some forgers used metal impressions of the sort of matrix used by royal officials, others merely removed the wax seal from writs or documents issued in the normal manner and attached them to documents drawn up by, or on behalf of, themselves. The latter method was favoured by Philip Burden, a chaplain, who in 1324 purchased two writs of the sort normally used to establish the legal possession of property (one a close writ of novel disseisin, the other a writ patent in agreement with it) from the Chancery. Having had two forged writs made out against several of his enemies, Philip took the seals from the authentic writs and attached them to the forgeries. At his trial before the Court of the King's Bench, it was suggested that Philip belonged to a gang which in fact possessed an imitation of the royal stamp, and whose members specialised in fraudulently obtaining money and real estate by producing faked credentials or instructions and by serving false writs on people.

No less ingenious than some of the frauds perpetrated by medieval fakers of seals and documents were some of the ruses resorted to by confidence tricksters. At Barnstaple, in Devon, on March 7, 1354, Gervase Worthy, William Kele and Geoffrey Ipswich called on the wife of Roland Smalecombe and told her that, although now they were Christians, they had formerly been pagans and were possessed of magical powers. If Mrs Smalecombe would care to produce any valuables she had in the house, the three men knew of a way in which their quantity might be doubled. Impressed by the men's boasted knowledge of the future and excited by their proposal, Mrs Smalecombe lost no time in gathering together all her gold and silver trinkets. These the men put in a linen bag, which they then locked in a box. All Mrs Smalecombe needed to do, said Gervase Worthy, who took charge of the key, was to go to church and have three masses a day celebrated for nine days; on the tenth day he and his companions would return, and there would be twice as many precious articles in the box as had been put into it. But that, needless to say, was the last the woman ever saw of the three magicians. When eventually she broke open the box, she discovered that the linen bag contained nothing but lead and stones; whereupon, according to the indictment of the presumed thieves (who were said to have extorted more than 200 marks out of honest Devon folk by similar methods), the wife of Roland Smalecombe fell ill, and, soon afterwards, died.

Another and more commonly employed method of persuading the gullible to part with money was for a person in a position of authority—say the agent of an important magnate or a priest, whether bona fide or an impostor—to offer to use his influence to further the interests of those whom he managed to talk into believing that his intervention on their behalf might be to their advantage. Particularly adept, it would appear, in this line of trickery, was Master Robert Colynson, a priest who had been banished from Cambridge University because of his erroneous and seditious sermons, and who was accused by Ralph Lord Cromwell of having extorted money from people by having made them promises which he had never had any intention of keeping. On one occasion, for instance, in 1450, Lord Cromwell claimed that Colynson had gone to the Prioress of Swine Abbey in Yorkshire and, having assured her that he had been sent there by Cardinal Kemp, succeeded in extracting 20s 8d from the nuns, in return for a promise to get them absolution from the Papal Court at Rome. On another occasion the priest was alleged to have defrauded a woman of Hedon, near Hull, of a considerable sum of money, with which she had been hoping to buy herself a place in an Abbey: Colynson, it was said, had hood-winked the woman into handing over the money by promising her that, once he had said a mass for her at the church of Scala Coeli, her soul would be free forever from pain. But despite these and other charges brought against him before the King's Council, Colynson was never tried, as he should have been, by an ecclesiastical court; until his death he retained the rectorship of Chelsfield in Kent while, in March 1460, the Pope presented him with the Irish bishopric of Ross.

The guarantees of absolution offered by Colynson are remi-niscent of Berthold of Ratisbon's sermon denouncing the penny-preacher who 'murdered right penance' by using 'all manner of deceit whereby he may coax pennies from his hearers, and their souls into the bargain': a sermon in which Berthold also speaks of 'a certain sin which hinders us far and wide from the sight of the true sun. This sin is called covetousness for wealth—filthy lucre . . .' Among the 'many folk . . . who strive for filthy lucre, and gain filthy lucre . . . are deceivers in their trade and handi-work'.[19] In other sermons Berthold makes more specific mention of shopkeepers who cheat their customers by selling them hats through whose brims the rain will pour down into the purchasers' bosoms and other sub-standard and virtually useless goods; of piece-workers and day labourers who cheat their employers, either by working too fast, without attention to quality, or by idling away the hours for which they are being paid to work; of traders who, to the accompaniment of many dreadful and blasphemous oaths, underpay and oversell; of dishonest vintners, corn merchants, butchers and bakers, who offer for sale corrupt wines and mouldy corn, rotten meat and unwholesome bread; of vendors of all sorts of goods who use faulty scales or otherwise give short measure. In the opinion of Berthold, as of many other medieval writers, wherever merchants foregathered, there was likely to be 'so much fraud and falsehood and blasphemy that no man can tell it'.[20] And indeed, as towns became both more numerous and more populous, so did the authorities find it necessary to introduce more and more laws ordering the pillory and increasingly heavy fines for dishonest traders and shop-keepers. But from the frequency with which they were reiterated it is clear that these measures must have been largely ineffectual. 'There is one merchant in these days,' Chaucer's friend, John Gower, writes in his *Mirour de l'Omme*, some hundred years after Berthold of Ratisbon's outburst, 'whose name is on most men's tongues: Trick is his name, and guile his nature: though thou seek from the East to the going out of the West, there is no city or good town where Trick doth not amass his ill-gotten wealth. Trick at Bordeaux, Trick at Seville, Trick at Paris buys and sells; he hath his ships and his crowds of servants, and of the choicest riches Trick hath ten times more than other folk. Trick at Florence and Venice hath his counting-house and his freedom of the city, nor less at Bruges and Ghent; to his rule, too, hath the noble city on the Thames bowed herself, which Brutus founded in old days, but which Trick stands now in the way to confound, fleecing his neighbours of their goods: for all means are alike to him whether before or behind; he followeth straight after his own lucre, and thinketh scorn of the common good.'[21]

Although the majority of crookedly inclined salesmen may have gone no further in their dishonesty than to rely on a combination of glib speech and misrepresentation to defraud the unwary of small or large sums of money, there were nevertheless some who only used the tricks of the market place as a prelude to more vicious crimes. According to Guibert of Nogent, for instance, some townspeople of Laôn resorted in the early years of the twelfth century to a 'practice, which occurring amongst barbarians or Scythians, men having no code of laws, would be regarded as most iniquitous. When on Saturday the country people from different parts came there to buy and sell, the townsfolk carried round as for sale beans, barley, or any kind of corn in cup and platter and other kind of measure in the market place, and when they had offered them for sale to the country men seeking such things, the latter having settled the price promised to buy. "Follow me," said the seller, "that you may see the rest of the corn that I am selling you, and when you have seen it, may take away." He followed, but when he came to the bin, the honest seller, having raised and held up the lid, would say, "Bend your head and shoulders over the bin, that you may see that the bulk does not differ from the sample which I showed you in the market place." And when the buyer getting up on the pediment of the bin leaned his belly over it, the worthy seller standing behind lifted up his feet and pushed the unwary man into the bin, and having put the lid down on him as he fell, kept him in safe prison until he had ransomed himself'.[22]

Probably Guibert's 'honest seller' was no merchant at all, but simply one of the increasing number of professional thieves who found it more profitable, and often safer, to operate and to live in towns, than to lurk in the forest. For despite curfews and a wide variety of other measures intended to discourage criminal activity in the towns—like insisting, as many town councils did, that strangers, beggars and other undesirables should spend the night outside the city gates, or imposing a communal fine on citizens who failed to produce those who committed crimes in their neighbour-hood before the courts—it was seldom difficult, either for locals who turned to crime, or for fugitives from other areas, to become absorbed into the shifting underworld of thieves, beggars, fences, pickpockets and receivers of stolen goods which no medieval town of any size was without.

As might have been expected, among the favourite haunts of such people were the taverns, which often doubled as brothels, and of whose landlords' and landladies' tendency to consort with and to harbour criminals the authorities were well aware. In 1285, the Statutes for the City of London explain that it is forbidden to keep open house after curfew 'because . . . offenders . . . going about by night, do commonly resort and have their meetings and hold their evil talk in taverns more than elsewhere, and there do seek for shelter, lying in wait and watching their time to do mischief'.[23] Half a century later, 'An Inquest as to Evildoers and Disturbers of the King's Peace' tells the same story over and over again: to give but one example from the report covering this general round-up of criminals, Thomas Whiteheved, Joan la Tapstere and William atte Pond were presented by the jurors of Broad Street and adjacent wards as being persons of ill-fame; their House in Apcherche Lane 'Atte pye on the hope' was a brothel and, with the neighbouring brew-house, a resort of bad characters.[24] Eighty years later again, King Henry V ordered a similar series of raids to be made on London's underworld. Typical of the sort of evils recorded by Henry V's team of investigators are the following: 'Item: Behind the Pye [a tavern] in Queenhythe is a privy place which is a good shadowing for thieves and evil bargains have been made there: and many strumpettes and pimps have their covert there . . . Item: in Crepulgate they indite Gerard Clayson and his wyfe of the Estewehous in Grub Street as evildoers and receivers and main-tainers of harlotry and bawdry . . . and of strumpettes and other malefactors. . . .'[25]

Little different, it seems, from the sort of men and women who were alleged to have frequented Gerard Clayson's establishment in Grub Street, were some of those who, at the turn of the thirteenth and fourteenth centuries, had been in the habit of spending their evenings boozing with John Senche, the Keeper of both the Palace of Westminster and the Fleet prison, and William of the Palace, his deputy. Often these drunken junketings were held in the Keeper's lodge of the royal Palace itself; and here it was that a number of monks from Westminster Abbey first met, in 1302 or 1303, Richard

31 A thief stealing from a coffer in church.

Pudlicott, a dealer in butter, cheese and wool, who had come to London, so he said later, in order to sue for the return of £14.17s. due to him as a result of his having been arrested in Flanders as surety for debts left there by King Edward I. Finding the merchant congenial company, the monks sometimes asked him to dine with them in their refectory—thus providing Pudlicott with the opportunity to familiarise himself with the Abbey's layout, and most particularly, at this stage, with the whereabouts of its silver plate. One night in March 1302, a window of the chapter house was forced, and a quantity of valuable plate hustled out through it.

On the proceeds of this burglary, Pudlicott was able to continue carousing with his intimates till towards the end of the year. But by December the money was beginning to run out and it was then, according to his confession, that Pudlicott hit upon the ambitious idea of robbing the royal hoard of treasure, which he knew to be stored in the crypt under the chapter house of Westminster Abbey. Since 1298, when Edward I had moved the law courts, the Chancery and the Exchequer to York (so, incidentally, making a nonsense of Pudlicott's claim to be in London to initiate legislation for the recovery of monies owing to him), more and more officials had gone north to be nearer their royal master, most of whose energies were devoted between 1298 and 1303 to fighting the Scots. Only a skeleton staff remained at Westminster; and with several of its members Pudlicott was by now well acquainted.

Again according to his own highly improbable confession, rather than enlisting the help of the friendly sacrist, Adam of Warfield, who could easily have admitted him to the sacristy from which a door led into the crypt, Pudlicott preferred to pass many winter nights hacking a way through the outside wall of the chapter house, which was in some places as many as thirteen feet thick. In doing this he was assisted, so the indictment claims, by masons and carpenters; while, in order to conceal what must have been the increasingly apparent evidence of his activities, he himself later said that he had sown quick-growing hemp seed. On April 24, 1303 he achieved his goal; but not until the 26th did he emerge from his Aladdin's cave, laden down with so much treasure that he had to stop and bury some of it in St Margaret's churchyard. Then, after two nights of drunken celebration at a house which was actually inside the compound of the Fleet prison, he and some of his cronies set out, armed, for the wardrobe treasury, and were back again before dawn, with as large a haul as they could carry.

Although contemporary estimates put the value of the goods stolen from the crypt at about £100,000, it was not until some of the loot began to find its way into the hands of London's metal-workers and money-changers, and precious dishes and cups were discovered in St Margaret's churchyard and in the fields round Westminster, that anyone seems to have suspected that the royal treasury might have been robbed. So why, then, did Pudlicott and his drinking companions not return to their tunnel? The answer is, in all probability, a very simple one: that the tunnel had never existed. For by the time the Keeper of the Wardrobe arrived at Westminster on June 20 to check his inventories, articles identified as having come from the treasury had been recovered, not only from Pudlicott's lodgings, but from several Westminster monks, including Adam of Warfield, and from under William of the Palace's bed. That such people should have been in possession of a share of the royal treasure would seem to imply at any rate complicity, if not indeed—as some believed—that the robbery had been an inside job, master-minded by the sacrist, Adam of Warfield, and that Pudlicott's 'confession' was merely used, by royal officials and ecclesiastics alike, as a screen behind which to hide their own guilt. Be that as it may, on June 25 Pudlicott was taken from sanctuary in St Michael's Church, Candlewick Street, and soon afterwards indicted, together with William of the Palace, the Abbot and forty-nine monks of Westminster Abbey, and thirty-two laymen. Of these, most were released on bail; but in November the King ordered a new commission of investigation, and at sessions held from January through to March 1304 Pudlicott, Adam of Warfield, William of the Palace, and several monks and laymen were pronounced guilty of having been involved in the robbery.

William of the Palace and five other laymen were hanged that same year while Richard Pudlicott, who had tried to join Adam of Warfield and the monks in claiming benefit of clergy, was similarly executed a year later, in October 1305.

Still more questionable, evidently, than the behaviour of some of Edward I's household officials, who were left behind at Westminster during his long absences in Northern England and Scotland, had been the conduct of many officers of the French Crown in the period preceding King Louis IX's return from six years spent on Crusade in 1254. For, as a first step in 'the reform of his kingdom' after he 'returned to France from oversea', Joinville tells us that Louis found it necessary to promulgate a number of detailed ordinances, in an attempt to put a stop to various abuses of their authority by 'Our bailiffs, sheriffs, provosts, mayors, and all others, in whatever matter it may be, or whatever office they may hold . . .' While all royal officials were to take an oath 'that, so long as they remain in office, they will do justice to all, without respect of persons, to the poor as to the rich, and to men from other countries as to those who are native-born . . .', it was also enacted 'that, on vacating office, all bailiffs, sheriffs, mayors, and provosts shall remain, either in person or by deputy, for a further forty days in the district where they have exercised their functions, so that each may answer to the incoming officer with regard to any wrong done to such as wish to lay a complaint against him'. As for the important provostship of Paris, the King 'forbade the selling of the office . . . and arranged for a good and generous salary to be given to those who should hold it in future', because it had 'invariably happened that those who bought this office condoned all offences committed by their children or their nephews, so that these young delinquents became accustomed to relying on those who occupied the provostship. In consequence people of the lower classes were greatly downtrodden; nor could they obtain justice against the rich, because of the great gifts and presents the latter made to the provosts'.[26]

It was against this background of corruption in high places and among those generally, both lay and ecclesiastical, who were expected to set an example, that thousands of poorer people had been persuaded, when Louis IX was captured by the Saracens after his defeat at Mansura in 1250, to join the ranks of the so-called Pastoureaux, or the Shepherds' Crusade. And it was because their members had reached the pessimistic conclusion that the first concern of anyone put in authority over others must be to feather his own nest, that many Italian City Councils had begun, in about 1200, to appoint men from other cities, who had no local ties or interests, to be their chief magistrate or 'Podesta', each for a carefully limited number of years. But whereas Kings and City Councils could always try, at least, to remedy what struck them as an unsatisfactory state of affairs by introducing new laws, the only means of righting things which seemed to be available to the more militant poor was to do as the Pastoureaux eventually did, and attempt to wipe out those people whose wickedness they imagined to be responsible for their sufferings.

In the case of the Pastoureaux, the enemy on whom the popular fury came to focus was the 'avaricious' and 'luxurious' Church. But, like so many other quasi-religious popular movements in the later Middle Ages, the Crusade of the Shepherds had started as one thing, and ended up as another. First preached by three men in Picardy at Easter 1251, the leadership of the Shepherds' Crusade was soon assumed by a renegade monk by the name of Jacob, who was also known as the 'Master of Hungary', whence he was supposed to have originated. A forceful and eloquent speaker in French, German and Latin, Jacob claimed, like others both before him and after him, to have been visited in a dream by the Virgin Mary, who had given him a letter as token of her having instructed him to encourage good and humble people—like the simple shepherds to whom the news of the Nativity had first been made known—to go to the relief of their captive King and to free the Holy Sepulchre. Within a matter of weeks only, Jacob had attracted to his banners depicting his visitation by the Virgin a horde of men, women and children, which included, as well as shepherds and cowherds, the inevitable complement of apostate clerics, prostitutes, thieves, murderers and other desperadoes who were always eager to lend a hand in such enterprises. This force Jacob divided into fifty companies; and proceeding, as about half their number did, armed with knives, pitchforks, axes and daggers, towards Paris, the simple 'Shepherds' struck as much fear into the hearts of the authorities in some areas through which they passed as they did joy into those of the destitute, the oppressed and the restless, many of whom hastened to join them.

But, the uncouth appearance and the often openly menacing attitude of the Pastoureaux notwithstanding, at Amiens the townspeople were so impressed by their holiness that the crusaders were supplied with free food and drink, while the Master of Hungary was besought to help himself to any of their belongings which might be so fortunate as to take his fancy. And again, when the crusaders reached Paris, the Queen Mother seems to have been so touched by Jacob's eloquence, and by the thought of these simple souls going to her son's rescue, that the leader was showered with presents and the crusade given her blessing.

Perhaps Jacob had thought it best to conceal from the pious King's mother that he considered the Papal Court to be a sink of iniquity, friars to be hypocrites and vagabonds, Cistercians to be obsessed with land and with property, Premonstratensians to be vainglorious gluttons, and canons regular no better than semi-secular fast-breakers? Perhaps he had omitted to tell her that in his opinion the murder of a priest might be atoned for by drinking some wine? And perhaps, too, the favour shown him by the Queen Mother had gone to his head? For no sooner had Queen Blanche given him leave to do as he chose in Paris, than Jacob's followers set about murdering as many clerics as they could lay their hands on—the students of the University narrowly escaped massacre by closing the bridge which led to their quarter on the left bank of the Seine—while their leader took to preaching in churches, dressed up as a Bishop, and performing weird ceremonies of his own devising with holy water.

On leaving Paris, the Pastoureaux went first to Tours, where the delighted populace applauded them as they whipped friars through the streets, looted the church of the Dominicans and launched an attack on the Franciscan friary. Next, at Orléans, where the Bishop had had the city locked and barred against the Pastoureaux but the townspeople had thrown the gates open again, a scholar who had the effrontery to argue with Jacob was cut down with an axe. Houses in which the clergy were thought to have taken refuge were broken into, looted and burned. Priests, monks, friars, University teachers and scholars were, along with several laymen, either hacked and stabbed to death, or drowned in the Loire. News of these events spread widespread alarm among the clergy; wherever churchmen heard that the Pastoureaux were approaching their district, they made themselves scarce.

By the time the crusaders arrived at Bourges, where the citizenry defied an archiepiscopal order to refuse them entry into the town, there was hardly a cleric to be found. However, when he saw that his followers had been deprived of their accustomed victims, on whom the local populace could also usually be relied upon to turn, the resourceful Jacob preached a sermon instead about the Jews: and, once they had destroyed the sacred scrolls belonging to the town's Jewish community, it was not long before the crusaders were killing not only Jews but Christian burghers, whose houses they pillaged and whose women they raped. But by now reports of the Shepherds' activities had travelled to Paris, and the Queen

Mother had finally been persuaded to outlaw the movement upon which, earlier, she had bestowed the royal blessing. On learning that their crusade had been outlawed, large numbers of Pastoureaux deserted, but Jacob, with a hard core of supporters, continued to urge the townsfolk to seek out and to exterminate the clergy, until one day a man presumed to contradict something he had said, and the infuriated Master of Hungary struck him dead with a blow from a sword. At last the burghers lost patience. The Master of Hungary was ridden down and slashed to pieces, while many of his supporters were rounded up by royal officials and hanged. Of the survivors, some eventually appeared at Aigues Mortes and Marseilles, where they intended to take ship for the Holy Land, but were in fact hanged; another group, which made its way to Bordeaux, met with a similar fate at the hands of Simon de Montfort, then Governor of Gascony. One of the Bordeaux band who managed to escape to England, and collect a small following at Shoreham, was in the end torn limb from limb by his own men.

In 1315, a year when bad harvests were reported to be driving some of his less fortunate subjects to cannibalism, King Louis X of France announced that, since every man was according to natural law born free, he intended to free all the serfs of the royal demesne. But as this freedom had to be bought—and at fairly high prices—the royal decision only added to the hardships caused by the famine: and when, therefore, in 1320, Louis's successor, King Philip V, was unwise enough to suggest a new expedition against the Infidel, his proposal, although dismissed as being altogether impracticable by the Pope, was received with wild enthusiasm by the very same sort of desperate people who had in 1251 thrown in their lot with the Master of Hungary. Once again, in 1320, it was in Northern France that a renegade monk and his colleague, a defrocked priest, began to preach the crusade; once again the first to answer the call to battle were poor country people, cowherds, swineherds and shepherds; and once again, as they made their way towards Paris, the ranks of the crusaders were swelled by outlaws and beggars, by professional criminals and unemployed men and women from the towns through which they passed.

When the 1320 band of Pastoureaux arrived at Paris, they broke into the Châtelet and assaulted the Provost. Next, on being told that troops were to be used to disperse them, they arranged themselves as if for battle in St Germain-des-Prés. But the authorities made no move. Disappointed, the Pastoureaux set off south-westwards, in the direction of English-held Gascony. Although officially all Jews had been expelled from France in 1306, wherever the Pastoureaux managed to find Jews, they encouraged the local populace to join them in murdering them and in looting their property. After the Jews, it was the turn of the clergy. Fearing that the Pastoureaux might attack the Papal Court at Avignon, Pope John XXII, after excommunicating the crusaders, called upon a military force commanded by the Seneschal de Beaucaire to move against them. The populace, which had so far tended to side with the Pastoureaux, was ordered, on pain of death, not to open town gates to them or give them any food. As a result of these measures, many Pastoureaux died of hunger, while for three months the military continued to harass them, capturing large numbers of them and stringing them up from trees. Finally, the few remaining Pastoureaux straggled through the Pyrenees into Spain, where they went on hunting out and murdering Jews until they were routed by an armed force led against them by the son of the King of Aragon.

Although European Jewry had provided a regular butt for the zeal of rank and file crusaders since the days of the First Crusade in 1096, it is significant that in 1320, as in 1251, the Pastoureaux and the urban proletariat should have found common cause too in their hatred of the clergy. For what the growing commercialism of the later Middle Ages made more immediately apparent to town-dwellers and to countrymen alike, was not only the widening gulf that divided poor men from rich men, but the enormous wealth of the Church; and, as more and more laymen seem to have come to the sad conclusion that the Church was more intent upon accumulating still greater riches than it was interested in fulfilling either its spiritual duties or its obligations towards the needy, so did increasing numbers of poor people hasten to follow popular leaders whose rantings against the ecclesiastical establishment tended to make the authorities regard them as heretics.

In theory a convicted heretic was supposed to be burned to death, whereas an ordinary rebel or insurgent might be punished in any number of ways. But in practice the dividing line between the two types of criminal was sometimes a blurred one; for, since it was from among those who were worst affected by changing economic and social conditions that many heretical sects recruited the majority of their adherents, it not infrequently proved impossible to say whether the inspiration of a popular movement was primarily religious, or whether its origins and aims were chiefly political. Indeed so closely, in particular, did eschatalogical and millenarian heresies become bound up with social unrest in the last centuries of the Middle Ages, that it is almost always in anticipation of the Last Judgement, or of the Millennium—and very often on the fringe of larger but less radical movements for reform—that a few people are to be found advocating the sort of thoroughgoing social revolution which was in general uncharacteristic of the Middle Ages.

Prominent among later medieval thinkers whose revolutionary ideas seem to have influenced the programmes of people more actively militant than themselves were two mid-fourteenth-century writers, the Franciscan, Jean de Roquetaillade, and the English scholar, Wyclif. Kept in ecclesiastical prisons for the last twenty years of his life, and several times threatened with being burned as a heretic, de Roquetaillade produced his *Vademecum in tribulationibus* in 1356, the year of King Jean II of France's capture at the Battle of Poitiers, and two years before the peasant uprising known as the Jacquerie. The *Vademecum* prophesied great upheavals throughout the whole of Christendom. Between the years 1360 and 1365, the populace would take up arms against the rich and the powerful, and rob them of the riches which they had acquired at the expense of the poor. In the midst of floods, tempests, plagues and Infidel invasions, with two Antichrists disseminating false doctrines from Rome and from Jerusalem, rulers and people would unite to massacre all greedy churchmen and take away their property. Then, in 1367, peace would be restored. An ever-victorious King of France would be elected Emperor and, with the help of a reforming Pope, this new Charlemagne would put an end to heresy and idolatry, so making of the whole world one Christian community, the most marvellous characteristic of which would be the dedication of everyone in it to the pursuit of holy poverty. After the death, within two years, of the Pope and the Emperor, the reign of peace would endure for another thousand years, until the end of the world.

While it is unlikely that many of the villeins who terrorised central France in 1358 would even have heard of de Roquetaillade's *Vademecum*, the work was nonetheless sufficiently popular to be translated into Catalan, English and Czech, and it seems reasonable to assume therefore that some inkling of the views put forward in it must gradually have filtered through to a very much larger public than would actually have been able to read it. And the same was probably true also of Wyclif's treatise *De civili dominio*, written at Oxford in 1374, in which the teacher argued: 'Firstly, that all good things of God ought to be in common. The proof of this is as follows: Every man ought to be in a state of grace; if he is in a state of grace he is lord of the world and all that it contains; therefore every man ought to be lord of the whole world. But, because of the multitudes of men, this will not happen unless they all hold all things in common: therefore all things ought to be in common.'[27] Almost immediately Wyclif goes on to say that such a theory cannot, of course, be applied to everyday secular life, in which good men must put up with irregularities and, trusting in God's inscrutable wisdom, leave the unjust in possession of their ill-gotten power and wealth. But even if this brief sortie into the world of communistic theory may have been no more than an academic exercise in syllogistic logic, Wyclif was an influential teacher and there are in fact echoes of the passage quoted from his *De civili dominio* to be found in the sermons of, for instance, one of the most radical of the English rebel leaders in 1381, as reported both by Froissart and the English chronicler Thomas of Walsingham. 'Good people, things cannot go right in England and never will,' Froissart tells us John Ball was in the habit of informing the audiences he mustered in the cloisters or graveyards as they came out of church on Sundays after Mass, 'until goods are held in common and there are no more villeins and gentlefolk, but we are all one and the same.'[28]

Like de Roquetaillade's *Vademecum in tribulationibus*, Wyclif's works too were well known in Bohemia, where moves originally aimed at reforming an immensely rich and, at the higher levels, a largely foreign-staffed ecclesiastical establishment eventually led, in the early fifteenth century, to the setting up of a series of progressively smaller, but more and more extreme, anarcho-communist communities. As early as the 1360s the corruption of the Bohemian Church had prompted a number of popular preachers to identify the times in which they were living with the Age of Antichrist and to announce the imminence of the Second Coming. But John Hus, who became the chief spokesman of the reformers at about the turn of the fourteenth and the fifteenth centuries, took a more moderate line. Rector of Prague University and a self-proclaimed admirer of Wyclif, he did no more than oppose the indiscriminate sale of indulgences and maintain that, when papal laws contravened the Eternal Law of God, as laid down in the Scriptures, it was the duty of the good Christian to ignore them. Yet this for the Council of Constance was enough. When in 1414 Hus answered a summons to appear before the Council, and refused to recant his opinions, he was burned as a heretic.

In his home country, where for some years now growth in unemployment had been matched by a corresponding upsurge of Czech resentment of the wealthy Germans who owned large tracts of land and held many important positions in Bohemia, the news of Hus's execution had the effect of uniting King Wenceslas, the Czech nobility and those who had been agitating for Church reform in a co-operative attempt at implementing some, at least, of the changes for which Hus came to be thought of as having given his life. During the four or five years that this uneasy alliance lasted, a relatively calm atmosphere pervaded both capital and countryside. But then, in 1419, King Wenceslas was prevailed upon by his brother Sigismund, who was Emperor of Germany, and by Pope Martin V, to change sides; and, when in July of that year he ordered all Hussite councillors to be dismissed from the 'New City' district of Prague, the predominantly Hussite populace of the area responded by breaking into the town hall and flinging the new royal nominees out of the windows.

A month later King Wenceslas died, reputedly from shock at the mob's treatment of the anti-Hussite councillors. But although the July insurrection succeeded in wresting the government of the 'New City' from the hands of the old patrician families, and placing it in those of the Hussite-controlled guilds of artisans, there were many Hussites whose reaction to the German-inspired persecution of their movement was to demand very much more radical changes than those proposed by the comparatively prosperous guild-members. From the name of 'Mount Tabor' which some of them gave to a hill beside the river Lužnica on which they installed themselves to await the Second Coming, the more radical Hussites, who were drawn chiefly from the lowest strata of the urban and rural proletariats, soon became known as 'Taborites'; and in the early months of 1420, at Písek in Southern Bohemia, the Taborites launched their first experiment in 'returning', as some of their leaders put it, to a communal way of life, in which all goods were to be held in common, all men would be bound together by brotherly love and none was to be subject to the control of another. Converts to the Taborite movement were urged to sell all their possessions and to deposit the proceeds in the community chests administered by the Taborite priesthood, while at Mount Tabor itself the private ownership of any property whatsoever was held to constitute a mortal sin.

Almost certainly the best-known Taborite was John Zizka, a member of the lesser nobility and the commander of the Czech nationalist forces, who, in March 1420, moved his headquarters from Plžen to Tabor. Called away soon afterwards to help fight off the army which the Emperor Sigismund had sent against the non-Taborite Hussites of Prague, Zizka and the Taborites who served under him did not return to Tabor until September, by which time the funds in the community chests had run nearly dry. Concessions made in the spring to the peasantry of areas controlled by the

Taborites were withdrawn. Taxes, services and dues were not only reimposed, but increased. Bands of Taborites, who seem to have expected to be fed like Adam and Eve in Paradise by the hand of Providence, had taken to pillaging the countryside.

Exhausted by the fight against the Emperor's forces, and disappointed by the failure of their efforts to create a truly egalitarian society, the more moderate Taborites now began to abandon their communistic principles and, while still insisting on 'Utraquism' (or the taking of communion in both kinds), to revert to a way of life little different from that which they had led before they became Taborites. But not so the more hysterical and fanatical Taborite splinter groups, several of which were in fact suppressed, not by the Catholic authorities, but by the order of John Zizka. In April 1421, for instance, it was Zizka who captured Peter Kanis and some seventy-five of his 'Adamite' followers, and burned them as heretics. And again, in October of the same year, it was a force despatched by Zizka which finally succeeded in exterminating the remainder of the Adamites, whose particularly fanatical blend of religious and political convictions evidently required them, when they were not prancing naked round bonfires chanting hymns, to wage a 'Holy War', at first against priests and the rich, but in the end against virtually anybody who had the misfortune to live within striking distance of their last stronghold on an island in the river Nezarka.

As in England in 1381, so in Bohemia in 1420–1, the most extreme revolutionaries made their appearance when a significant proportion of the population was already agitating for reform; as in England, during the course of the Peasants' Revolt, the idea of an egalitarian community seems to have fired the imaginations mainly of people who were more interested in the destruction of the old order than in building anything new; and as in England, those men who were thought to have popularised such ideas were denounced by both Church and State as being heretics, and dealt with accordingly. But although medieval advocates of an anarcho-communistic society may have met with little success in turning their visions into any sort of political reality, their failure in no way undermined, or even shook, the popular belief in the Day of Judgement as a day when the rich and the mighty, who had misused the powers entrusted to them, would be cast down from their pinnacles into the lowest pits of Hell, and the poor and the humble received into the Life Everlasting in the Kingdom of Heaven.

Comforting as the prospects of eventual redress and a place in Heaven might be supposed to have been, they did not, however, prevent many of the poorer inhabitants of medieval Europe from doing as Wat Tyler's English peasants or the Prague Hussites did, and resorting to physical violence as a means of improving their material lot in the world here below. But whereas concerted moves on the part of skilled workers like the Flemish weavers, or the members of the Prague artisans' guilds, may from time to time have succeeded in seizing control of a town council from the rich merchants, who owned the lion's share both of urban real estate and of the capital invested in manufacturing processes and commerce, the disorganized rebellions of unskilled labourers and journeymen seldom achieved anything more than their own bloody suppression. For, while the unemployed and the unemployable could usually be relied upon to support any revolt of the skilled workers against the rich capitalists, the skilled workers, on the other hand, were inclined to view the motley insurrections of the very poor with no less apprehension than the wealthy merchants; and as a rule, therefore, when the unskilled proletariat showed signs of becoming restive, the skilled workers would unite with their sometime enemies, the important capitalists, to make sure that the poor man whose 'belly is hollow' did not 'hack down', as the fourteenth-century German poet Suchenwirt put it, 'the rich man's doors and burst in to dine with him'.[29]

In the unsettled economic and social climate of the later Middle Ages—and in a world, moreover, where a woolcarder could be hanged, as was Cinto Brandini at Florence in 1345, for defying the influential Arte della Lane by trying to form his wretchedly-paid fellow unskilled workers into a guild and calling them out on strike—it is hardly remarkable that unskilled members of the proletariat should have made a substantial contribution to the urban crime rate. But no less of a menace to the good order of most medieval towns and cities was the tendency of their better-off inhabitants to use violence, or the threat of violence, as a means either of furthering their business interests or of settling differences with their political or personal enemies. For the street fights between Shakespeare's Montagues and Capulets were no more unique to Verona than to Italy. In London, when Andrew Bucquinte was put on trial for having made an armed raid on a rival merchant's house, John Screex, who was generally reckoned to be one of the richest Londoners of his day, was among those whom Bucquinte accused of having taken part in the affray. (Bucquinte was unlucky: his offer of 500 marks for a 'free pardon' was refused, and he was hanged.) Then too there were the more discreet burghers, who preferred to hire professional criminals to do their dirty work for them. And then again, in addition to the wide variety of rivalries and animosities which might prompt one layman to try to harm the person or property of another, there was the by no means always passive hostility which larger and larger numbers of laymen of all classes and conditions felt towards churchmen.

In few places was anti-clerical prejudice more pronounced than in University towns, where lay resentment of the privileges enjoyed by the clergy was considerably exacerbated by the ease with which it seemed to laymen that both students and teachers could, in most cases when they were accused of breaking the law, avoid being tried in the secular courts by pleading benefit of clergy. Nor are there many medieval documents which better describe the sort of trouble to which this resentment might lead than an early four-teenth-century petition addressed by the Roman Senators to the absentee Pope at Avignon. 'Know indeed, most Holy Father,' the Senators write, 'that many in the city [of Rome], furnished only with the shield and privilege conferred by the first tonsure, strive not in honesty of manners, but rather, are ordinarily guided by the rule of horrible misdeeds; wandering armed from tavern to tavern and other unhonest places; sometimes going on to quarrel or fight in arms with laymen; committing manslaughter, thefts, robberies and very many other things that are far from honesty. For which things'—and here is the familiar lay complaint against benefit of clergy—'no safeguard or remedy is applied by the ecclesiastical judges holding the place of your most Holy See; but rather, when [these evildoers] are accused of the aforesaid misdeeds in our courts, they compel us to release them from our examination, saying that they themselves will see to the infliction of a fine upon them; and thus, under the cloak of such assertions, these so nefarious and most criminal men, hateful both to God and to man, pass unpunished.' That such 'miscreants who call themselves clerics and yet comport themselves as layfolk . . . are . . . not punished out of their evil courses,' say the Senators, redounds to the discredit both of the Papacy and themselves. 'Wherefore we most piously beseech your Holiness, with all humility and devotion, that if it should so befall that our rigour should go so far as to punish them in virtue of our office as judges, then you would vouchsafe (if it so please you) to permit this unto us and to support us in future with the authority of your Holiness.' Not of course, the canny Senators are quick to reassure the Pope, 'that we are on this account minded to go so far as to touch clerics in possession of church benefices, whom we are purposed and ready to treat with all due reverence, since we are unwilling to do anything derogatory to ecclesiastical liberties'. But what they fear is that 'if the aforesaid impious fellows are not controlled to some extent by the secular arm, then the people of Rome will grow to such horror of these their misdeeds as to rise up in wrath and fury not only against these, but even against the aforesaid clerics who are zealous for the orthodox faith'.[30]

One of the earliest recorded Town versus Gown riots occurred at Paris, in 1200, when the servant of a young German student called Henri de Jacea was assaulted in a tavern and a group of German scholars from the University retaliated by beating up the tavern-keeper. When the Provost of Paris was told of this, he resolved to teach all unruly scholars a lesson. Having summoned a number of citizens to arm themselves and come with him, he stormed the hostel in which the Germans had their lodgings; and among the students killed in the ensuing battle was de Jacea, who turned out to be not only an Archdeacon, but the Bishop-Elect of Liège. Understandably, the Masters of the University were outraged. Unless they were granted proper redress, they told King Philip Augustus, who no doubt valued the University as a useful recruiting-ground for government servants, they would leave Paris altogether: and it seems to have been in response to this threat that the King gave instructions for the drawing up of the University's first extant Charter of Privileges, a document in which it was laid down that all future Provosts must swear on oath to try to see that the scholars' privileges were respected. As for the Provost who had been responsible for the attack on the hostel, he was duly sentenced to spend the rest of his life in prison (this unless he preferred to submit to trial by the ordeal of fire or water: if cleared by one of these, he would be banished from Paris; if convicted, he would be hanged). Anybody else who had joined in the attack, and who was unable to persuade the injured scholars to intercede on his behalf, was also condemned to life imprisonment; if such a person succeeded in evading arrest, his house was to be razed to the ground.

Another celebrated clash between the city police and University of Paris has come to be known as the affair of the Pet-au-Deable (Devil's Fart or, more substantially perhaps, Devil's Turd), a name it takes from that of a colossal boundary stone, which, on an autumn day in 1451, some University students dragged away from outside the house of the widow of one of Charles VI's notaries and re-erected, as a sort of totem around which to frolic and roister, on the Mont St Hilaire. Within a week of the theft, the widow had reported her loss to the city authorities, and the stone was with great difficulty removed from the Quartier Latin to what was thought to be the safety of the courtyard of the Palais Royal. But before the end of the following week the Pet-au-Deable was back in the students' quarter. On November 15, 1451, the Parlement of Paris instructed Jehan Bezon, the Criminal Lieutenant of the Provost, to look into the matter.

As a result of his investigations, which occupied him on and off for more than a year, the Criminal Lieutenant was able to rehearse a long list of grievances against members of the University, when, nearly two years later, he and thirteen other officials connected with the Châtelet, including Robert d'Estouteville, the Provost, were accused before the Court of Parlement of having acted in flagrant contempt of the University's privileges.[31] To start with, Jehan Bezon told the Court on Tuesday, June 5, 1453, the students had not stolen one boundary stone, but two. The second stone they had set up on the Mont Ste Geneviève, referring to it as 'La Vesse', forcing passers by to salute it and dancing 'round it every night to the sound of flutes and drums'. On other occasions, bands of scholars had stolen meat hooks from the butchers of Ste Geneviève, poached fowls from St Germain-des-Prés and 'taken away by force a young woman at Vanves'. They had also created terrible disturbances by roaring through the streets at night, tearing down or smashing tavern and inn signs and shouting, 'Kill, Kill!' One night, when several scholars were trying to take the sign of 'The Spinning Sow' (which they intended to 'marry' to 'The Bear'), the ladder up which the would-be thief had tried to climb had proved to be too short and the young hooligan had fallen to his death, 'so it was said'.

At last Robert d'Estouteville's patience in the face of this mayhem gave out. On December 6, 1452, he sent some of his men with a cart to take the Pet-au-Deable away from the Quartier Latin. According to Counsel for the University at the trial in 1453, the scholars made no attempt to prevent their prize from being removed. So imagine their astonishment when a group of the Provost's Serjeants, quite suddenly as it seemed to the innocent youths, went berserk. First, these officials started shoving the students about. Then, on the pretext, so they said, of flushing the thieves of the signs and butchers' hooks out of their hiding-places, they battered their way into the house of a priest, who was out saying mass, and ransacked it. 'Break everything, take everything,' the Criminal Lieutenant was alleged to have urged his men on, 'and kill anybody who stands in your way.' Next, the Serjeants stove in the doors and windows of another house, and drank all the wine they discovered inside. And finally they burst in on a lecture being delivered by Master Darian, a distinguished teacher, and seized some forty young men from among his audience.

For five months the prisoners taken by the Serjeants remained in custody, while the members of the University pondered their next move. Then, on May 9, 1453, a procession of close on a thousand unarmed Doctors, Masters and students marched behind the Rector to Robert d'Estouteville's house in the Rue de Jouy. The prisoners, said the Rector, should be handed over to the ecclesiastical authorities; this would be done, said the Provost: and all might perhaps have been amicably settled if the academics had not, in turning about, come face to face with a band of Serjeants, which was proceeding in the opposite direction up the Rue de Jouy towards them. According again to the University's evidence, it was a Serjeant named le Fèvre who, with no provocation whatsoever, as the two groups were passing one another, suddenly called out to his companions to come to his rescue, and so precipitated a bloody riot in which the Rector narrowly avoided being murdered and a young Master of Arts called Raymond de Mauregart was killed.

At the trial of the Provost and his officers before the Parlement, the Court accepted the University's claims that the students who had stolen the fowls from St Germain had long ago been punished by the Bishop's Court, and that the alleged theft of butchers' hooks and abduction of the young lady from Vanves (who had herself proposed the visit to the students in question and had, when she made it, proved most reluctant to leave their hostel) were fabrications on the part of the Lieutenant. It also agreed with the University that while those students who had stolen tavern signs or boundary stones certainly deserved to be punished, the punishments should have been meted out by the proper authorities and there should not have been any bloodshed. Indeed, although the University was forced to concede that some of the forty prisoners arrested by the Serjeants had not in fact been clerics, the academic party had good reason to be pleased with the view that the Court took of the affair. Of the fourteen people charged with having violated the scholars' privileges, only Robert d'Estouteville escaped unscathed. On June 16, Serjeant Charpentier, who was said to have killed de Mauregart and to have threatened the life of the Rector, was ordered to make 'amende' to the University, by kneeling, with a rope round his neck, in various public places, and there humbly begging forgiveness of the King and the University. In addition, he was sentenced to have his right hand cut off and to pay a fine of 400 livres Parisis. The other defendant Serjeants were banished from Paris and, still more gratifying to the scholars on the subject of whose alleged misdemeanours he had compiled his weighty dossier, the courts recommended that Jehan Bezon be removed from the post of Criminal Lieutenant.

Among those admitted Masters of Arts at Paris University during the course of that summer, when the Pet-au-Deable provided a focal point for student revelry on the Mont St Hilaire, was the poet, François Villon. Born François des Loges or de Montcorbier (the latter after his father's native village in the Bourbonnais) in 1431, Villon later took the name of his relative and guardian, Guillaume de Villon, a respected and, in matters concerning his ward, a most indulgent priest, whose household in the cloister of St Benoît-le-Bientourné in Paris the future poet seems to have entered when he was about seven or eight years old. Since the by-then fatherless boy was, as his poor mother had perceived with some relief, quick-witted, Master Guillaume undertook—as, presumably, the mother had hoped he might—to supervise and, when necessary, to sponsor his education. Probably in about 1443, the young François de Montcorbier would have begun his studies at the University, where he was in 1449 received a Bachelor and, three years later, a Licentiate and Master. Yet, whatever company de Montcorbier, *dit* Villon, may have kept until his twenty-fourth year—and, to judge by the picture of the man which emerges from his poetry, this was unlikely to have been of the most salubrious sort—there is no official record of his having fallen foul of the law before 1455, when, at about nine o'clock on the evening of June 5, he mortally wounded a priest called Chermoye, with whom he had become involved in a fight. As soon as his own wounds had been dressed by a barber named Foucquet, Villon prudently fled from Paris; and remained out of the city until, in January of the next year, the efforts of his friends to obtain a Letter of Remission for him met with such success as to procure two of these pardons, the first of them awarded to 'Master François des Loges, otherwise known as Villon' and the second to 'Master François de Montcorbier'. In both Letters Villon is represented as having acted in self-defence while, in the second, the expiring Chermoye is reported to have told an officer of the Châtelet that he forgave Master François any injuries he had done him.

Thus triply pardoned, Villon returned to Paris, where the next crime in which he was accused of having had a hand was committed on or about Christmas Eve 1456, between the hours of 10 p.m. and midnight. Having dined 'at the sign of the Mule', the poet and another Master of Arts named Guy de Tabarie, two talented pick-locks called Colin des Cayeulx (also a clerk) and 'Petit-Jehan', and a lapsed Picard monk known as Dom Nicolas made their way to an empty house which shared a party wall with the Faculty of Theology's headquarters in the College of Navarre. Here, de Tabarie was posted sentinel, a ladder was propped against the wall, and the others disappeared into the College. Two hours later the four emerged again. From a rifled coffer in the sacristy they had extracted a haul of about a hundred crowns, they told de Tabarie, to whom they gave ten crowns as his share of the night's takings. Then they divided up the rest of the money among themselves, afterwards giving de Tabarie another two crowns, with which they suggested he buy himself a good dinner on the morrow. Not until the following day did Master Guy learn that the amount stolen had in fact been between five and six hundred gold crowns, and that the others had pocketed more than a hundred crowns each.

Such was the version of the College of Navarre robbery offered by Master Guy de Tabarie at his examination by the Bishop's Official on July 5, 1458, a month after his arrest and some eighteen months after the events described had taken place.[32] Obviously, de Tabarie was more frightened of the tortures to which he might be—and, indeed, subsequently was—put, than he was of reprisals on the part of those whom he had incriminated. Of these, the real villains of de Tabarie's piece, it is known that François Villon had left Paris in time to spend Christmas 1457 at the court of the poet-Duke, Charles of Orléans, at Blois, and that almost four years after the robbery, on September 26, 1460, Colin des Cayeulx, having been pronounced so incorrigible a rogue that he had forfeited his right to benefit of clergy, was hanged by the secular authorities for highway robbery and rape; of Petit-Jehan and the renegade monk, Dom Nicolas, no further record survives.

From what he himself says in his verse, and most particularly in his chef d'oeuvre, *Le Grand Testament*, it seems that Villon spent the four years following this, his second flight from Paris, roaming from town to town, living by his wits. For even if he may have been flush at first with the share of the College of Navarre's treasure which Guy de Tabarie was to tell the Bishop's Court he had received, by the poet's own account it is clear that he was all too soon reduced to depending on what he could steal or scrounge. True, at St Généroux, near Parthenay, there were good times to be had with two jolly girls; at Blois, for a while, the liberality of the ducal kitchens and, possibly, a small stipend, later cut off; at Moulins a loan of six crowns from Duke Jean II of Bourbon, maybe more. But at Bourges there was some sort of trouble with the authorities and, for the most part, Villon seems to have lived the life of the vagabond:

32 A group of mendicants on their travels.

sleeping in ditches, swiping poultry, pilfering and spending the
occasional lucky windfall on women and wine.

When, on July 17, 1460, the two-and-a-half-year-old daughter of
Duke Charles, the little Princess Marie, made a progress through
Orléans, among those prisoners released from the town goal in
celebration of this 'joyous event' was François Villon, who had for

some unknown crime been condemned to death earlier in the summer and had spent the past few weeks gloomily waiting for a noose to be slipped over his prematurely bald head. A year later, he was back in gaol—this time at Meun, where he seems to have been submitted to the water torture and the rack. Again the crime with which he was charged is unknown; and again he was saved by a 'joyous event'. On October 20, 1461, the new King, Louis XI, stopped at Meun, on his way from Paris, via Orléans, to Bordeaux: and Master François Villon was the happy recipient of a plenary pardon, in which all his past offences against the law were forgiven him.

No sooner had Master Guillaume had this new Letter of Remission confirmed by the appropriate authorities in Paris, than his errant protégé was back in his old room in the house in the cloister of St Benoît. But, whatever new leaves the younger Villon may have promised to turn over, the first week of November found him standing trial before the Court of the Châtelet, accused of having committed a minor theft. In the event, the Court declared the charge to be unproven; but, just as Villon was about to be released, Master Jehan Collet, the Procurator of the Faculty of Theology, stepped in with an application for a writ of *Ne exeat*. His request was granted. Villon was again brought before the Court and, when examined about the part he had played in the College of Navarre robbery, made a full confession. For a transcript of this confession, the Grand Beadle of the Faculty of Theology, Master Laurent Poutrel, who was also a Canon of St Benoît-le-Bientourné, paid over eleven sols Parisis; and, armed with this document, hastened round to confront his dear colleague, Master Guillaume. Very likely Master Guillaume would have pleaded the Letter of Remission: and very probably Master Laurent would have reminded him how easy it was, with a Letter of Remission, for a clever lawyer to find some irregularity in the wording which might be held to make the pardon invalid. As it was, however, the Faculty was not so much interested in the criminal aspect of the robbery as in initiating civil proceedings, which Letters of Remission did not cover. Now, in the case of de Tabarie, the Faculty had agreed to drop all charges against him on condition that his mother stood surety for him to repay fivefold, in two yearly instalments, the ten gold crowns which he admitted to having received as his share of the loot. But since Master Guillaume was, after all, such an old friend . . .

On a day between November 2 and 7, 1462, François Villon was released from the Châtelet prison, in return for his written undertaking, guaranteed by poor, long-suffering Master Guillaume, to repay, in three annual instalments of forty crowns each, the one hundred and twenty gold crowns which he had confessed to having stolen from the Faculty of Theology. But before the end of the month he was back in the same gaol, wrongly accused of having been involved in a brawl (from which he had in fact fled before it had properly begun), but with too familiar a face by now to be able to interest the officers of the Châtelet in his protestations of innocence. Indeed, from the way in which they handled his case, it is clear that Pierre de la Dehors, the new Criminal Lieutenant, and Jacques Villiers de l'Isle-Adam, the Provost, had decided the time had come to settle this pestiferous clerk once and for all. Of Villon, like des Cayeulx in 1460, the Bishop seems at last to have washed his hands. After being submitted to the water torture in the question-chamber of the Châtelet, perhaps once, perhaps twice, the poet was hauled before the Provost and sentenced to be hanged by the neck.

Only in one direction did there lie the smallest hope of obtaining a reprieve. From the Conciergerie prison, to which he had been transferred to await execution of sentence, Villon applied for leave to appeal to Parlement; and, almost incredibly, as it must have seemed to him in view of the Provost's evident determination to see him hanged, he was given permission to do so. On January 3, 1463, the Court of Parlement announced its decision in the matter: the sentence of death by hanging was annulled but, because of Villon's notoriously bad character, he was forthwith banished from the town, Provosty and Viscounty of Paris for ten years. Very humbly, the haggard poet asked if he might be allowed three days' grace, in which to say his goodbyes and to try to scrape together some money for his journey? Yes, this would be in order, the Court told him. And no more is known about Master François Villon.

As so often happens with people whom subsequent generations have endowed with semi-legendary status, it is sometimes impossible to distinguish, in all that has been said in the last five hundred and more years about Villon, between fiction and fact. But since seven of his poems are written in the 'jargon' of the so-called 'Coquille' (literally a shell, so possibly by derivation a sword-hilt, or maybe in some way connected with the shell which a person who wanted to pass himself off as a pilgrim might carry), there does not seem to be any reason to question the tradition which holds that, at some time before he was banished from Paris, the poet had joined the ranks of this association of criminals, the style of whose life is most expressively described, in the year 1455, by Jehan Rabustel, the Procurator-Syndic and Clerk to the Tribunal of Dijon.[33] 'The case is thus,' runs Rabustel's evidence against those members of the Coquille whom he and a band of heavily-armed men had captured in a night raid on a brothel run by one Jacquot de la Mer, a suspected receiver of stolen goods: 'For two years past there has infested, and still infests this Town of Dijon, a number of idle and vagabond companions who, on their entry and during their stay in the said town, do nothing except drink, eat, and squander money at dice, at cards, at "marelle", and other games. Most usually, and especially at night, they hold their assembly at a brothel, where they lead the filthy, vile, and dissolute life of ruffians and scoundrels, often losing and squandering all their money till they have left not a single dernier. And then, when they have taken all they can from the poor common prostitutes they frequent in the said brothel, some of them disappear in directions unknown, and are absent some for fifteen days, some for a month, some for six weeks. And they then return, some on horseback and some afoot, well clothed and harnessed, with plenty of gold and silver, and once more begin, with those who await them, or with new arrivals, their accustomed games and debaucheries.'

Nor was the Procurator-Syndic in any doubt as to how 'the said gallants [who] call themselves the Coquillards' came by their gold and silver. 'It is also a fact, as is affirmed, that some of the said Coquillards are picklocks of coffers, chests and treasuries. Others work with their fingers in cheating over the changing of gold to small money and back again, or in the buying of goods. Others make, carry, and sell false ingots of gold, and chains resembling gold: others carry and sell false jewels in place of diamonds, rubies, and other precious stones. Others lie at an inn with some merchant and rob themselves and him alike, passing the booty to a member of their gang; and then they lodge a complaint in company with the said merchant. Others play with loaded dice and win all the money of those who play with them. Others practise such skilful tricks at cards and "marelle" that no one can win money of them. And what is worse, most of them are footpads and bandits in the woods and on the highroads, robbers and assassins, and it is to be presumed that it is thus that they are able to lead such a dissolute life.'

For those who broke down under torture and confessed, or who were otherwise found guilty of the more serious crimes with which they were charged by Rabustel, the end had come. They were either boiled alive or hanged. But, for those who were lucky enough to escape with minor convictions and were banished from Burgundy, there can have been little difficulty in joining—as Villon may well have done after he was banished from Paris—another regional

33 French beggars in the fifteenth century.

division of this redoubtable freemasonry of criminals, all of whom
were believed by the Procurator-Syndic of Dijon to owe allegiance
to a mysterious figure, who was, 'as it is said, a king, called the King
of the Coquille'.

Also mentioned in the Procurator-Syndic's evidence is the 'fact
that the said companions use among themselves a certain jargon
and other signs by which they know each other'. Whatever the
'other signs', it is clear from Villon's *Ballads of the Jargon* that the
'certain jargon' of the Coquillards was in fact a version of the 'argot'
or 'jobelin' (from Job, the patron of beggars), which was current
among the lower echelons of French criminal society. But although
several attempts have been made at updating this language—
which was, like any other slang, always changing—the argot
remains for the most part untranslatable, either into modern French
slang or into any other tongue. From 'pain', bread, came the argot
word 'pantière', meaning mouth; legs were 'quilles', ninepins, and
arms were 'lyans', literally binders. Some words were ordinary
French words, either lengthened or shortened; many words were
used metaphorically or metonymically, often in an ironic sense; and
some words were given a new meaning because of their similarity
in sound to the word which would ordinarily have been used, as in
Cockney rhyming slang. Then, in addition to words of French
origin, at least one philologist has claimed to have discovered in the
argot words taken from the language of the Gitanos or Gypsies, an
unfamiliar people of whom nobody was quite sure what to make
when a band of them appeared at Lüneberg in 1417, but who soon

succeeded in acquiring the reputation of being accomplished liars, swindlers, sneak-thieves and tricksters. According to M. Francisque Michel, sheets were known in the argot as 'limans', and a chambermaid as a 'limogère', from the Gypsies' word 'lima', meaning a shirt; similarly, a rich man was called a 'rupin' and a knife a 'chourin', from the Gypsies' words 'rup' and 'chori', meaning silver and knife.[34]

Not to be confused with Jehan Rabustel's 'king, called the King of the Coquille', is the Grand Coesre, or King of the Beggars, a monarch who generally held court at Paris, in one of the thieves' meeting-places known in France as 'Cours des Miracles', and whose subjects throughout the country paid an annual tax. Immediately below the Grand Coesre in the criminal hierarchy over which he presided were the Cagoux, whom he appointed to look after his interests in the provinces. And beneath the Cagoux, there were the Archisuppôts, whose job it was to train new recruits, who were usually required to serve an apprenticeship—and quite often, in the manner of the apprentice to a regular craft-guild, to produce (or more accurately, perhaps, to commit) an 'épreuve de maîtrise' or masterpiece—before being admitted to full membership of the brotherhood. In return for initiating the apprentices into the secrets of their profession, the Archisuppôts were allowed to beg in any way that they chose, and without paying taxes to the Grand Coesre; while, in addition to being similarly exempted from paying fees, the Cagoux, whose duties included the collection of monies due to the Grand Coesre and the sorting out of freelance operators who refused to recognise his authority, were allowed to take a share of any property stolen from persons whom they had ordered to be robbed.

As for the rank and file member of this French beggars' Mafia, he or she would be expected to stick to his or her special line in mendacious beggary, and the amount which he or she paid to the Grand Coesre would be determined by what this line was. Thus the Marcandiers, who tried to excite sympathy by pretending to be merchants who had been robbed, or been ruined by wars, were required to pay one écu. But the Francs-Mitoux, on the other hand, who affected to fall down in public places in fainting fits, were only taxed to the tune of five sous. Among the other descriptively named categories of dishonest beggars to which an 'Argotier', or a subject of the Grand Coesre, might belong, there were the Malingreux, who made themselves up to look as if they were suffering from dreadful swellings and sores; the Piètres, who hobbled or crawled about on crutches and sticks; the Sabouleux, also known as the Poor Sick of St John, who daubed themselves with blood and sucked and blew on pieces of soap, to give the appearance of frothing at the mouth; the Polissons, who went about as good as naked, begging for clothes; the Courtauds-de-Boutanche, who carried the tools of a particular trade with them and pretended to be out of work; and the Hubins, who displayed forged certificates announcing that they had been bitten by a mad dog and were on their way either to or back from seeking a miraculous cure at the Shrine of St Hubert.

In an age when the sort of havoc wrought by plagues, famines and wars was forever throwing more and more people out of work, and so leaving them dependent on the charity of their more fortunate neighbours, it is not difficult then to understand why later medieval governments should have become increasingly fierce about insisting, not only that people should stay in their own neighbourhoods, where they were known, but that travellers should carry with them papers stating who they were and why they had undertaken their journey. For, although no other country seems to have possessed quite so highly organized a confraternity of thieves and petty criminals as France, the methods by which the subjects of the Grand Coesre sought to pass themselves off as deserving of charity were known to able-bodied beggars and vagabonds throughout Western Europe. In London, for instance, in 1380, John Warde of Yorkshire and Richard Lynham of Somerset were found guilty of having fraudulently collected alms by pretending to be merchants who had had their tongues torn out with an iron hook and a pair of pincers, both of which instruments they showed people—together with a tongue-shaped piece of leather inscribed 'This is the tongue of John Warde', and to the accompaniment of strange rattlings and roaring sounds which they had learned to make in their throats.[35] Then again, in Italy, there were the Affrati, who pretended to be poor monks or priests; the Allacrimanti, or weeping ones, who burst into what they hoped were deeply touching floods of tears; and the Accosti, who said they had recently escaped from slavery, and begged for money to ransom fellow-Christians who were still in the hands of the Turks or the Saracens. But few medieval thieves or beggars can have succeeded in assuming a more unlikely character than a contemporary of St Bernardino's, who, at night, used to tie a bag round his thighs and a bell round his neck and, thus disguised as one of the six pigs who were Siena's answer to the garbage problem, steal corn and flour from the market-place, around which he rootled and snorted, on his hands and his knees.

6

Prostitutes

CARNAL PLEASURE was, in the opinion of the Church, an invention of the Devil, the direct result of Man's Fall from Grace and a mortal sin. Before the Fall, says St Augustine, the sexual organs had, like all the other organs, been under control; so that if Adam and Eve should at this time have performed the sexual act—an event which Augustine is quite certain never took place—then that act would have been 'entirely decorous'. With the Fall, though, 'the lust that excites the indecent parts of the body' escaped from the mind's control to assume power 'not only over the whole body, and not only from the outside, but also internally', disturbing the whole man and resulting, if gratified, in a pleasure so intense 'that when it reaches its climax there is an almost total extinction of mental alertness'. Must not 'any friend of wisdom and holy joys', who lives a married life, asks St Augustine, prefer, if possible, to beget children 'without lust of this kind'?[1]

If sex was, unfortunately, necessary to the reproduction of the human species, the Church declared, it was nonetheless very wicked to derive any enjoyment from this animal function. Pope Gregory the Great, in the eighth century, thundered his condemnation of such base pleasures and some churchmen went so far as to demand that there should be restrictions on sexual intercourse even within marriage—an attitude that was to be responsible for the appearance in the later Middle Ages of the chemise cajoule, a sort of thick nightshirt with a strategically placed hole in it, through which a pious husband might impregnate his wife with the minimal risk of experiencing pleasure in the discharge of his duty.

While it is doubtful that this extraordinary garment was ever in great vogue, the views of such influential thinkers as St Thomas Aquinas were, in any case, by the thirteenth century, rather more balanced. The urge towards coital pleasure was, as it had always been, said the angelic doctor, the result of the Fall but, since God had created man's nature, it was not a sin in itself; only if it was pursued for itself and 'in such a way as to submerge reason' did it become sin.

So much for the theory of the matter: a theory whose main achievement seems to have been the introduction of a novel frisson of sinfulness into what had hitherto been regarded simply as a healthy and highly pleasurable diversion. It was St Augustine himself, in a more practical mood, who had said that if prostitution were to be suppressed, capricious lusts would then overthrow society; and this sentiment was reiterated in the later period by Aquinas, who wrote in his *Summa Theologica*, apropos of prostitution, that if you were to take away the sewer, the whole palace would soon be filled with corruption.[2] Prostitution was, in other words, a necessary evil.

Of the sumptuous brothels and bathing establishments, however, in which the Romans had been accustomed to satisfy their sometimes gross sexual appetites, few escaped the general destruction of the barbarian invasions. The prostitutes of the earlier Middle Ages were to be found rather amongst the scavenging bands of fugitives from justice and serfs of both sexes who had run away from their masters—bands which would trail along in the wake of merchandise being transported to markets, or of armies on the march. Others of this motley society would attach themselves to the groups of pilgrims on their journeys to the Holy Places while, if St Boniface is to be believed, the lady pilgrims themselves often fell literally by the wayside, losing sight of their original devout goal and embarking instead on a new and most ungodly career. It was a great scandal to the Church, Boniface advised Cuthbert, Archbishop of Canterbury, in a letter of 747, that so many English women and nuns should be allowed to set out on the pilgrimage to Rome for very few of them returned intact and there was scarcely a city in Lombardy or in Gaul where you could not find several of these English pilgrims turned prostitute.[3]

For as long as there was slavery in Western Europe, the slaves were, of course, available to slake the sexual appetites of their owners and their owners' friends. But, as the Church met with more and more success in its campaign to eradicate slavery, the traffic in women, in particular, became increasingly frowned upon and its operation gradually confined to the inhabitants of the wilder

34 *A prostitute in a sea port beckoning from her door.*

fringes of Christian influence, and beyond: to the Rani of the island of Rügen and the Pomeranians who sold women captured in special raiding parties to the East; to the Vikings who sometimes sold their more dissolute womenfolk to the Arabs; and to the pre-Conquest English, who, according anyway to William of Malmesbury's somewhat prejudiced account, followed a 'custom repugnant to nature. . . ; namely to sell their female servants, when pregnant by them and after they had satisfied their lust, either to public prostitution, or to foreign slavery'.[4] Within the frontiers, meanwhile, of the Carolingian Empire, where a man discovered with a prostitute was required to carry her upon his shoulders to the whipping bench, accusations of trafficking in women—and, in the case of the Jews, Christian boys too, whom they were believed themselves to have castrated—were levelled chiefly at non-believers: at Jewish and Arab merchants, and most especially at Arab horse-dealers.

In this earlier period of turbulence and generally weak government, prostitution was not, on the whole, organised. But, with the rebirth of the towns, organised prostitution began to revive. For, while the dregs of the profession continued to travel in the baggage of the armies or to throw in their lot with bands of mercenaries or criminal gangs, the advantages to a prostitute of life in the more settled environment of a prospering mercantile community were obvious. From the eleventh century onwards a growing number of strollers', who had hitherto plied a peripatetic trade, absconding serfs and outlaws flooded into the burgeoning towns, where the shrewd mercantile mind soon tumbled to the fact that some of these women were doing very well for themselves, and that a tax on their earnings might provide a useful addition to the community funds. Nor was it long before this desire to participate in the ladies' good fortune, together with the necessity of supervising their activities, with a view to maintaining both order and hygiene, led to the setting up, usually just outside the city walls, of official brothel areas, known in France and Germany as 'women's quarters'. The inhabitants of these quarters, who were often required to wear some distinguishing ribbon, cloak or bonnet, thus became licensed and were taken under the protection of the authorities; whereas unauthorised operators and freelances (such as the 'crazies', who would, under pretence of being possessed, strip off in the marketplaces and outside churches to display their wares), from whom it was less easy to obtain a cut of the profits, were to be taken to the city gates, birched and formally exiled. In many places the use of the brothels was forbidden to certain classes of person: to priests, of course, everywhere; often to Jews; sometimes to married men; and, in the case of Vienna, to the city bakers as well.

An early example of legislation designed to regulate, and so tacitly condoning, prostitution is the 'Ordinaunces touching upon the Government of the Stewes of Southwark under direction of the Bishop of Winchester.'*5 That these 'stewes' should have belonged to the Bishop of Winchester need not surprise us for, although most ecclesiastical bodies sought, as the Bishops of Winchester had done in the earlier twelfth century, to avoid charges of direct participation in the management of their brothels by subletting them, the most

---

* The fashion of bathing, so much enjoyed by the Romans, is thought to have been revived by the returning crusaders, who had sampled the pleasures of the Eastern hammams. As early as 1100, there is evidence of hot baths or 'estewes' having been set up on London's Bankside; although, to begin with, these establishments were segregated, by the time of the Ordinaunce a 'stewe' was simply another name for a brothel.

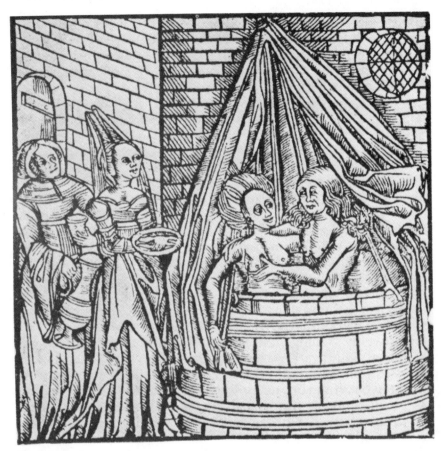

35 *A 'stewe'*.

cursory glance at the records will reveal that all through the Middle Ages many bishoprics, abbeys, monasteries and even the Papacy—which towards the close of the Middle Ages could hope to make in a good year as much as 20,000 ducats from its premises leased out to brothel-keepers—included whorehouses, amongst their properties. Disputes between religious foundations and lay powers over the revenue from bawdy-houses are no rarity, while, in 1309, we find Bishop Johann of Strasbourg building, at his own expense, a magnificent new brothel in that city.

Of greater interest, therefore, than the Bishops of Winchester's ownership of London's main brothel area are the actual provisions laid down by Henry II's 'dyvers ordinaunces and constitutions' for the regulation of what is referred to as 'orrible synne'. All of these are, says the preamble to the legislation, old customs that have

applied 'oute of tyme of mynde'. But lately, 'to the gret displesuir of
God & gret hurte unto the lorde King', they have been ignored.
Horrible sin has multiplied, the poor tenants of the manor of
Southwark have had a rough time of it, women are being kept in
brothels against their will . . .

'For th'eschewing of this inconvenientes', the King ordains that
no stew-holder is to prevent a single woman from coming and
going as she pleases; nor is he to insist on her living on his premises;
nor, if she should choose to live in, is he to charge her more than
fourteen pence a week for her room. If a woman should want to give
up whoring, no stew-holder is to stop her. Nor must he receive a
woman who is visibly pregnant or married women or nuns. Nor,
under pain of expulsion from the parish, must he open his establishment on religious festivals or other Holy Days. No woman was
to take money from a man unless she lay with him all night. If a
customer refused to pay, he was on no account to be detained in the
stew-house but must be taken to the Lord of the Manor's prison.
Although the whores might sit at their doors, they were forbidden
to solicit or to throw stones at passers-by. A stew-holder who kept a
woman in his house who had 'any sikeness of brennynge' was to be
fined twenty shillings. No stew-holder was to own a boat (the
Manor of Southwark was on the opposite bank of the Thames,
across the river from the City of London), to keep more than one
washerwoman and one male ostler or to lend more than six shillings
and eightpence to any woman. If the Parliament was sitting at
Westminster or if the King was holding a meeting of the Privy
Council, all the women must leave the lordship for the duration of
the session.

The ordinance also provided that the Bailiff should make weekly
visits of inspection, to check whether any of the women had become diseased or if there were any who were being kept there
against their wishes. This Bailiff, whose own job was strictly regu-
lated lest he should try to defraud either the King or the Lords of the
Manor of their just revenue by taking bribes or holding back for
himself any part of their dues, was further instructed to ensure that
both the women and the stew-holders had been observing the
regulations by asking each group, on his weekly visits, a specially
prepared set of questions. Breaches of the various rules were to be
punished by a graduated system of fines, ranging from three shillings and fourpence for minor infringements to much stiffer penalties for offences such as the failure of a stew-holder to report to the
Bailiff or his officers a woman who had come clandestinely to his
establishment. In this latter case, the stew-holder was to be fined

forty shillings and the woman, who was also to be set three times upon the cucking-stool and then thrown out of the Manor, twenty shillings.

A remarkable feature of Henry II's legislation, and one in which it differed from its continental counterparts, was its insistence on the brothels themselves being sober and utilitarian places. The customer was to be served with a woman—a whole night of her, indeed—and a woman only, for no stew-holder was permitted to offer his customers any ale, bread, meat, fish, candles, 'nor any othere vitaill'. From the exasperated tone, however, of the many subsequent reiterations of Henry's ordinances, it is clear that this improbable attempt at turning the roistering Southwark stewes into lugubrious sex-shops met with little success.

Equally unsuccessful were the efforts of the Papacy, some seventeen years later, to remind a new crop of crusaders of the holy nature of their mission and so to try to dissuade them from taking with them an unseemly complement of prostitutes. In 1188, Roger of Hoveden tells us, Pope Clement III wrote the Kings of France and England, the Count of Flanders and other leaders of the proposed expedition a letter, in which he urged 'that no one was to take any woman with him on pilgrimage, unless, perhaps, some laundress to accompany him on foot, about whom no suspicion could be entertained . . .'[6] Of the number of prostitutes who actually accompanied the crusaders on the journey we have no record, but an Arab writer has left a highly-coloured description of a boat-load of 'three hundred lovely Frankish women, full of youth and beauty, assembled from beyond the sea and offering themselves for sin', who followed soon after.*[7]

'They were expatriates come to help expatriates,' writes 'Imad ad-Din, 'ready to cheer the fallen and sustained in turn to give support and assistance, and they glowed with ardour for carnal intercourse. They were all licentious harlots . . . singers and coquettes, appearing proudly in public . . . tinted and painted, desirable and appetising . . . like tipsy adolescents, making love and selling themselves for gold . . . with nasal voices and fleshy thighs, broken-down little fools. Each one trailed the train of her robes behind her and bewitched the beholder with her effulgence. She swayed like a sapling, revealed herself like a strong castle, quivered like a small branch, walked proudly with a cross on her breast, sold her graces for gratitude, and longed to lose her robes and her honour.'

* These girls would not necessarily all have been French, for to the Arabs as to the Byzantines, Western Europeans were known generically as 'Franks'.

'They arrived', Imad continues, 'after consecrating their persons as if to works of piety and offered and prostituted the most chaste and precious among them. They said that they had set out with the intention of consecrating their charms, that they did not intend to refuse themselves to bachelors, and they maintained that they could make themselves acceptable to God by no better sacrifice than this.' Hoping thus to win the approval of their Maker, 'they set themselves up each in a tent or pavilion erected for her use, together with other lovely young girls of their age, and opened the gates of pleasure. They dedicated as a holy offering what they kept between their thighs; they were openly licentious and devoted themselves to relaxation; they removed every obstacle to making of themselves free offerings. They were permitted territory for forbidden acts, they offered themselves to the lances' blows and humiliated themselves to their lovers'.

As might have been expected, the girls 'plied a brisk trade'. They were 'Imad tells us, by now quite carried away by his own powers of imagery, 'the places where tent-pegs are driven in, they invited swords to enter their sheaths, they razed their terrain for planting, they made javelins rise towards shields, excited the plough to plough, gave the birds a place to peck with their beak, allowed heads to enter their ante-chambers and raced under whoever bestrode them at the spur's blow . . . They interwove leg with leg, slaked their lovers' thirsts, caught lizard after lizard in their holes, disregarded the wickedness of the intimacies, guided pens to inkwells, torrents to the valley bottom . . . They contested for tree trunks, wandered far and wide to collect fruit and maintained that this was an act of piety without equal, especially to those who were far from home and wives. They mixed wine, and with the eye of sin they begged for its hire.'

Could Clement II have read this account, he would doubtless have turned in the grave to which he had by this time been consigned. But it is significant (despite the obvious exaggeration and despite 'Imad's purple prose) that some of these girls were as happy, apparently, 'making of themselves free offerings' or selling 'their graces for gratitude' as they were to 'sell themselves for gold'. For herein lay one of the major obstacles to efficient legislation about prostitution: there were so many semi-amateurs or occasional practitioners that it was impossible to keep track of them. Already in Henry II's ordinances of 1161, as we have seen, heavy penalties were prescribed for 'women who come clandestinely to

36 *Monks in a bath-house 'to the great dishonour of the City'.*

37   *A young gentleman visits a German brothel, accompanied by a jester.*

the brothels' while in 1338 we find one William de Dalton, a London spicer, being committed to prison for keeping a House of Ill-fame, to which married women had resorted. A later ordinance, sponsored by Henry V and issued by the Mayor and Aldermen of the City of London, in 1417, for the Abolition of the Stews within the City of London refers, in its preamble, to the same evil. After lamenting the many 'grievous abominations, damages, distur-bances, murders, homicides, larcenies and other common nuisances' that have resulted from the harbouring of 'lewd men and women of bad and evil life' in stews within the City and in its suburbs, the preamble goes on: 'and what is worse . . . the wives, sons, daughters, apprentices and servants of the respectable men of the City . . . are oftentimes drawn and enticed thereto [the stews] . . . to the great dishonour of the City . . .'[8]

If even the wives and daughters of respectable citizens were in the habit of repairing to these 'sinks of iniquity' to quench their sexual appetites, and perhaps to earn a little pin money, how much more tempting must it not have been for a poor girl from the country or for the mother of a starving family to jump at the opportunity of alleviating her own or her children's miserable condition by selling her body? 'Be very wary,' the Goodman of Paris advised his young wife, of girls wanting positions as maids who come with references from their previous employers, 'as often-times such women from distant parts of the country have been blamed for some vice in their own district and this it is that brings them into service at a distance'; and, on the sort of money sensible people like the Goodman saw fit to pay them, we can be sure that not a few serving girls, whether or not they had been 'blamed for some vice in their own district', resorted to part-time whoring in order to supplement their meagre wages. But would they, on this account, have thought of themselves as prostitutes? Would they, any more than the randy wives and daughters of their masters, have considered presenting themselves to the appropriate authorities and becoming officially registered?

Of all medieval monarchs, the most concerned about prostitution from the moral point of view was almost certainly St Louis of France, whose grandfather, Philip Augustus, had shown no signs of being bothered by any such anxiety. Indeed, very much the opposite: when the growth of Paris University was accompanied by a marked increase in prostitution, King Philip II had smiled upon it. For Philip's particular sexual bugbear was homosexuality; and since, in his opinion, more readily available prostitutes must necessarily mean less unnatural vice, the whores and their help-mates he reckoned his allies. That a large number of students should have spent their time pimping for the prostitutes of the Quartier Latin was, of course, unfortunate: nevertheless, the profession as a whole and, in particular, well-run 'bordels' (from the old French 'bordeau', originally a small house near water or an arbour) were encouraged; a new official, the Roi des Ribauds, was appointed to look after the interests of the 'corporation' of Parisian prostitutes at court; and the result, at least to the grandson's way of thinking, was disaster.

During the course of his long reign (1226–70), Louis was to make several attempts at reforming prostitutes by offering them induce-ments which he hoped might persuade them to give up their trade. On one occasion, he promised a pension to any whore who would repent her ways and withdraw herself from the market; and, in addition to founding and endowing a good many new houses of béguinage for the accommodation of women who decided to dedi-cate their lives—or what was left of them—to practising the virtues of chastity, he also built, the Sire de Joinville tells us, 'another establishment outside Paris, which was called the Maison des

Filles-Dieu. In this he placed a very large number of women, who, through poverty, had become prostitutes, and allowed them, for their maintenance, four hundred livres a year'.[9] But to Louis's surprise and considerable chagrin, very few whores seemed to want to be reformed. In the case of the pension offer, although a contemporary chronicler asserted (with some exaggeration, no doubt, since the total population of Paris was then about 150,000 persons) that there were at least 12,000 prostitutes in the capital, only 200 ladies came forward to claim their reward. And, even when a prostitute did profess herself desirous of amending her ways, there was still little anyone could do to ensure that she would in fact stick to her resolve. At the Maison des Filles-Dieu, for instance, it proved quite impossible to prevent some of the more incorrigible residents from making sorties to their old haunts, or worse, in that it set a disturbing example to the other inmates, from bringing clients back to the actual Maison itself.

In the face of such female perversity and general lack of stead-fastness, St Louis determined to introduce stricter measures. Although he did not go so far as the city fathers of Vienna—who were to order, in 1383, that a reformed tart who had married and then reverted to prostitution was to be flung into the Danube—in 1254 he issued an edict ordering exile from her parish and the confiscation of all her possessions for any woman who, having been once admonished, continued to prostitute herself. But the difficulties involved in enforcing this legislation turned out to be insurmountable; in so far as it achieved anything, the chief effect of the edict seems to have been to drive prostitution underground, thereby making any kind of official control still more of a problem.

But, except in the case of a few godly men like St Louis, the secular authorities' main objection to prostitution was not so much the immorality of the business as the tendency of the whores and their pimps and panders not only to provide a refuge for criminals, but all too often to aid and abet them in their various criminal activities. In London, in the thirteenth century, there were repeated complaints about bands of people who made expeditions across the river from the brothel area of Southwark to pick the citizens' pockets, to rob them and even to murder them. In 1285, Edward I decreed that 'whereas thieves and other . . . light persons of bad repute are . . . more commonly harboured in the houses of women of evil life within the City than elsewhere, through whom [are perpetrated] evil deeds and murders . . . and great evils and scandals', any 'common whore' found dwelling within the walls of the City was henceforth to be imprisoned for forty days. Boatmen were to keep their boats moored on the City side of the river after sunset, 'nor may they carry any man nor woman neither denizens nor strangers into the Stewes except in the daytime, on pain of punishment . . .'[10] In 1417, the same year in which, as we saw earlier, the Mayor and Aldermen of the City had maintained that the harbouring of 'lewd men and women of evil life' was giving rise to 'many grievous abominations, damages, disturbances, murders . . . etc.', complaints were also made about protection gangs, who were demanding 'imposts' from . . . 'the poor common people who time out of mind have fetched and carried their water and washed their clothes and done other things for their own needs . . .'[11] In France, at about the same time, François Villon tells us that he and his fellow criminals were constantly in and out of Paris brothels like Fat Margot's (where Villon himself sometimes acted as an attendant, serving the clients with 'pots and wine . . . cheese and fruit and bread and water as they please');[12] while at Dijon in 1455 it was, as we have seen, in a brothel that the Procurator-Syndic succeeded in capturing a large number of the local Coquillards.

But much as they all of them deplored the high incidence of crime among prostitutes and those with whom they associated, there were very few medieval Kings, Popes, Bishops or town councils who were prepared to deprive themselves of an important source of revenue by seeking, as St Louis did, to get rid of prostitution altogether. As a rule, therefore, what the authorities tried to do rather was to bring prostitution more and more directly under their own control; and, by tightening up the regulations designed to confine the trade to controlled areas, to reduce the chances both of their being cheated of their share of the profits, and of such official brothel areas, at any rate, becoming infested with criminals. Thus in France, for instance, St Louis's impractical edict was replaced in 1367 by a more sensible ordonnance which restricted prostitution to specific districts, where the whores were required to wear distinctive clothing and subjected to medical inspections.*

* The names of the medieval brothel areas were often explicit, and some of them have lingered on, in a contracted form, into the twentieth century. In fourteenth-century London there were Slut's Hole, Gropecuntlane and Codpiece Alley, the last two still persisting as Grape Street and Coppice Alley; without the city walls was Cokkeslane. Mary Stuart, it is said, used to faint, whenever, in Paris, her route took her through the rue Trousse-Puteyne (literally Whore's Slit Street); while the French capital also boasted a rue Grattecon (Scratchcunt Street), a rue du Chapon (for those who preferred boys, presumably?) and, just outside the town limits, a rue du Poil au Con, today the rue de Pélécan, where there were to be found prostitutes who refused to comply with a city regulation requiring them to shave their private parts.

38 *Another brothel, complete with open air theatre on the first floor.*

Although syphilis was unknown as such in Western Europe until the diagnosis of the first recorded case at Naples in January 1496, the prevalence of other forms of venereal disease in the Middle Ages made some sort of medical supervision extremely important. For popular ignorance and irresponsibility with regard both to venereal diseases and sexual hygiene were often quite appalling. In his account of the Black Death of 1348–9, the chronicler Knighton reports, for example, that while many Englishmen thought sexual intercourse prevented catching the plague, others actually believed that the contraction of a venereal disease would work as an antidote: with the result that, once the general terror of the epidemic had subsided, the greater part of the population, from the highest-born noble to the meanest labourer, abandoned itself to wanton and utterly reckless promiscuity.*

In times of panic like these—when, if the chroniclers are to be believed, a sort of desperate profligacy seems to have become the rule of the day—it was, of course, difficult to enforce any laws, let alone those by which it was hoped to control prostitution. But once the immediate threat of a fatal epidemic or of an invading army (which often had much the same effect on the people exposed to it) was removed, the authorities would return to the fray with a new spate of legislation prescribing punishments for unlicensed prostitution and curfews, special clothing and medical examinations for the licensed ladies. Although no precise date is given, Jacob's *Law Dictionary* suggests, in a section entitled 'Subnervare', that at an early period in England it had been the practice to punish women

* In Knighton's opinion, it was just this sort of immorality which had encouraged God to punish the world by sending the plague. Thus he writes that, in the earlier part of 1348, there had arisen 'a huge clamour and outcry among the people, because when tournaments were held, almost in every place, a band of women would come as if to share the sport, dressed in divers and marvellous dresses of men—sometimes to the number of 40 or 50 ladies, of the fairest and comeliest (though I say not of the best) among the whole kingdom. Thither they came in parti-coloured tunics, one colour or pattern on the right side and another on the left, with short hoods that had pendants like ropes wound round their necks, and belts thickly studded with gold or silver—nay, they even wore, in pouches slung across their bodies, those knives which are called 'daggers' in the vulgar tongue; and thus they rode on choice war-horses or other splendid steeds to the place of tournament. There and thus they spent and lavished their possessions, and wearied their bodies with fooleries and wanton buffoonery, if popular report lie not . . . But God in this matter, as in all others, brought marvellous remedy; for He harassed the places and times appointed for such vanities by opening the floodgates of heaven with rain and thunder and lurid lightning, and by unwonted blasts of tempestuous winds . . . and that same year and the next came the general mortality throughout the world.' (Henry Knighton, *Chronicle*, II, 57, A.D. 1348— trs. G. G. Coulton, *A Medieval Panorama*, Vol. II, pp. 128–9.)

found guilty of whoring by cutting the sinews of their thighs and legs, or in other words by hamstringing them; and in some parts of France, in the twelfth century, it was still not uncommon for 'mulieres rixosas' (literally 'brawling women') to be exhibited to the public in cages before being either mutilated or ducked to death in a river or pond. But in the later Middle Ages it was more usual for the occasional offender to be punished by some sort of public humiliation, such as having her hair cropped, being tied, naked or half-dressed, to the pillory, paraded in a cart or placed in the cucking-stool; while unauthorised operators who persisted in whoring were either punished in one or several of the above ways, branded, publicly whipped, imprisoned or fined, in addition to being expelled quite often from the town or region in which they had been apprehended.

So far as medieval armies were concerned, in the case of the earlier militia or feudal levies, the soldiers' need for a sexual outlet was as a rule supplied by the freelance whores who attached themselves to the armies or, less willingly, by the women of the country through which the soldiers passed. Despite a growing body of legislation aimed at preventing such behaviour, looting and rape continued, throughout the medieval period, to be an inevitable accompaniment to warfare. In 1379, for instance, the army of Sir John Arundel, Marshal of England, before embarking for the French Wars (which it never reached, being driven westwards by contrary winds, and shipwrecked off the coast of Ireland), paused en route, still on their own home ground, in Sussex, to rape, 'a convent of virgins', pillage the countryside and rob the church altars of their plate. But, with the decline of the feudal army and the increasing use of professional soldiers, most military commanders seem to have recognised the advantages to be gained—both from the point of view of discipline and of combating the spread through the ranks of contagious diseases—by enlisting the services of official prostitutes on whose activities they, like the civilian authorities, hoped to be able to keep a check. In the French crusading forces led by St Louis, things were, of course, different: at Caesarea, the Sire de Joinville reports, a knight arrested in a brothel was given the choice between being led through the camp by the prostitute with whom he had been discovered 'in his shirt and shamefully bound by a rope, or to surrender his horse and arms and be dismissed from the army'.[13] But in general, from the thirteenth century onwards, a medieval army would include the military equivalent of the Parisian Roi des Ribauds, a Whore's Serjeant, whose job it was to keep order among the officially licensed army

39 Soliciting next door to a gymnasium.

prostitutes, as well as to supervise any other duties—such as tending the sick, doing the laundry, cleaning out the latrines or filling in potholes in the roads—which these ladies might also be required to perform. At the siege of Neuss (1474–5), Duke Charles the Bold of Burgundy, who was as rich as he was irascible, provided the besieging force with one woman to every four men.

In 1347, the year before she sold the town to the Papacy, Queen Joanna of Naples had ordered the prostitutes off the streets of Avignon and into a splendid new supervised brothel quarter, which she had had specially built for them. In this Maison de Débauche, or house of carnal dissipation, over which presided an 'Abbess', there were weekly medical inspections and offences against the regulations were punished by birching; whores who became pregnant were obliged to have their babies, for whose education and proper bringing-up provision was also made; on certain Holy Days, and always on Fridays, the gates were locked.

Other luxury brothels soon followed—at Toulouse, Angers, Strasbourg and elsewhere—and it was, as a rule, these superior establishments which supplied the women who were offered, free of charge, to visiting dignitaries or displayed naked in the pageants with which medieval towns sometimes honoured their more important guests. In Ireland, in the seventh century, the Queen of

Ulster and the ladies of her court had sought to appease the wrath of the conqueror, Cuchalainn, by advancing to meet him bare-chested and then, when close to him, raising their skirts 'so as to expose their secret places'. But, in the later Middle Ages, ladies of rank and title were spared these indignities. Such services were performed instead by prostitutes and things were, on the whole, more decorously arranged. In the fourteenth century, for example, the city worthies of Antwerp tried to ingratiate themselves with the Emperor Charles V by sending the choicest of the municipality's prostitutes round to the imperial lodgings; while, in 1431, King Henry VI of England, then aged ten, was greeted at the St Denis Gate of Paris by the spectacle of three nude 'mermaids' splashing about in a fountain, which had, as its centrepiece, a representation of the fleur de lys. With a tableau vivant seen thirty years later, at the entry of Louis XI into Paris in 1461, the author of the *Journal dite Chronique scandaleuse*, Jean de Roye, was delighted. 'And there were also,' he reports, 'three very handsome girls, representing quite naked sirens, and one saw their beautiful, turgid, separate, round and hard breasts, which was a very pleasant sight, and they recited little motets and bergerettes; and near them several deep-toned instruments were playing fine melodies.'[14] Less erotic was a 'Judgement of Paris' with which Charles the Bold was welcomed in 1468 by the citizens of Lille: in this 'humorous' variation on a favourite theme, Venus was hugely fat, Juno emaciated, and Minerva a hunchback.

While it seems improbable that the three ladies employed in this last display would have come from one of the smarter brothels, many of the women who made their way across Europe to Constance in 1414 most certainly did. For here, at the Council of the highest Church dignitaries, called to end the Great Schism and to pronounce sentence on such heretics as Wyclif and Hus, there were, apparently, some great beauties among the 1,500 odd prostitutes said to have been on offer. One of them was reputed to have made as much as 800 ducats for a single night; while at nearby Baden, during the four years that the Council lasted, a certain Poggio of Florence was said to have made a fortune out of the entertainments he provided in the thermal baths.

With the dawning of the Renaissance, in the fifteenth century, and in Italy especially, a new age of great courtesans was about to break; an age of women who could play the harp or the lyre and read, write and sing; of women like Imperia Cognata, who sat for Raphael's 'Parnassus'; of women who, like the fifty prostitutes who were present at a feast in the rooms of Cesare Borgia in the Papal

40 *The eternal punishment of pimps, panders and seducers in Hell.*

Palace on October 30, 1501, were 'of the kind known as *corteggiane* and who are not of the common people'. At this party, which was given in honour of Cesare's father Pope Alexander VI, the courtesans, according to Johann Burchard, 'danced with the servants and the others who were present. At first they wore their dresses, then they stripped themselves completely naked. The meal over, the lighted candles, which were on the table, were set on the floor, and chestnuts were scattered for the naked courtesans to pick up, crawling about on their hands and knees between the candlesticks. The Pope, the Duke and his sister Lucrezia all watched. Finally a collection of silk cloaks, hose, brooches and other things were displayed, and were promised to those who had connection with the greatest number of prostitutes. This was done in public. The onlookers, who were the judges, awarded prizes to those who were reckoned to be the winners'.[15]

But despite such junketings at the Vatican, and despite even the glorious careers of some of these ladies who were 'not of the common people', prostitution in general remained, throughout the Middle Ages, closely linked with poverty, misery, crime and disease—a fact of which one, at least, of the ladies present at the 'Chestnut Ballet' would seem to have been well aware: for Tullia d'Aragona, a famous courtesan who had been at Cesare Borgia's banquet, is known to have been among the most generous of the contributors to the paving of the Strada del Populo in Rome, to which the poor peasant girls still flocked in from Southern Italy in the hope of screwing some sort of a living out of the lower end of the market.

7

Homosexuals

'IF A MAN lie with mankind, as with womankind,' declares Leviticus XX, 13, 'both of them have committed abomination; they shall surely be put to death; their blood shall be upon them'. No mention is made of how the execution is to be carried out but the Talmud, which goes no further in the case of ladies who 'have practised lewdness with one another' than to forbid them to marry priests, prescribes the usual Jewish method of death, by stoning.

From the severity of this sentence, the gravest that Judaic law could inflict, it is clear that the Hebrew attitude to male homosexuality was hostile, but it is nonetheless interesting that the Old Testament does not include a single instance of an execution for this particular crime. Homosexuality was rather the sort of 'abomination' in which worshippers of graven images were accused of wallowing and imputations of it were frequently included in the lists of depravities ascribed to idolaters. So, too, does St Paul, in his Epistle to the Romans (I, 26–32), write of those people who preferred to adore false idols rather than worship the true God and who, therefore, God 'gave up unto vile affections; for even their women did change the natural use into that which is against nature. And likewise also the men, leaving the natural use of the woman, burned in their lust, one towards another: men with men working that which is unseemly . . .' 'God,' says St Paul, gave them over to a reprobate mind', for they knew 'the judgement of God, that they which commit such things are worthy of death.'

As the chosen race had come, during the course of the three centuries before the birth of the Christian Saviour, into closer contact with the pagan civilizations of the Greeks, whose love of boys was famous, and of the Romans, who could enjoy official taxed male prostitutes,* the attention of Jewish writers had been drawn to the subject, and the crime of the Old Testament Sodomites, which in earlier references does not appear to have had any sexual overtones, was invested not only with sexual, but more especially with homosexual connotations.† By the time of Josephus, who wrote towards the end of the first century A.D., the 'two angels' of the Old Testament had become young men of amazingly beautiful appearance, whom the Sodomites, when they set eyes on them, determined to ravish.

With the dawning of the Christian era, the homosexual interpretation of the Sodom story soon took its place in the main body of theological tradition. Although John Chrysostom—who with Tertullian and Eusebius agreed that homosexuality was more reprehensible than fornication, since the latter was at least 'natural'— does not make any reference to Sodom in a sermon complaining about pederasts who came to church only to leer at good-looking youths, St Augustine, in his *Confessions*, declares that 'those sins which are against nature, like those of the men of Sodom, are in all times and places to be detested and punished'.[1]

This same interpretation of the Sodomites' crime may well have influenced the formulators of Codex Theodosius IX vii 6, which decrees that 'all people who have the shameful custom of condemning a man's body, acting the part of a woman's, to the sufferance of an alien sex (for they appear not to be different to women) shall expiate a crime of this kind in avenging flames in the sight of the people'. The 'avenging flames' are very probably an echo of the fire with which the Divine Justice had visited the sins of the Sodomites but it is not until a novella of Justinian's, dealing with 'blasphemers and *sodomists*' and dating from the year 538—some thirteen years after an earthquake had destroyed several imperial cities—that the connection is explicitly made in secular legislation. 'It is because of such crimes,' says the novella, 'that there are famines, earthquakes and pestilences.' A subsequent novella of

* In the year 235 A.D., the Emperor Alexander Severus enacted that these taxes should no longer be paid to the treasury but be used instead to augment the special 'entertainment' fund set up to restore the Circus, the Theatre, the Amphitheatre and the Stadium; fourteen years later, the Emperor Philip pronounced male prostitution illegal.

† The Rev. D. S. Bailey (*Homosexuality and the Western Christian Tradition* pp. 1–6) considers that the original crime of the Sodomites was that in insisting forcibly on 'knowing' Lot's two visitors they had violated the rules of hospitality. The interpretation of the relevant text, Genesis, XIX, 1–11, depends on the precise meaning given to the Hebrew word 'yadha' = to 'know'.

41 *Dante and Virgil meet some homosexuals in Hell.*

544, which urged strict enforcement of the Theodosian penalties on those sodomists who would not be persuaded 'to reform and repent', expressed the principle of the matter more succinctly still: the Theodosian penalties must be enforced, the novella explained, because 'instructed by the Holy Scriptures, we know that God brought a just judgement upon those who lived in Sodom, on account of this very madness of intercourse, so that to this very day that land burns with inextinguishable fire'.

A desert the land of the Sodomites may in the sixth century have been; a land burning with 'inextinguishable fire' it was not. But, whatever the geographical facts, the crime of the Sodomites was by now generally accepted, by theologians and legislators alike, to have been that of male homosexuality; and death by burning was to remain the penalty most often prescribed by secular authorities for its persistent practice throughout the Middle Ages.

We have now, of course, no means of discovering how often the full penalties were inflicted; but the official policy of the Church, as laid down in the decisions of Church Councils and the penitentials or manuals for the guidance of private confessors, was as emphatic in its condemnation of those who committed mortal sin by practising homosexuality as was that of the Imperial legislators. In 305–6 the Council of Elvira forbad the sacrament even at death to the debauchers of boys while the penances recommended by the penitentials are as a rule equivalent to those imposed for such other crimes as incest, bestiality and idolatry.

St Basil, who, towards the end of the sixth century, reckoned homosexuality to be on a par with adultery, was a man at the same time acutely aware of its temptations. 'If thou art young in either body or mind,' he writes in his *Renunciation of the Secular World*, 'shun the companionship of other young men and avoid them as thou wouldst a flame. For through them the enemy has kindled the desires of many and then handed them over to eternal fire, hurling them into the vile pit of the five cities under the pretence of spiritual love . . .;' at meals, it is advisable to choose a seat far from other young men; when lying down to sleep, it is better to have an old man between you rather than run the risk of touching a young man's clothing; and, if a young man should speak to you, 'lest perhaps by gazing at his face thou receive a seed of desire sown by the enemy and reap sheaves of corruption and ruin . . .', it is best to reply to him with your eyes fixed firmly upon the ground.[2] In the letter of 375, which had bracketed sodomy with adultery, St Basil recommended that those found guilty of homosexual practices should be debarred from Holy Communion for a period of up to fifteen years in the case of those in the most important positions.

While most subsequent authorities quoted in the penitentials followed the familiar pattern of imposing heavier penances for clerics than for laymen, for mature men than for youths, many made the distinction between habitual and occasional offenders and several attempted even to distinguish between the varying degrees of physical contact involved. Such a man, who would appear to have made a very thorough investigation of the potential avenues of satisfaction available to male homosexuals, was Cummean. His penitential of *c*.650 suggests that, where the offender is under twenty, an appropriate penance for simple kissing would be six special fasts, for licentious kissing but without ejaculation eight special fasts, for kissing with ejaculation or 'embrace' ten special fasts; where the guilty party was over twenty, Cummean suggests that he be made to live in continence, at a table apart, on bread and water, and be excluded from church— although for how long he omits to specify. The catalogue then carries on, with increasingly rigorous penances in each succeeding case, through mutual masturbation, interfemoral connection and fellatio to sodomy proper, for which Cummean considered a penance of seven years to be suitable atonement.[3]

As to the precise term of penance, the compilers of the penitentials continued to differ. Only a generation, for instance, after

Cummean, we find the *Penitential of Theodore* advising that 'he who commits fornication with a man or with a beast shall do penance for ten years',[4] and it was left to Pope Gregory III (731–41) to sum up the situation, with regard to clerics at least, in a judgement which declared that if any ordained person had been 'defiled with the crime of sodomy . . . let him do penance for ten years, according to the ancient rule'. 'Some, however,' the judgement goes on, 'being more humanely disposed, have fixed the term at seven years. Those who are ignorant of the gravity of the offence are assigned three years in which to do penance. As for boys who know that they are indulging in this practice, it behoves them to hasten to amend; let them do penance for fifty days, and in addition let them be beaten with rods; for it is necessary that the crop which has brought forth bad fruit be cut down.'[5]

For such evidence as we have of the barbarian attitude to homosexuality it seems clear that the Northern races who overran Roman Europe were likewise opposed to such practices. In 650, for example, an edict of the Spanish Visigothic king, Kindasvinth, ordered that those found guilty of homosexual activities should be castrated before being handed over to the Church, while the opinion of the thirteenth-century English jurist known as Fleta, that sodomists should be buried alive, would seem to suggest that according to Teutonic law homosexuals were punished like cowards and 'notorious evil-doers', as Tacitus describes, by being plunged into marshes. As the marauding tribes converted to Christianity, none of them appears, in any case, to have quarrelled with the Christian view of the matter and most of them, at a later stage, actually incorporated the Roman law punishment for the crime into their own legal codes.

On the subject of female homosexuality, meanwhile, the secular law was silent. Although St Paul, in his Epistle to the Romans, had denounced both male and female practices and St Augustine had, in 423, found it necessary to remind a convent of nuns, over whom his sister had been the superior, that 'the love which they bore to one another ought not to be carnal but spiritual', the prospect of women 'practising lewdness with one another' does not seem to have excited the same horror as that of men. If some medieval law-makers may have refused to believe, like Queen Victoria in the nineteenth century, that women could indulge in such activities, this comparative lack of legal interest in lesbianism as opposed to male homosexuality is probably due rather to the survival until the sixteenth century of the primitive superstitious reverence for semen, as a precious fluid which should on no account be wasted,

42 *A crowd of Sodomites in Hell; most are monks and one is a bishop.*

and to the essentially inferior role allotted to women, not only in society as a whole but even in the process of producing a child. For, whereas the male sperm was credited, on the authority of Aristotle himself, with the potential possession of a sentient soul, the menstrual fluid of a woman (whose contribution to the generation of a child was considered to be little more than the provision of a convenient incubator in which the all-important male egg could develop) was thought to contain only the potential parts of the body and a merely nutritive soul.

Not many penitentials, either, touch on the question of female homosexuality, but those that do are in general similar to that of Theodore, which, as we have seen, imposed a penance of ten years on those found guilty of male homosexuality. 'If a woman practises vice with a woman,' Theodore's penitential stipulates, 'she shall do penance for three years.' And 'if she practises solitary vice, she shall do penance for the same period'.[6] The various degrees of intimacy are not, as they are for men, differentiated while the activity itself is not in this case deemed to be any worse than masturbation.

All forms of homosexuality were, then, from the Church's point of view, deserving of correction, while secular legislators agreed that male homosexuality was a crime meriting the severest of penalties. It is, therefore, all the more remarkable that there should be, as there is, a general dearth in the records of specific cases being brought before the authorities, a dearth from which we can only conclude that the vast majority of cases were never reported. It is, as a result, very difficult today to try to determine just how widespread homosexuality may at any given period of the Middle Ages have been.

This obstacle notwithstanding, homosexual proclivities have, at one time or another, been attributed in particular to the Franks, to the Vikings, who spent much time at sea without their womenfolk, and to the crusaders, who by some are believed to have 'discovered' the vice in the East; but this last opinion, at least, is challenged by the testimony of Peter Damiani's *Liber Gomorrhianus* in 1051, which claimed that homosexuality was rampant among the clergy; by the amount both of secular legislation and of penitentials also predating the First Crusade; and possibly even by poems like that of a Veronese cleric, who, in the ninth century, praises thus the physical charms of the boy who has forsaken him for another:

> O thou eidolon of Venus adorable
> Perfect thy body and nowhere deplorable!
> The sun and the stars and the sea and the firmament
> These are like thee, and the Lord made them permanent.[7]

Sympathetic references to homosexuality in what survives of medieval literature are, however, a rarity. While, occasionally, a poet may, in imitation of the classical models, address a verse or two to some 'Ganymede', or even compose a metrical debate, such as that ascribed by E. R. Curtius to Bernard Silvestris, during the course of which it is asserted that 'the best people' have often fancied the smooth thigh of a boy whereas country clowns are fit only to befoul themselves with women,[8] far more usual are the denunciations. Peter Damiani's mid-eleventh-century tirade against the rifeness of homosexuality * is followed, for example, in the early twelfth century, by Ordericus Vitalis's complaint that after the death of William the Conqueror 'effeminates set the fashion in many parts of the world: foul catamites, doomed to eternal fire, unrestrainedly pursued their revels and gave themselves up to the filth of sodomy . . . They parted their hair from the crown of the head to the forehead, grew long and luxurious locks like women, and longed to deck themselves in long overtight shirts and tunics'.[9] Again, towards the end of the same century, we find the Frenchman, Alanus de Insulis, in his *de Planctu Natura* lamenting how the human race, having lost sight of its noble origins, commits monstrous acts in its union of genders and perverts the laws of love by a practice of extreme and abnormal irregularity; while a later Oxford MS. (Bodleian Digby 166 f.91.93), after referring back to the *de Planctu Natura*, declares that so many 'are straying in error, leaving the good way, hankering after the rose-coloured way, hunting out the bristling stalk . . .' that the author has decided to take the

---

* It is interesting to note that Pope Leo III, while accepting the dedication of this tract, replied that he thought Damiani's recommendation that clerics found guilty of homosexual practices be degraded from their Order too severe a punishment, for the occasional offender at any rate.

initiative and call them back, both in prose and in verse, from such ruinous paths.

From these and other outbursts in the same vein, we might be led to suppose that homosexuality was, from the tenth century onwards, generally on the rampage. But still there is little evidence of actual prosecutions for the crime—in a total, for instance, of fifteen hundred recorded judgements made by the French Parlement under Louis IX there is only one passing reference to the crime of sodomy—and, once again, it seems that the medieval tendency to exaggerate, especially where anything gloomy or sinful was involved, must preclude us from assuming that any of these diatribes inveighing against the ubiquity of homosexuality provides a reliable contemporary indication of its prevalence.

The continuing absence from the records of homosexual cases brought to trial does not mean, however, that the authorities had lost interest in such practices or that they had ceased to pass laws condemning them. In 1102, in England, where the court of the late King William Rufus had, according to William of Malmesbury, been followed by troops of pathics who, 'enervated and effeminate, unwillingly remained what nature had made them',[10] the Council of London pronounced excommunication upon those who committed 'the shameful sin of sodomy', while a statute of Edward I, in 1285, prescribed the familiar formula of burning alive for those who were taken in the act and publicly found guilty of either bestiality or sodomy.

In 1120, from the Latin kingdom of Jerusalem, at the other extremity of Christian influence, there comes a similar enactment. 'If any adult,' says Canon 8 of the Council of Naplouse, which opens with a sermon attributing the disasters of the times to evil living, 'be proved to have defiled himself with sodomitical vice, whether actively or passively, let him be burnt.' Reluctant victims of homosexual attentions are to do penance, although anyone forced to commit the crime who does not inform a magistrate is to be treated as if he had consented to the act; the instigator of the crime is, in all cases, to be consigned to the flames. Only 'if the sodomist comes to his senses', before he is accused, and if he does penance, swearing to abjure 'that abominable vice' shall he be received back into the Church.

In France, likewise, under St Louis, the prescribed punishment for sodomy was death by burning and the confiscation of the offender's goods; but here, as in the late thirteenth-century treatise on French customary law compiled by the Sire de Beaumanoir, which recommends the same penalties for the man 'who errs against the faith like an heretic who is unwilling to see the way or he who commits sodomy,[11] the crime of sodomy is expressly linked with heresy. For where St Paul and the Old Testament had, in associating sodomy with idolatry, shown the lead, those people bent on the eradication of the later medieval heresies were not slow to follow. Indeed, so indiscriminate did the lists of atrocities ascribed to heretics become that it is difficult to decide which, if any, of the sects or societies even tolerated, let alone encouraged, in its adherents the practice of homosexuality.

However ill-founded, though, these accusations may have been, we know from the records that many heretics were burned as a result of convictions on charges including that of sodomy while even in the case of Gilles de Rais, who was convicted in 1440 of the sexual murder of one hundred and forty male children and young men, the charges of sodomy were inextricably bound up with those of heresy and apostasy. In fact, so close was the connection in the popular mind between the separate crimes of heresy and sodomy that the word bugger, deriving from Bulgar and originally used to describe a member of one of the Manicheean sects (who disapproved of the continued generation of the corrupted human race and may or may not, as a corollary of this distaste, have considered homosexual practices less invidious than routine copulation), soon came to be thought of as meaning, as it does to this day, a male homosexual.

Charges of homosexuality were then, as a rule, brought in conjunction with other charges, to add ballast to the case against the defendant and to assist in the task of discrediting religious or, more rarely, political opponents. Such adventitious accusations could, in a doubtful prosecution, shift the balance of opinion; and a King who made full use of this ploy was Philip IV of France, who included allegations of homosexuality not only in the heresy charges he levelled at Pope Boniface VIII and Guichard, Bishop of Troyes, but also in his thoroughly successful campaign (1307–1312) to defame the Order of the Knights Templar. In this last instance, Philip's unavowed purpose was to get his hands on the Templars' fabled riches, which he could do only by proving the whole Order guilty of heresy and so achieving the forfeiture to himself—and, to a lesser degree, to the Church—of the Order's entire property. In his determination to secure this lucrative judgement, the rapacious monarch would have no stone left unturned: the Inquisitors appointed to examine the individual Knights of the Order were duly instructed to accuse them of, amongst other sinister things, performing at their admission ceremony a variety of obscene rites

43 *The execution of Gilles de Rais.*

involving kisses on the navel, 'on the point of the spine', 'on the virile member' and on the anus, as well as enjoining upon new candidates the practice of 'unnatural vices' as being, whether actively or passively performed, no sin and therefore permissible, if not, indeed, desirable.

Apart, however, from cases where accusations of homosexuality were thrown in for good measure and where persons who had never known any kind of homosexual experience may well have been committed to the flames as a result of convictions on blanket charges, there is, as we have remarked, little evidence in the Middle Ages of secular persecutions, and the punishment of those homosexuals who were ever reported appears to have been left, in the main, to the Church. While most medieval people might have agreed, therefore, with St Thomas Aquinas that 'sins against nature' were sins against 'right reason' and thus the worst 'sins of the flesh', and while Kings, Councils and Parliaments pronounced themselves outraged by 'unnatural vices' and prescribed the direst of penalties for them, it would, nevertheless, seem safe to conclude that the awful fate of Edward II of England—reputedly a bugger and reputedly despatched, by an assassin possessed of a truly medieval sense of the appropriate, with a red-hot poker thrust up his anus—was exceptional; that the full rigour of the law was seldom invoked; and that even those vicious boys of whom San Bernardino had heard, 'who paint their cheeks and go about boasting of their sodomy and practise it for gain' (for whom it was 'a grave sin to make a doublet reaching only to the numbril and those with only one small patch in front and one behind, so that they show enough flesh to the sodomites')[12] were, on the whole, left alone to make such 'gain' as their physical endowments might permit.

8

Heretics

FROM JUDAISM Christianity inherited an obsession with orthodoxy. Yet despite the anathemas and the accusations of
wrong-belief which a bewildering variety of early Christian
communities and sects levelled at one another in the three centuries
following the death of their Saviour, it was not until St Paul's
'Catholic' brand of Christianity was given the seal of Imperial
approval in 313 A.D. that large numbers of Christians began to go in
mortal fear of other Christians on account of their beliefs. For,
whether or not he may have seen a miraculous sign in the sky
shortly before his victory over the usurper Maxentius at the Battle of
the Milvian Bridge in 311, the Emperor Constantine was politician
enough to appreciate that for an alliance with the commendably
paternalistic and authoritarian Catholic Church to be of maximum
use to him, in helping to keep an unruly and far-flung Empire in
order, it was essential that the Catholic Bishops should command
the obedience of as many Christians as was possible.

Thus from the moment Constantine and his co-Emperor Licinius
granted legal recognition to the Catholic Church—and long before
Christianity became the official State religion of the Empire—the
Emperors were as eager as the Catholic Bishops to secure uniformity of Christian belief. Accordingly both Church and State
insisted that, when a properly authorised synod, or Council of
Catholic Bishops, had pronounced judgement in a doctrinal issue,
it was the duty of every devout and God-fearing Christian to accept
the synod's decision in the matter as an unquestionable article of
his faith. If any man or woman dared to do otherwise—if, for

instance, he or she presumed to believe with Arius that God the Son must have had a beginning in time since he was born of God the Father—then that man or woman was a heretic. And in order to deal with heretics the State now presented the Catholic Church with a very powerful new weapon: the right to call upon the secular arm to inflict physical penalties on anyone who refused to renounce beliefs which the Catholics considered unorthodox. In 382, a law of Theodosius I made heresy punishable by death.

Among those whom the Catholic Church could henceforward hope to terrorise into admitting the incontestable rectitude of the Catholic interpretation of the Scriptures were the members of many splinter-groups and sub-sects of two earlier gnostic sects, the Montanists, who scandalised the Catholics by claiming that the perfect Christian actually became God, and the Marcionites. According to Marcion, the real God had sent the merciful and loving Jesus into an evil world to bring men the direct knowledge of the Divinity which the cruel and vengeful God of the Old Testament, when he created the world, had withheld from them. Marcion himself claimed to be the Paraclete and preached sermons extolling the virtues of a pure and simple life. However, because the Marcionites were known to abhor the wicked material world of the Old Testament God, they were accused by their enemies of holding it to be so awful that it justified them in indulging in all manner of illegal and vicious behaviour.

Similarly preoccupied with the problem of why there should be so much evil in a world supposedly created by God was a mid-third-century ecstatic who lived in Persia and described himself as 'Mani, the Apostle of Jesus Christ'. In constructing his highly complicated theology, Mani seems to have borrowed chiefly from Marcionite Christianity and from the Zoroastrian Dualism of the Persians. The Manichees, as Mani's followers came to be called, were divided into two classes: the Elect, of whom there were very few, and the Hearers The Elect could not work or own any property. Their needs were supplied by the Hearers, who sustained them and confessed to them, but who could never be saved. Manicheeism spread as far East as China and one of its catechumens, in his youth, was none other than the Father of Western orthodoxy himself, St Augustine of Hippo, who later wrote a long denunciation of the sect. By the sixth century, the movement seems to have lost much of its original impetus. But after various vicissitudes and alterations at the hands of sects like the seventh- and eighth-century Armenian Paulicians and the ninth- and tenth-century Bogomils in the Balkans, a new form of Manicheeism would, in the late twelfth and thirteenth centuries, lead to hysterical violence and mass murder in Southern France.

While most of the earlier Christian heterodoxies had been inspired by a craving either for asceticism or for a more personal and immediate knowledge of the Deity than the Catholics allowed to be possible, the association of the increasingly dictatorial Catholic Church with the Roman establishment soon began to produce a type of heretic whose reasons for rejecting the orthodox line were partly religious and partly political. In North Africa, for example, in 311 A.D., the Donatist heresy was sparked off by the unwillingness of eighty-odd Numidian Bishops to recognise the newly appointed Bishop of Carthage, on the grounds that he had been ordained by a Bishop who, they claimed, had forfeited his Church Orders by handing over Holy Books to be burned during the recent persecution of Christians. When this new Bishop, Caecilian, refused to resign, his opponents elected another Bishop, a man named Donatus. And, when in 313 the Emperor Constantine made his momentous switch from persecutor to protector of the Church, both sides sent in their appeals to him. After lengthy consultations with those who were equipped to expound the orthodox line on whether or not, and in what circumstances, a man might be deprived of his Holy Orders, the Emperor finally came down on the side of Caecilian; whereupon, there rose up in Africa a fiercely Punic-nationalist and anti-Imperial Donatist army, an army which claimed to believe that the end of the world was fast approaching, and the more fanatical members of which burned down and devastated the houses and crops of rich (and especially Roman) landlords, while offering their protection to the poorer peasants and demanding freedom for all slaves.

Nor was the cause of Catholic orthodoxy greatly helped in these early centuries by the summoning of the synods which were supposed to settle, once and for all, such tricky questions as whether God the Father and God the Son were made of the same substance, or whether they had one Holy Will between them or each had His own? Of the Emperor Constantius II (d. 361) his contemporary Ammianus observes scathingly that by his 'vain curiosity' he succeeded in creating a chaotic jumble out of what was in reality a perfectly straightforward religion. Indeed so many synods did that Emperor convoke, and so great was the multitude of Bishops galloping all over the Empire to place their arguments before them, that 'the public establishment of the posts was almost ruined'.[1] But, despite the objections of sensible men like Ammianus to these councils at which the highest Church dignitaries were apt

to fly at one another like fishwives, thus creating still more confusion and discord, generation after generation of Eastern
churchmen continued to throng the synods, frantic in their efforts
to establish or anathematise some new interpretation of the sacred
texts. Increasingly dissimilar, however, to the history of the
Catholic Church in the East was the history, after the invasion of the
Western provinces of the Empire by the predominantly pagan
barbarians, of the Catholic Church in the West. In fact, in the Dark
Ages, as the Eastern and Western Churches drifted steadily further
and further apart, and especially when the Eastern Patriarchs
refused to acknowledge the supremacy of the Pope, the most
violently-phrased anathemas of the Roman Church were as a rule
reserved for the Churches of the Eastern Mediterranean. At home
in the West, meanwhile, where the Church's first concern must be
to convert its new secular masters to Christianity, there was
obviously little point in Popes or Bishops uttering curses or threats,
which were now, in the absence of effective sanctions, largely
meaningless and empty.

For as long as the future of Christianity in Western Europe was in
any way doubtful, the Church does not seem to have paid too much
attention, therefore, to maintaining rigid orthodoxy of belief among
its steadily multiplying flock of new adherents. But this is not to say
that any wrong-believing Christian, or 'impostor', who sought to
attract a following in the Dark Ages, was automatically dismissed as
a harmless crank or a poor misguided simpleton. In his *History of the
Franks*, under the year 591, Gregory of Tours reports how a certain
man of Bourges went into a glade to cut wood, and was there
encompassed by so large a swarm of flies that he was for two years
quite out of his wits. After some time spent in ascetic retreat in a
forest near Arles, the man eventually reappeared, dressed in skins
and accompanied by a woman whom he called Mary. He was, he
said, the Messiah; and, as if to prove it, performed many
miraculous cures. According to Gregory, this man soon had a
following of 3,000 people, some of whom were priests, and all of
whom he encouraged to prostrate themselves in prayer before him,
and then to rise up and 'adore him'. Further, this Messiah gave
orders to his disciples that the rich were to be robbed, so that he
might redistribute the stolen property among 'those with no
possessions'. At last this troupe of robber-ascetics arrived at le Puy,
where the leader 'disposed his men like an army, as if to attack
Aurelius, at that time Bishop of the Diocese'. But for a while nothing
happened. Then, a day or so later, the Messiah sent before him to
the Bishop 'as messengers to announce his arrival, naked men who

leaped and performed antics as they went': a display to which the astonished Bishop responded by instructing several 'stout fellows' to surround the Messiah, while one of them bowed down before him, as if to kiss his knees. This was done; and, as soon as the Messiah was tightly held, the 'stout fellows' cut him to pieces. When afterwards the woman whom he had called Mary was put to the torture, 'she disclosed all his visionary schemes and his tricks'.[2]

On reflecting upon this and several other instances of people who had succeeded in 'attracting to themselves by such deceptions weak women who in a frenzy proclaimed them to be saints', Bishop Gregory was inclined to agree with many of his contemporaries that this sort of madness must be interpreted as signalling the end of the world. For, although St Augustine had been at pains to discourage speculation as to when this event would take place, large numbers of Christians still continued to believe, as St Paul in his day had done, that the end of the world was imminent. The three sources of eschatological and millenarian information on which medieval theories were based were the Old Testament Book of Daniel, the New Testament Book of the Revelations of St John the Divine and the more widely disseminated, though uncanonical, corpus of so-called 'Sybilline Oracles', which foretold a bloody contest between Antichrist and a hero who was usually presented as a kind of Warrior-Saviour or a great Christian Emperor of the Last Days; and, despite many differences as to detail, all of these authorities were agreed that the final victory of the Powers of Righteousness over the Powers of Evil must be preceded by many strange and dreadful portents, and a period of universal chaos.

Having witnessed some of the excesses committed in anticipation of the Millennium by the anti-Roman Donatist army of 'circum-cellions', or self-styled 'Saints', in North Africa, St Augustine had gone to considerable lengths to try to explain away scriptural texts which might be interpreted by a fanatical group of dissidents as a justification for leading the purge of what they considered to be a sin-laden world hovering on the brink of final destruction. In so far as the prophecies dealing with the inauguration of the Last Age of the world's history were concerned, these were to be interpreted in an allegorical sense: and according to this, the correct interpretation, they had been fulfilled by the founding of the Christian Church, with which the Last Age had already begun. As for the other prognostications of the prophet Daniel and the inspired utterances of St John of Patmos, although 'that last persecution, to be sure, which will be inflicted by Antichrist, will be extinguished by Jesus, himself, present in person', to ask when this would happen was 'completely ill-timed. For had it been in our interest to know this, who could have been a better informant than the Master, God himself, when the disciples asked him?'[3] Yet, his enormous prestige notwithstanding, in this matter the Saint's warnings went unheeded. The speculation continued, not only among fanatical dissidents, but in the most exalted ecclesiastical circles. And few people were in any doubt but that the world would end sooner rather than later. On June 22, 601, for example, no less a personage than Pope Gregory the Great is to be found writing to 'our excellent son, the most glorious King Ethelbert, King of the English' that 'we would . . . have Your Majesty know what we have learned from the words of Almighty God in holy Scripture, that the end of this present world is at hand and the everlasting Kingdom of the Saints is approaching'. As a necessary prelude to this happening there would occur 'unprecedented things'—such as 'portents in the sky, terrors from heaven, unseasonable tempests, wars, famines, pestilences and widespread earthquakes'. Although, in Gregory's opinion, 'not all these things will happen during our own lifetimes, but will all ensure in due course', his purpose in writing is to reassure Ethelbert that, 'if any such things occur in your own country', the newly Christian King is not to be anxious, 'for these portents of the end are sent to warn us to consider the welfare of our souls and remember our last end, so that, when our Judge comes, He may find us prepared by good lives'.[4]

After the terrors of the ninth- and tenth-century wars against the Infidel, it was inevitable that, as the tenth century began to draw towards its close, people should have come to fix on the year 1000 A.D. as the year in which 'this present world' must come to its appointed end. But, in the event, 1000 turned out to be a year very much like any other: and many millenarians had already transferred their expectations to 1033, the thousandth anniversary of the Crucifixion, when, quite suddenly, in 1009, the Caliph Hakim ordered the Holy Sepulchre at Jerusalem to be utterly destroyed. To large numbers of Frenchmen in particular, this seemed to be the sign for which they had been waiting. While at home in France some Christians sought to prepare the way for the return of the Saviour by forcibly baptising or murdering Jews, from all over the country there set out, in 1010, a mass pilgrimage of men and women whose intention it was to be ready and waiting in Jerusalem, having washed away their sins in the water of the Jordan, at that glorious moment when Christ would rise again on the very spot where the year before the Caliph had destroyed the shrine of the Holy Sepulchre.

In 1010, as in 1000, the millenarians were to be disappointed; and again in 1033, although that year began promisingly with famine and appalling floods—portents which soon had another horde of pilgrims heading for Jerusalem. Yet the repeated failure of the Millennium to materialise did nothing to stanch the increasingly feverish belief in its imminence. Wherever a popular preacher, or 'propheta', turned up to announce the approaching end of a world which had fallen into the clutches of evil men, and to urge his audience to repent now, at once, before it was too late, he could be sure of an enthusiastic response. But, whereas in the eleventh century the evil men against whom such men had railed had generally been Infidel pagans, Moslems or Jews, by the early years of the twelfth century an alarming number of prophetae were beginning to preach against the worldliness and the corruption of the Catholic Church.

Ironically enough, the spread of heresy in Western Europe can in part to be attributed to the more ambitious schemes of eleventh-century Popes like Gregory VII for ecclesiastical reform, and in part again to Pope Urban II's efforts to promote peace by encouraging the more restless and refractory elements in Western society to go East and fight a Holy War against the Infidel. For one of the things which Gregory VII's call for a purified and spiritually revitalised ecclesiastical establishment had done was to awaken, in the hearts of many Christians, expectations which the Church proved quite incapable of fulfilling. And however successful Urban's Crusade may have been in ridding the West, in the short term at least, of many of its more unruly and fanatical inhabitants, what that Pope does not seem to have reckoned with was the danger that the survivors of such an expedition might, like other travellers to the East, return to the West as the conscious or unconscious disseminators of heterodox beliefs with which they had come into contact during their sojourn abroad.

Since St Augustine had dealt at such length with the errors of the Manicheean sect, to which he had formerly belonged, it was not uncommon for medieval people to use the word Manichee in a general sense, to mean any kind of heretic. Thus it is impossible to say whether in 1015, when Bishop Gerard of Limoges spoke of introducing severe measures to deal with Manichees, he was referring specifically to people holding some sort of gnostic-dualist beliefs, or whether he was using the word in its looser sense. Nevertheless, rumour in Limoges had it that the heresy which the Bishop was so anxious to suppress had been imported from Italy, where in 1030 the word Cathar was first used to describe a community of heretics whose beliefs were generally supposed to have been similar to those of the tenth-century Eastern European heirs of Mani, the Dalmatian and Bosnian Bogomils. And it may well be therefore that a group of Manicheean heretics, properly so-called, was active in Southern France as early as the first decade of the eleventh century.

Be that as it may, whatever the precise date at which gnostic-dualist beliefs of the kind associated with the Manicheean sects of the East first took root and began to flourish in the West, it is clear that by the middle years of the twelfth century several popular preachers had become acquainted with some part at least of their dogma. For instance, very definitely Manicheean in emphasis according to Guibert of Nogent, who had read St Augustine on the subject, was the heresy of the brothers Clement and Everard, which 'is not a heresy that openly defends its faith, but condemned to everlasting whispers, spreads secretly'. Despite this secrecy, Guibert manages to present a fairly detailed account of what 'is said to be the sum of it'. The heretics were accused of calling the mouths of all priests the mouths of Hell, and of holding the mysteries of the Catholic Church to be so much nonsense. The rule of the Son of the Virgin they were said to dismiss as having no reality. Instead, they believed in imitating the lives of the Apostles and spoke of 'God's own Word which came into being through some rigmarole or other'. Marriage and propagation they held in abhorrence, and any food which was the product of sexual generation they would not eat. As had happened almost a thousand years earlier, with the Marcionites, this distaste on the part of the followers of Clement and Everard for the material world once again led their detractors to suppose them guilty both of unnatural vices, 'men with men and women with women', and of living with women without marrying them, calling them wives 'but not keeping to one only'. And, as if this was not enough, they were further accused of holding 'assemblies in vaults or secret sanctums, both sexes together indiscriminately. Then they light candles, uncover their breasts, and, in the sight of all (it is said), shove the candle up the rear of some slut on her hands and knees. This soon snuffs the candles, whereupon they all call on the King of Hell, and everyone couples with the woman who first comes to hand'.

When two members of this group were brought before the Bishop's Court at Soissons in 1115, they did not deny that they held meetings but, in Guibert's opinion, the answers which they gave to questions about their beliefs were 'most Christian answers'. Subsequently, however, while one of the accused was found guilty of heresy by the water ordeal—'Clement being then thrown into the tun floated on the top like a stick'—the other 'confessed his error', and both were cast into prison, there to await the decision of a Council held at Beauvais as to what should be done with them. But their wait was to be a short one: for 'in the interval the faithful people fearing weakness on the part of the clergy, ran to the prison, seized them and having lighted a fire under them outside the city, burnt them both to ashes'. If the Church may not have been certain yet quite how it should deal with men like Clement, the populace clearly was. And Guibert was right behind them. 'To prevent the spreading of this cancer,' he says with approval, 'God's people showed a righteous zeal against them.'[5]

Another early twelfth-century heresiarch whose teaching seems to have had certain characteristics in common with the Marcionite and Manicheean traditions is Eudes de L'Etoile, a *propheta* who was burned to death by the authorities at Rouen in 1148. Like so many freelance preachers who were to come after him, Eudes had called for a return to the asceticism of the early Christians and was soon considered by his followers to be, if not a reincarnation of Christ himself, then at least a near-Divine messenger. William of Newburgh records that Eudes and his disciples went on a looting tour of Brittany; he also records that they gave some of the proceeds to the poor. And then again, in the earlier part of the twelfth century, there is the case of a revivalist named Tachelm, who went about the neighbourhood of Antwerp surrounded by an armed bodyguard, and who preached that the Church was so corrupt that to take the eucharist from the hands of a priest was meaningless. His followers drank his bath-water instead. Yet, although they were pleased to do him this reverence, Tachelm did not claim to be Christ. He was, however, possessed of the Holy Spirit—and thus like Christ, and, therefore, God.

Whether or not any of these *prophetae* may have come into direct contact with Eastern heretics, or whether perhaps they had spoken with returned pilgrims or crusaders who had picked up some knowledge of the heretical doctrines of the East, there is no means of telling. But far more numerous than the bands of men and women who had attached themselves to these leaders, and unquestionably the Western heirs of the gnostic-dualist tradition of the Manichees, were the Cathar heretics of Southern France, commonly known as the Albigensians. Also referred to sometimes as Bogomils, Paulicians, Publicans, Paterenes, Bulgars, Manichees, Marcionites and occasionally even Arians, the Albigensians claimed that, since God was the pure spirit of good, then the God of the Church, who had entrapped the soul in the flesh, must be none other than the Devil. Like the original followers of Mani in the third century, the Albigensian Cathars were divided into two groups: the 'perfecti', an elite few, who were the Cathars' alternative to the worldly Catholic priesthood, and the general mass of 'believers', who were free to marry and to lead ordinary lives, and who did not receive the 'consolamentum' from one of the perfecti until they were about to die. Ideally, the profoundly pessimistic Cathars maintained, the only possible solution to the appalling situation in which mankind had been placed was mass-suicide. But this, until their work on earth had been done, they deemed to be impracticable.

In the opinion of St Bernard of Clairvaux (d. 1153), an influential preacher and advocate of austerity, one of the main reasons for the extraordinary popularity of Catharism was the widespread dissatisfaction of both rich and poor with the lack of piety or enthusiasm for pastoral duties among the regular Catholic clergy. But, although as early as 1145 a progress through Southern France had convinced the Saint that in many areas Catholicism had virtually disappeared, it was not in fact until sixty-three years later that affairs there came to a ghastly head. In the interim, the orderly and well-organized Cathar Church seems to have existed side by side with the Catholic Church and to have included in its congregations many members of a local nobility which was in those days the most highly civilized in Western Europe. From time to time efforts were made to woo the Cathars away from their wrong beliefs. And from time to time the Counts of Provence shifted their allegiance from one faction to the other. But then, in 1208, came the murder of Peter of Castelnau, a Papal Legate who had evidently been meeting with some success in converting Cathars to orthodoxy. Infuriated by this attack on a papal official, and exasperated by the apparent unwillingness of Count Raymond VII of Toulouse to do anything about it, Pope Innocent III appealed to the French King for help. And the result, in the autumn of the same year, was the first in a series of particularly horrible 'crusades', in which the Church, for its part, offered a plenary indulgence to any zealot, opportunist or hoodlum, who would undertake to fight for the cause of orthodoxy in Southern France.* The resistance was ferocious. But in 1209 the crusaders captured the town of Béziers and, much to the joy of the Papal Legate, Arnold Aimery, he was able to send word to the Pope that

---

* As usual the announcement of this plenary indulgence was accompanied by certain provisos; but many people seem to have been unaware of the conditions under which the indulgence was offered, and the Church's efforts to enforce them were in some cases bitterly resented.

the 'heretics' had been killed indiscriminately, at least fifteen thousand of them, so he reckoned.

As the bloodbath continued, the hysteria mounted. Before the Albigensian Crusades, there had been many churchmen who had decried the burning of heretics and urged that the ecclesiastical authorities should show compassion towards those of the flock who had had the misfortune to fall into error. But, so fiercely did the heretics defend themselves against their assailants that, in the aftermath of the Albigensian Crusades, anybody who advocated such tolerance was in danger of himself being thought to be a heretic.

Having set in motion these Crusades against the Cathars in Southern France—the dualism of the Cathars was to linger on as a distinctive brand of heresy in Lombardy and even in some parts of France until the early years of the fourteenth century—the Pope began to look about for ways in which the Church might in future be able to prevent any heretical sect from attracting so large and so resolute a following. As a first tentative step in this direction, in 1210, Innocent decided to grant official papal recognition to the ministry of the charismatic *poverello*, Francesco Bernardone of Assisi. By doing this he hoped to provide an orthodox outlet for the religious cravings of the growing number of Christians whose fervent desire it was to dedicate their lives to the pursuit of holy poverty. But, although it is greatly to Innocent's credit that he should have tried to direct this fervour into orthodox channels, it is indicative of the sort of problems with which the Church was now faced that, within a generation only of St Francis of Assisi's death in 1226, the governing body of the Franciscan Order was demanding the execution, as heretics, of fellow Franciscans who had in fact done little more than try to practise to the letter the asceticism and self-abnegation advocated by their founder.

Had things gone slightly differently for Francesco Bernardone, or had he lived earlier, longer or later, he might well have been condemned as a heretic rather than canonized. For what was today heretical might well tomorrow be orthodox, and vice-versa. Nor was there any sure means of telling in which way the Catholic establishment would react to any new outbreak of religious enthusiasm or revivalism. In about 1170, for example, what later became known as the Waldensian movement had been founded by

44 A dispute between the Catholic clergy and Cathar heretics: the orthodox text leaps out of the fire while the Albigensian documents are consumed by the flames.

Peter Waldo, a merchant of Lyons. Like so many of his contemporaries, Waldo had become convinced that the true Christian must abandon all thought of earthly power and wealth and live a life of poverty in imitation of the Apostles. So, in order to learn more about the Apostles' lives and Christ's own teachings, he had sponsored the translation into the vernacular of various parts of the Holy Scriptures: and in these had been overjoyed to discover a God who bore little resemblance to the merciless judge who scowled stonily down on his congregations as they gathered to grovel before him in the great Romanesque cathedrals, but who was instead the Saviour and Redeemer of mankind, a God who brought good news not only to monks and to churchmen but to any man or woman who, with a pure heart, would follow in his poor footsteps. Yet although this God whom Peter Waldo had worshipped is obviously very much the same God as the God in whom St Francis believed—and even though the Waldensians had set themselves especially to preach against the Cathars—in 1182 all Waldensians were excommunicated as heretics. As so often and tragically happened when the plans of would-be reformers were rejected by the ecclesiastical establishment, rather than try to become reconciled to that establishment, many Waldensians had soon begun to preach against it. Indeed, it had not been long before some of them were claiming that, since there was no authority in the Gospels for either the Sacraments or the existence of Purgatory, then the Church which had invented these lies, and which insisted on their reality, must be the Congregation of the Devil.

Six years after St Francis of Assisi and eleven companions had been authorised to be 'roving preachers of Christ in simplicity and lowliness', in 1216 the Papacy formally approved the foundation of the great Order of Friars Preacher, the Dominicans. Of St Dominic himself it has been said that he was 'a man of remarkable attractiveness of character and broadness of vision; he had the deepest compassion for every sort of human suffering; he saw the need to use all the resources of human learning in the service of Christ . . .'[6] Nevertheless, from 1206, when he had accompanied his Bishop from Spain to Languedoc, until the founding of his Order in 1216, St Dominic had been involved in trying to win the Albigensian heretics away from their false beliefs by the force of his arguments. And although he himself had always advocated the preaching of the true faith as the best means of converting heretics to orthodoxy, it was inevitable that once the authorities' attitude to heretics began to follow that of the people in becoming more and more hysterical, later members of an Order which had been founded with the express intention of combating heresy should have been led to use methods rather less compassionate than those recommended by St Dominic.

In 1230, nine years after St Dominic had died at Bologna, the first permanent tribunal to deal with heresy was set up at Toulouse by Pope Gregory IX. Officered and administered by Dominican friars (who were many of them educated in the increasingly militant theology of their Order at the newly-founded University of Toulouse), the Inquisition, or Holy Office, was intended to put a stop to the sort of injustices which were alleged to have occurred as a result of the confused nature of earlier legislation about heresy. But what in fact the Inquisition did was to multiply such injustices. For the most important job of the Inquisition was to sniff out and to stifle any manifestation of heresy before it could spread. Accordingly, when the Inquisitors arrived in an area where there were believed to be heretics, every male over the age of fourteen and every female over twelve was forced to take a public oath, affirming his or her own orthodoxy and promising to denounce anyone whom he or she suspected of heterodoxy. Informants and denouncers remained anonymous. Persons accused of heresy before the Inquisition were not told the names of those who had so accused them, or of those who were prepared to testify against them. Nor were they allowed to defend themselves, or to appeal against the Court's decision to any other authority than the Papacy. Thus, although a relatively small proportion of the large numbers of people accused seem actually to have been burned to death, as Gregory IX directed all convicted heretics were to be from 1231 onwards, there was little chance that a person who was denounced to the Inquisition as a heretic would escape without some sort of punishment. In cases where the interrogatory methods of the Inquisitors succeeded in extracting a 'free confession', and the confession was, as usually happened, followed by a 'conversion' to orthodoxy, the normal penalty was life imprisonment. But quite often such penalties might be shortened, or even quashed, in return for the names of other 'heretics'. The system was designed to secure convictions: and this it did from the very beginning, although not unnaturally there was a most encouraging rise in the number of 'free confessions' extorted after the Bull of 1252 in which Pope Innocent IV authorised the use of torture, 'as it was applied in cases of robbery or theft', in cases of suspected heresy. After torture, the most favoured method of obtaining the confession of heresy without which the victim could not be convicted—and so forfeit all

45 *A number of women are seduced away from the True Faith by male heretics*

his possessions—was to make the suspect answer a list of specially prepared questions, which he or she could not understand.

Even before the founding of the Inquisition, there had been instances of people abusing the laws against heretics to achieve their own ends. In his *Verbum Abbreviatum*, for instance, Petrus Cantor (d. 1197), a one-time Rector of the Cathedral School at Paris, describes how 'certain honest matrons, refusing to consent to the lasciviousness of priests "of the seed of Canaan" have been written by such priests in the book of death, and accused as heretics, and even condemned by a certain notoriously foolish zealot for the

Christian faith, while rich heretics were simply blackmailed and suffered to depart'.[7] But as one after another thirteenth-century Pope strove to outdo his predecessor in endowing the Holy Office with the sort of extraordinary powers which allowed the Inquisitors to conduct their proceedings, not only in secret, but in a manner that was often forbidden by the ordinary law of the land, so did hatred of those who were charged with administering the heresy laws and, by extension, hostility towards the Papacy, and the Church of which it was head, became more and more pronounced. In some countries, among them England, the ecclesiastical authorities backed the secular authorities in refusing to admit the Inquisitors into their territories at all; yet, even in those countries into which the Holy Office was denied entry, there was from the middle years of the thirteenth century onwards a growing tendency for discontented and desperate people actually to take up arms, as the Pastoureaux did in France in 1251, not merely against the officers of the Inquisition or papal emissaries, but against the clergy in general.

It is again ironic, and at the same time significant of the kind of situation in which the medieval Church so frequently found itself, that no less than three Popes should have besought Joachim of Fiore, a Calabrian abbot and mystic, to write a book whose description of a new scheme of world history was to play a decisive part in encouraging still more people to see the established Church as their enemy. For, although Joachim may not have meant to contradict what St Augustine had had to say about the Millennium, that is precisely what his book did. And, in the fifty years following Joachim's death in 1202, his new eschatology was to take its place beside the earlier prophecies contained in 'Daniel' and 'Revelation' and the Sybilline Oracles.

According to the revelation of the true meaning of the Scriptures which had been vouchsafed to Joachim, the history of the world had been planned by the Deity to pass through three distinct ages, each of which was to be preceded by a preparatory period of incubation. The first two ages, the Age of the Father (or of the Law) and the Age of the Son (or of the Gospel), had already run their course—as too, almost, had the third period of incubation, which had begun with St Benedict (c.480–c.547), the father of Western monasticism. If Joachim's calculations were correct, the last age, the Age of the Spirit, would begin at some time between the years 1200 and 1260, and would endure until the coming of a second Antichrist and the Last Judgement. But, before this could happen, certain events must occur. Under the leadership of a great teacher, a 'new Elias' or 'novus dux', and his twelve apostles, a new order of monks must carry the Gospel into the furthest corners of the Earth, converting even the Jews to Christianity and persuading all men to abandon material things for the sake of things spiritual. And there must appear too the first Antichrist, who was to be a secular King and would inflict great sufferings on the faithful, although he would also scourge the corrupt ecclesiastical establishment and duly destroy it. The reign of this Antichrist would last three and a half years, until he himself was overthrown and the whole of humanity would be united, in the Age of the Spirit, in mystical adoration of the One True God.

Especially novel in the Joachite scheme of world history (and altogether incompatible with the Bishop of Hippo's dismal pronouncements on the subject) was the idea of a preliminary struggle with a first Antichrist and, in its sequel, an age of universal Christianity and peace, which was to precede, rather than to follow, the series of disasters and upheavals which the Books of 'Daniel' and 'Revelation' foretold would usher in Doomsday and the end of the world. And such was the excitement generated in some circles by this new interpretation of the eschatological texts that Joachim's own writings were soon almost obscured beneath the weight of interpretations, exegeses and pseudo-Joachite tracts, in which men and women identified themselves and their enemies with the various characters in a drama which they confidently expected to find themselves any minute helping to enact. In the minds, for instance, of the Franciscan Spirituals, who were eventually expelled from the Order, there could be no doubt but that they themselves were the monks whose mission it was to take over the control of the Church from the Roman Curia and to lead the new truly Christian community into the Age of the Spirit. To other people, it seemed obvious that the Emperor Frederick II, who was excommunicated at least three times for perjury, blasphemy and heresy, must be Antichrist. But then to others again it seemed equally clear that Frederick II was the Emperor of the Last Days or Warrior Saviour of the Sybilline Oracles. In parts of Germany it seems that, in addition to being regarded as the Emperor of the Last Days, Frederick was further credited with being the 'novus dux' of whom Joachim had spoken. Nor did it make much difference even when, in 1250, Frederick died without having fulfilled his role. The Sybilline Oracles abounded in stories of Emperors who were asleep in forests or behind mountains, and who would on the appointed day return to the centre of the world stage. While the French were awaiting the reappearance of Charlemagne, future generations of German dissidents could usually be counted upon to answer the call of prophetae who claimed to be the resurrected Frederick. And, always prominent on the agenda of these Fredericks, was the task which both those who had seen him in his lifetime as Antichrist and those who had seen him as the 'novus dux' were all of them agreed he had been sent to perform: the purging of an avaricious and a luxury-loving ecclesiastical establishment.

It is no accident that it should have been towards the end of 1260 that there occurred the first outbreak of public self-flagellation. For 1260 was the date by which Joachim had foretold that the Age of the Spirit would have begun, and his prophecies had been lent additional credence by a famine in 1258 and plague in 1259. Like the Camaldolian hermits who had introduced self-flagellation into their rigorously ascetic routine at some point in the early eleventh century, it seems that those people who took part in the flagellant processions of the later Middle Ages were trying to achieve two things. On the one hand they sought to imitate and so to participate in the sufferings of their Redeemer while, on the other hand, they hoped that, by inflicting this severe form of penance on themselves, they might avoid the far worse punishments which were to be meted out by God on the Day of Judgement.

Starting in Perugia in November 1260, the flagellant craze quickly spread south to Rome and north and westwards across the Alps.* But, whereas in Southern Europe the flagellants were for the most part orthodox believers, whose processions were usually led by equally orthodox priests, in Germany and the Low Countries the leadership of such movements was more often assumed either by laymen or by renegade priests, monks or friars. Indeed, in South Germany and the Rhineland in particular, the flagellant movements soon became the virtual monopoly of very much the same sort of people as had joined in the People's Crusade of 1096, or the movements of the Capuchonnés and the Pastoureaux in France in 1183 and 1251. And it does not come as much of a surprise, therefore, to learn that by the end of 1261 the leaders of the German flagellants were claiming to be in possession of yet another Letter from Heaven, in this case a copy of a message which an angel had recently read out from a tablet, in God's own writing, that had appeared on the altar of the rebuilt Church of the Holy Sepulchre at Jerusalem. Although God was angry with the world, the Letter

* One of the countries in which the mania for flagellation did not catch on was England. In 1348–9 a boatload of flagellants from the Low Countries arrived in London, where they stripped and began to scourge themselves with metal-tipped lashes and thongs. But few Londoners seem to have been moved to emulate the flagellants' example.

said, He had been persuaded by the Holy Virgin and the angels that mankind should be given one last chance. If men would mend their ways, plagues, famines and other disasters would all cease; if men would turn their backs on usury, adultery and blasphemy, God would reward them with a golden age of peace and abundance; and, in order that everyone should be apprised of this last opportunity to escape the wrath that must otherwise surely come, the angel had instructed those assembled in the Church of the Holy Sepulchre that they must go on a flagellant procession lasting thirty-three-and-a-half days, the same number of days as the Saviour had spent years on this Earth.

Inevitably, what the Heavenly Letter produced was not one march of thirty-three-and-a-half days but an unending series of marches. As one march succeeded another, so did the hard core of flagellants, many of whom had left their homes forever, become more and more overtly hostile to the Church. By 1262 the disturbances which these people were causing had made it clear to the German authorities, lay as well as ecclesiastical, that the flagellants must be suppressed. But, although the Bishops and the secular princes were determined to disperse the 'heretics', as the German flagellants now became, all they seem to have done is to drive the movement underground; for, whenever in the next two hundred and fifty years there was social strain or unrest, new groups of flagellants would spring up, apparently out of nowhere, and almost always brandishing a version of the Heavenly Letter.

The largest flagellant movement of the Middle Ages was precipitated by fear of the Black Death, which had begun to reach the ports of Southern France and Italy by the early months of 1348. At Avignon, in May of that year, Pope Clement VI personally instituted flagellation sessions in which both men and women were encouraged to take part; but, only seventeen months later, in October 1349, the same Pope issued a Bull directing that all flagellants were henceforth to be treated as heretics and that the leaders, who had deceived their followers by preaching false doctrines, were to be arrested, examined and burnt.

The main reason for Pope Clement's change of heart was the way in which the German flagellants had, once again, slipped beyond the reach of official ecclesiastical control. For in Germany, in 1348–9, it was not long before many common people were hailing the flagellants as the true followers of Christ, who had come to deliver the poor from the extortions and exactions of the 'pastors of the Church [who] behave not like pastors but like wolves'.[8] Wherever the flagellants turned up in their special white, hooded uniforms,

46 *A group of German flagellants.*

with red crosses on them, chanting mournful hymns in the vernacular tongue and twice daily changing into the strange skirts in which they publicly scourged themselves, 'foolish women', Froissart tells us, 'had cloths ready to catch the blood and smear it on their eyes, saying that it was miraculous blood'.[9] Nor do the flagellants themselves seem to have discouraged this sort of adulation. While some announced that they were absolved from all sin, and so certain of a place in the Everlasting Kingdom of Heaven, others claimed to be able to cure the sick, to expel demons, to resurrect the dead or to have regular conversations and even meals with Christ and His Mother. With all this the populace was delighted. And as the ranks of these 'Armies of Saints' continued to be swelled by a steady influx, on the one hand of hysterical religious fanatics and on the other hand of outlaws and criminals, so did many of these maniacal bands begin physically to attack the enemies of God and the people. At Mainz, Cologne, Frankfurt, Brussels and elsewhere, what by then remained of the Jewish communities was systematically massacred, while in many parts of Germany the flagellants seized Church property, beat up

Dominicans or any other orthodox churchmen who tried to argue with them and, in at least one case, exhorted a frenzied audience to stone the clergy. News of the atrocities perpetrated by the German flagellants travelled quickly: so that when Pope Clement dispatched details of his Bull condemning the flagellants to the Archbishops and Bishops of Western Europe, neither these nor the secular rulers were slow to do what he asked of them. Indeed, quite large numbers of flagellants were not burned as heretics, but hanged or beheaded as criminal insurgents. And, although in later years flagellant movements were sometimes tolerated, the official attitude towards them was from now onwards a wary one.

Broadly speaking, the heresies of the later Middle Ages took one of three forms, although in some cases two of these, and in others all three, might coalesce. First, there were the millenarian movements, like those of the fourth- and fifth-century Donatists and the fourteenth-century German flagellants, which generally recruited the majority of their adherents from among the poor and which not infrequently ended up by demanding the violent purging, or even the destruction, of the Catholic Church. Secondly, there were the sort of heresies which had started as movements aimed at peacefully reforming the Church, and whose leaders very often urged both laity and clergy to pay closer attention to the lives of the Apostles and to the actual words of the Scriptures. When the authorities took fright at such people's proposals, as had happened in the case of Peter Waldo and would happen with Wyclif and Hus, they usually tried to silence them by denouncing them as heretics. And thirdly there were the gnostic heresies of the mystics and so-called 'Spirituals', who were mostly more interested in their own personal redemption, or even deification, than they were in the reform of an institutional Church whose authority many of them absolutely rejected. But on the whole it was rare for the authorities to seek to differentiate between one form of wrong-belief and another, and their attitude to the various heresiarchs and their suspected followers was therefore always roughly the same. Where violence or insurrection occurred, the secular authorities responded by using armed force; while, if no such violence was offered, those accused of entertaining unorthodox opinions were generally examined by the ecclesiastical authorities and, if they refused to recant their heresy, handed over to the secular arm for execution of sentence.

An important heretical tract which came into the hands of the authorities in the early years of the fourteenth century, and was duly condemned in 1311–12 by the Ecumenical Council of Vienne, was a book called the *Mirouer des simples âmes,* or *Mirror of simple souls,* which set out very clearly some of the beliefs of a group of heretics who had come to be known as the Brethren of the Free Spirit. In so far as its ancestry can be traced, the heterodoxy of the Free Spirits seems to have been the descendant of the mystical gnosticism of the Messalian and Euchite 'holy beggars', who had begun to disturb the peace of the Church in Armenia as long ago as the fourth century. For, like the more extreme Free Spirits, the Euchites and Messalians had claimed to have so intimate a knowledge of God that they were free to do whatever they chose: and a variety of their antinomian mysticism may well have been transmitted to Western Europe by the brotherhoods of Moslem holy beggars, who were known as Sufis and were in the twelfth century active in Spain.

Whatever the channels through which the cult of the Free Spirit gradually infiltrated the West, there can be little doubt of the influence it had on the teaching of Amoury de Bene, a lecturer in logic and theology at the University of Paris, whose ideas in their turn had a profound effect on the thinking of fourteen clerics who were in 1209 interrogated by a synod presided over by the Archbishop of Sens. Of these, three recanted their false beliefs and were sentenced to life imprisonment, while the others stood firm in their convictions and were burned to death. But, although Amoury had been compelled to confess the error of his doctrines before he died in 1206 or 1207—and although in the opinion of Pope Innocent III his 'perverse dogma' was 'to be considered not so much heretical as insane'[10]—the sort of mystical pantheism professed by the fourteen heretics at their trial in 1209 was soon to prove just as troublesome a thorn in the flesh of orthodox Catholicism as that other import from the East, the Manicheean dualism of the Cathars.

In part the philosophical system of Amoury and his disciples seems to have been derived from the Arab commentaries on Aristotle, which were in their time being translated into Latin, and in part from Johannes Scotus Erigena's summary of Neo-Platonism, which had been written several centuries earlier. But, in the case of the Neo-Platonist Plotinus in particular, the Amourians ignored all previous attempts to render his pantheism compatible with the teaching of the Church Fathers. Rather than accept the orthodox interpretation of Plotinus, the Amourians chose to believe, as the philosopher himself had done, that the spirit or essence of all things was God, from which it had proceeded and to which it must, inevitably, return.

As a natural corollary to this proposition it follows, of course, that orthodox Christianity, with its belief in original sin and the whole process of redemption, must be nonsense and that all men must, of necessity, be saved. Yet, although many Free Spirits do seem to have come to precisely this conclusion, very few of them seem to have thought it anything but Christian to strive, as they all did, to become an 'adept', or a member of an elite whose souls had arrived at such immediate awareness of God that they were reabsorbed into that inactive and undifferentiated Oneness of the Spirit in which they had had their Divine Origin.

Of particular interest in this context is the description given by the *Mirouer des simples âmes* of the seven stages by which the soul of a would-be adept of the Free Spirit was supposed to attain its mystical goal. For of these the first five are similar to the stages by which an orthodox mystic might hope to achieve that moment of illumination, or mystical union, with which the Catholic Church had no quarrel. But then, at the sixth stage of its development, according to Marguerite Porete, the authoress of the *Mirouer*, who was burned as a heretic in 1310, the soul of the adept was not merely illuminated for a moment, as an orthodox soul might be, but actually lost itself in God, as a drop of water might be lost in the sea. And, having thus become God, it remained God, reunited for ever in a state of pristine innocence, and hence of absolute freedom.

If Marguerite Porete may not have gone so far in her manual of instruction as to say that it was incumbent upon a Free Spirit to commit either sins or crimes, she did, on the other hand, maintain that to the deified soul the concepts of sin and of the rule of law were alike without any meaning. And given the belief in the untrammelled freedom of the deified soul, it was only natural that other Free Spirits, both before Marguerite Porete and afterwards, should have drawn from it very much wilder conclusions than she did. Indeed, many Free Spirits held that there were no such things as eternal rewards and punishments, and that the only sin which a man or a woman could commit was to fail to recognise his or her own divinity and so continue to believe that any other form of sin existed. Accordingly, the commission of what the ignorant masses of people called sins or crimes was not merely permissible but desirable, since any such acts must be seen as steps towards the spiritual emancipation of the person who performed them. Especially to be recommended for this purpose, in the opinion of some Free Spirits, were what the foolish masses had been taught to think of as sexual crimes. Of the Amourians, several of whom had combined their roles as adepts of the Free Spirit with those of millenarian prophetae and rabble-rousers, the chronicler William the Breton had heard that 'they committed rapes and adulteries and other acts which give pleasure to the body. And to the women with whom they sinned, and to the simple people whom they deceived, they promised that sins would not be punished'.[11] Later Brethren of the Free Spirit were to claim variously that they had rediscovered the way in which Adam and Eve had made love; that a matron who had sex with an adept would regain her virginity; and that any tavern-keeper of whose food or drink an adept partook was so honoured thereby that he must on no account ask to be paid. Others again were to claim that, if a Free Spirit was ordered by an adept to commit fornication or murder, it was his duty to perform these acts; while, according to an early fourteenth-century Bishop of Strasbourg, there were also some Free Spirits who believed 'that all things are common, wherefore they conclude that theft is lawful to them'.[12]

Throughout the earlier part of the thirteenth century, the authorities reacted as swiftly and as fiercely to any manifestation of the cult of the Free Spirit as they had in the previous century to the preaching of Eudes de l'Etoile and Tachelm, either or both of whom might very possibly have had some knowledge of the cult's doctrines. Yet, despite the vigilance of the ecclesiastical and secular establishments, the heresy of the Free Spirit had an insidious way of spreading unobserved, covertly, as it were underground; and towards the end of the thirteenth century it was discovered that a large part of the missionary work was being carried out by heretical members of a sometimes sedentary but more often peripatetic multitude of holy beggars who had sprung up as a sort of unofficial version of the Mendicant Orders, and who were called Beghards or, in the case of the females, Beguines. Most active in Northern France, the Low Countries and Germany, the Beghards and Beguines begged for alms with a special cry of 'Bread, for God's Sake'. Many of them were strictly orthodox and in some areas they were the most efficient and effective social workers of their day, spending any money they themselves had, as well as that which they collected by begging, on looking after the sick and the poor. But already at an Ecumenical Council held at Lyon in 1274 there had been allusions to unorthodox religious practices amongst the Beguines, while even earlier in Germany, in 1259, a council of the See of Mainz had excommunicated Beghards and Beguines alike. By the time of the Ecumenical Council of Vienne in 1311–12, the Church was referring to the heresy of the Free Spirit as the 'errors of the Beghards': in the Bull *Ad nostrum*, which was promulgated at the Council, Bishops and Inquisitors were told to keep a close watch on all Beghards and

Beguines, and in particular to see that they did not subscribe to heretical views akin to those which their sister, the Beguine Marguerite Porete, had gone to the stake two years earlier still staunchly professing.

In a society built and controlled by men who firmly believed in their own superiority to women in virtually all respects save as incubators of children, it was not unnatural that many women should have felt frustrated by the way in which the medieval Church so emphatically endorsed this view, not only by denying them admission to the priesthood but, more generally, by regarding any sign of a spiritual awakening in a woman with the deepest mistrust. 'Just as in the human soul there is one element which takes thought and dominates, another which is subjected to obedience,' wrote St Augustine in his *Confessions*, 'so woman has been created corporeally for man; for though she has indeed a nature like that of man in her mind and rational intelligence, yet by her bodily sex she is subjected to the sex of her husband, much as appetite, which is the source of action, must be subjected to reason if it is to learn the rules of *right* action.'[13] But what of unmarried women, of maidens and widows? And what of the woman who would rather be 'subjected' to the 'reason' of God, than to that of any mortal man? As early as the second century Tertullian had ascribed a large part of the regrettable popularity of the Montanist heresy (which he later embraced) to the equality which it allowed to women; and, like Tertullian in the case of the Montanists, St Dominic in the thirteenth century had been quick to appreciate the importance of the fact that it was possible for a Cathar woman to become one of the Elect or 'perfecti'. St Francis too had recognised the problem: in 1212 he had drawn up with a distinguished contemplative, St Clare of Assisi, a way of life by which the first community of 'Poor Ladies' was to live wholly on alms, without possessing any property whatsoever. But, rich or poor, there were still many spiritually aroused women for whom life in a convent or nunnery had little appeal, and whose efforts to find some relief for their feelings resulted in their being accused of heresy. On the whole, as with men, the poorer of these tended to associate with the more violently inclined millenarian movements while it was usually those from better-off and especially urban backgrounds who went in for voluntary poverty, mysticism and sometimes, like Marguerite Porete, the cultivation of a Free Spirit.

After the Council of Vienne, strenuous efforts were made by the Church to try to absorb all Beghards and Beguines into the official Third Orders of the Franciscans and Dominicans, to which lay people belonged while still leading a normal life in society. But inevitably the more extreme Free Spirits managed to evade this control; and in Northern Europe, where some communities of Beguines continued to flourish, the male Free Spirits gave up begging in public and moved about from place to place secretly, quite often being harboured by Beguines to whom they acted as spiritual advisers and instructors. It was a pattern of which the authorities were well enough aware for them to have tortured large numbers of innocent Beguines, in the hopes of discovering the names or whereabouts of Free Spirits. Yet still the heresy of the Free Spirit went on attracting new adherents. In the 1360s, in the neighbourhood of Erfurt and Magdeburg in central Germany, the local Brethren of the Free Spirit were found by an Inquisitor named Walter Kerlinger to have close links with some other Thuringian heretics, a group of secret flagellants led by one Konrad Schmid, a millenarian who claimed to be the King of Thuringia, or in other words the resurrected Emperor Frederick, recently awakened from his slumbers in the Kyffhäusen Mountains. Half a century later, in 1418, it was from Tournai and Lille, on the borders of Northern France and the Low Countries, that about forty Free Spirits set out for Bohemia, then poised on the brink of the Hussite rebellion, to instruct some of the more radical Hussites in the mysteries of their cult. Throughout the fifteenth century and well into the sixteenth, the heresy was to crop up again and again, sometimes in isolated instances but more commonly, as time went on, in conjunction with millenarianism and where social discontent was more than usually pronounced.

It is revealing that among the complaints made about the Beguines at the Council of Lyon in 1274 was the charge that some of these ladies had in their possession vernacular translations of the Scriptures, which they presumed to interpret and, even worse apparently, to discuss in the street. For, ever since the eruption of the millenarian craze in the eleventh century, the Church had set its face more and more resolutely against popular perusal of texts into which it was becoming clear that those without a proper training in their interpretation might read the most irregular meanings. To St John Chrysostom, writing in the late fourth century, the Bible had been 'even as a safe door . . . [shutting out] heretics from entrance, setting us in safety concerning all the things which we desire, and not permitting us to go astray'.[14] Indeed, since the Scriptures contained the true meaning of Christianity, St John of the Golden Mouth urged all literate Christians, not merely to read them, but to 'search' them, in order that they might acquire the closest possible

47 The execution of some Knights Templar. The Order was pronounced guilty of heresy in the second decade of the fourteenth century.

understanding of their religion. But during the Dark Ages in Western Europe the ability to read and to write had become largely confined to the clergy, as too had a knowledge of the Latin tongue into which Western scholars had translated the Scriptures from the original Hebrew and Greek. Thus, by the time an increase in literacy was beginning to point up the dangers of people other than the clergy 'searching' the Scriptures, the Church was able to insist that what had in fact happened accidentally was what God had always intended. It was not difficult to find a justificatory quotation. In all four Gospels Christ is reported as having said 'Men shall see and not understand': and his words were now interpreted as meaning that God had appointed the Church to be the sole guardian of His

Holy Word.* Although these were probably not yet very numerous, vernacular versions of the Scriptures, and even of Mass Books, were from about 1080 onwards forbidden.

As might have been expected, it was not long before such clumsy attempts at preventing first-hand study of the Scriptures were leading disgruntled Christians to suspect that there must be things written, or perhaps not written, in the Scriptures, which the vain-glorious and money-grubbing Catholic Church did not want them to know about. Nor were they mistaken. We have already seen how, in the latter half of the twelfth century, the Waldensians had discovered that there was no mention in the Bible of the Sacraments or of any place even roughly approximating to Purgatory. Far worse was to follow. As more and more ecclesiastics as well as laymen became disillusioned with the Church, so did a growing number of them begin to look to the Bible, rather than to the Church Fathers or the orthodox priesthood, for the true meaning of their religion; and in the Bible, as Wyclif, Hus, Martin Luther and countless other later medieval churchmen besides were to point out, there was no authority whatsoever for many of those things on which the Catholic Church had by then come to depend for its livelihood. If there may have been no mention of the Sacraments or of Purgatory, there was no reference either to pilgrimages or indulgences, or to the veneration of relics. But, most important of all from the point of view of Luther and the early sixteenth-century Protestants, there were no conclusive arguments supporting the papal claims to head-ship of Christ's Church. Accordingly, since the Papacy refused to comply with their demands for reforms, the Protestants quite simply broke with it: and thus it was chiefly as a result of the Catholic Church's inability to fulfil the role which the Bible-reading dissenters thought it should play, rather than because of the spread of Eastern gnosticism or the agitation of fanatical revolutionaries, that the medieval Papacy's battle to preserve uniformity of religious belief in a total Christian society was finally lost.

---

* The text from which Jesus was quoting is to be found in Isaiah VI, 9–12, where the meaning is very different to that ascribed to Jesus's words by the medieval Church. In Isaiah the hearts of God's enemies are to be made fat, their ears heavy and their eyes shut,' *lest they* see with their eyes, and hear with their ears, and understand with their heart, and *convert and be healed.*'

9

Sorcerers and Witches

IN CLASSICAL TIMES little distinction was made between religion and science. They were merely different aspects of Man's attempts to understand and, if possible, to control the Universe. Thus in the ancient world a magician might be a respected and respectable member of society, and was sometimes a priest (the word magic derives from the Magi, the ancient priestly caste of Persia); while, as to the actual magic which the magician might seek to perform, this could be either 'high magic' or 'low magic'. The purpose of high magic was to achieve union with the Divinity, as the Pythagoreans and the Neoplatonists strove to do, whereas low magic was concerned with more mundane matters, such as divination, augury, influencing the course of love or the nature of the weather, curing illnesses and visiting disasters on the magician's enemies. In the Middle Ages people thought to be witches or sorcerers were almost always charged with practising a form of low magic.

According to Roman law, sorcery only became a crime when it was practised with evil intent and caused damage. But to the Church Fathers the idea that a man or a woman should, for any purpose whatsoever, try to control a Universe created by the omnipotent Deity was unthinkable. All the Christian could do in this life was to supplicate his God, with a humble and a penitent heart, in the hope that by his prayers and with the gift of Divine Grace he might avoid eternal damnation; if anyone claimed, therefore, to be able to compel the powers of the Universe, it was clear to the Church Fathers that he must be dealing with the spirits of evil, the Devil and his demons.

From certain books of the Apocrypha, Christianity had taken over the tradition of an angel who had led a rebellion against God, and so been cast out of Heaven, along with his host of supporters or demons. On being excluded from the heavenly society, this fallen angel or Devil had assumed control of the mortal world, and his dominion had lasted until that moment when he had committed the unforgivable crime, the Christians said, of allowing the Son of God to be nailed to a cross. For trying to inflict a mortal death on His immortal Son, God had decided to limit the Devil's power by putting him in chains. Yet, despite these metaphorical chains, the Devil's capacity to do evil by tempting men away from the worship of the True God would endure until the second coming of the Messiah, when the fallen angel and all his subjects would at last be overthrown.

The spiritual life of the Christian was thus a perpetual battle, which was waged within him, between the forces of evil and the forces of good. To help him in this battle, there were the Martyrs and Saints, and the holy relics and brandea, artefacts which had acquired a miraculous and godly aura from contact with the Martyrs' persons or with objects they had touched. But bitterly opposed to the forces of good, and intent on leading men into sin by every conceivable kind of trickery and deceit, was the Devil's army of greater and lesser demons, among whom were to be counted, the Church said, the gods of the pagans. While the more important chthonic fertility and hunting gods now became greater demons, the old Teutonic elves, hobgoblins and fairies were transformed into lesser demons, incubi and succubi. Hitherto, the behaviour of the gods of thunder and lightning towards mankind had been, like that of the spirits of woodlands, fountains and river-beds, sometimes capricious and even cruel, but at other times kindly and helpful. From now onwards, in the official Christian scheme of things, although by no means always in the popular view, they were utterly evil and the cause of all human misfortunes.

Determined as the Church was to discredit the pagan gods, there were nevertheless many early churchmen who realised that, if they were to succeed in converting the Teutonic and Celtic barbarians to Christianity, they must, to begin with at any rate, proceed fairly slowly. 'When by God's help you reach our most reverend brother, Bishop Augustine,' Pope Gregory the Great wrote to 'our well loved son Abbot Mellitus' on June 17, 601, 'we wish you to inform him that we have been giving careful thought to the affairs of the English, and have come to the conclusion that the temples of the idols among that people should on no account be destroyed. The idols are to be destroyed, but the temples themselves are to be aspersed with holy water, altars set up in them, and relics deposited there. In this way, we hope that the people, seeing that their temples are not destroyed, may abandon their error and, flocking more readily to their accustomed resorts, may come to know and adore the true God.' Nor was this all. 'Since they have a custom of sacrificing many oxen to demons,' the Pope continues, 'let some other solemnity be substituted in its place, such as a day of Dedication or the Festivals of the holy martyrs whose relics are enshrined there. On such occasions they might well construct shelters of boughs for themselves around the churches that were once temples, and celebrate the solemnity with devout feasting. They are no longer to sacrifice beasts to the Devil, but they may kill them for food to the praise of God, and give thanks to the Giver of all gifts for the plenty they enjoy. If the people are allowed some worldly pleasures in this way, they will more readily come to desire the joys of the spirit.'[1]

Equally pragmatic had been the missionary Church's attitude to the difficult question of miracles, or, in other words, seemingly inexplicable and therefore magical occurrences. In 390, when he wrote his *On the true faith*, St Augustine of Hippo had been of the opinion that God had granted the Apostles the special power to work miracles so that the Church might the more easily become established; and that since then this power had been withdrawn. But, by the time he came to write *The City of God*, the prevalence of the Donatist and Pelagian heresies had persuaded the Saint to abandon his earlier position and to affirm that God might still endow certain holy persons with the power to demonstrate the superiority of His magic to the pretended magic of any other gods by performing, extraordinary and wonderful feats. Apparent marvels 'contrived by malicious demons', the Saint writes, 'are to be seen as mockeries, seductions and hindrances'. They are 'things from which true piety must protect us'. To be contrasted with these are 'all the miracles which are effected by the divine power, whether by means of angels or in any other manner, so as to commend to us the worship and the religion of the one God, in whom alone is the life of blessedness'.[2] Two centuries later, it seemed to Gregory the Great that Christianity was like a tender young plant; until the plant had taken root—which it never did altogether, in the way that Gregory had intended—it would need watering with miracles.

Effective though such policies may have proved in winning new converts, it was only natural that they should have allowed the old pantheistic religions to exert a strong reciprocal influence on the development of medieval Christianity. And it was, moreover, most unfortunate that the Church should have been unable to provide any foolproof rules of thumb whereby the witness of an apparently miraculous happening could know for certain whether it was a true miracle or one of St Augustine's 'mockeries, seductions and hindrances, contrived by malicious demons.' In his *History of the English Church and People,* for instance, the Venerable Bede reports how St John of Beverley (d. 721), when he went into retreat one Lent, took with him a dumb youth who 'had never been able to utter a single word'. On the second Sunday of his retreat, St John, who was then Bishop of Hexham, asked the boy to show him his tongue. This the boy did. Whereupon the Bishop 'took him by the chin, and making the sign of the holy cross on his tongue, told him to retract it and to speak. "Pronounce some word," he said: "say Yea," which is the English word of agreement and assent, i.e. "Yes". The lad's tongue was loosed, and at once he did what he was told. The Bishop then proceeded to the names of letters: "Say A". And he said "A". "Now say B," he said, which the youth did. And when he had repeated the names of each of the letters after the Bishop, the latter added syllables and words for him to repeat after him. When he had uttered every word accordingly, the Bishop set him to repeat longer sentences, and he did so. All those who were present say that all that day and the next night, as long as he could keep awake, the youth never stopped saying something and expressing his own inner thoughts and wishes to others, which he had never been able to do previously. He was,' says Bede, 'like the cripple healed by the Apostles Peter and John, who stood up, leaped, and walked, entering the temple with them, "walking, and leaping and praising God", rejoicing in the use of his feet, of which he had been so long deprived.'[3]* This then was a miracle. But a century or so earlier many equally remarkable cures had been effected by the man from Bourges whom Gregory of Tours describes as having gone about the province of Arles dressed in skins, with a woman called Mary. In fact, it had been largely because of his healing powers that this 'Antichrist' had succeeded, so Gregory tells us, in convincing no less than three thousand people of his holiness.

* In addition to being dumb, this 'poor lad' had also had 'so many scabs and scales on his head, that no hair ever grew on the crown, but only a few wisps stood up in a ragged circle round it'. But these too, by the arts of a 'physician' and 'with the assistance of the Bishop's blessing and prayer,' were cured; 'and a vigorous growth of hair appeared. So the youth obtained a clear complexion, readiness of speech, and a beautiful head of hair, whereas he had formerly been deformed, destitute and dumb.'

Throughout the Middle Ages the Church was to insist that for a miracle to be a proper miracle it must be performed in the name of God, and that any magic which did not call on the Christian God or the Saints for assistance must therefore be the work of evil spirits. But there is little evidence to suggest that this view was necessarily shared, either by the populace at large or by those individuals who really did believe that they were magicians or sorcerers. For, although some would-be sorcerers may indeed have thought they were seeking to enlist the help of the Devil or demons, it is obvious that many others had no more intention of calling upon the forces of evil than did the thousands of ordinary Christians who accompanied the taking of a potion by chanting invocations addressed to Mother Earth, who had produced the ingredients from which the medicine had been made, to Mother Nature or to the Spirit of Healing.

Whatever the differences, though, between popular and ecclesiastical ideas about the nature and uses of magic, most early medieval secular rulers appear to have been agreed that sorcery was a particularly heinous crime, and that it deserved the direst of punishments. The Theodosian Code and Justinian's Code, the Emperor Charlemagne and King Alfred of England all prescribed death. Yet despite the severe penalties laid down by the law, and despite too the Church's horror of all magic that could not be shown to have proceeded from God, in practice the early medieval courts seem to have continued to apply the old Roman law distinction between beneficent magic and magic which was alleged to have done harm. Sometimes, even where damage was found to have been done—say to livestock or crops—if that damage was slight enough, the convicted sorcerer might escape with no more serious punishment than being required to compensate the injured party. But where the sorcerer was thought to have tried to kill somebody, and particularly if he or she was accused of trying to encompass the death of his sovereign or a member of the royal family, both the method of trial and the manner of inflicting the death penalty could be more than usually horrible. It had been the alarming number of such charges which were made in his day that had prompted the Emperor Constantius II to enact in 358 that no dignity of birth or station could exempt persons accused of sorcery or magic from the application of torture; and an important patrician who felt the full force of this law more than two centuries later in Frankish Gaul was Mummolus, a high-ranking official at the court of King Chilperic and his Queen, Fredegunda.

As with so many medieval accusations of sorcery or witchcraft, the charge of having been involved with witches was brought against Mummolus by an enemy who wanted to see him out of the way. In this case the enemy was a rival court official, who, in 584, told the King and Queen that if certain women of Paris were to be put to the torture, they would soon reveal to the royal couple why their young son had recently died of dysentery. Both Chilperic and Fredegunda were well known to be firm believers in witchcraft, so Mummolus's rival had little difficulty in persuading them to have the women arrested. In fact, to begin with, everything went smoothly and according to the rival's plan. On being tortured, the women confessed to having killed quite a number of people, the young prince included. 'We gave the life of thy son, O Queen, for that of Mummolus,' the 'witches' explained to Fredegunda, and were forthwith sentenced to death. Some were burned, some were put to the sword, and others were broken on the wheel. As for Mummolus, however, although he was stretched on the pulley, he would confess to no more than having obtained from the witches a special potion, by means of which he had succeeded in winning the royal favour. But, when he was at last taken down from the pulley, he made a foolish and, as it turned out, fatal mistake. He sent a message to tell King Chilperic that he had not felt any pain, a circumstance which to the King's mind proved that his former favourite must be a sorcerer after all. On being returned to his torturers, the wretched Mummolus was 'beaten with triple thongs', had 'splinters driven beneath the nails of his fingers and toes' and was further racked 'by rope and pulley'—until Queen Fredegunda intervened to save his life, not on any compassionate grounds, but in case by dying he should cease to suffer. As it happened, though, the mortal sufferings of Mummolus did not last as long as the Queen might have hoped: for shortly after he had been returned to his native city of Bordeaux, in the greatest possible ignominy, 'in a cart', the presumed sorcerer died.[4]

Along with the conviction that certain people possessed the power to work magic, the Middle Ages had inherited from both the classical and the barbarian worlds a popular folk-belief in the existence of a kind of person who flew through the air at night to sinister gatherings, at which, very often, human flesh was consumed. But during the earlier part of the Middle Ages the authorities seem to have viewed talk of indulging in this sort of activity with disapproval. In 906, for instance, when Regino of Prüm made a collection of decisions from earlier Church Councils and synods, these 'Canoni Episcopi' included a ruling that the wild night ride which some people claimed to make with Diana was in fact a delusion. A century later, in about 1010, Burchard of Würms went further and declared that any such belief was to be regarded as false.

In the earlier Middle Ages then, a certain amount of scepticism seems to have prevailed regarding some of the wilder fantasies commonly associated with night-witches or 'striga', while, in so far as sorcery and magic were concerned, few people appear to have thought that the practitioners of these arts were sufficiently numerous to require their systematic hunting out and persecution. But in the later Middle Ages all this was to change. Throughout the long series of doctrinal rows from which the Eastern and Western Churches had by now emerged as two effectively (though not theoretically) separate, self-regulating entities, it had been the habit of one side to pour abuse on the other, denouncing all those who disagreed with them as heretics, who had succumbed to the wiles of the Devil and so lost sight of the True God. And, since the Church had always maintained that witchcraft and sorcery were performed through the agency of evil spirits, it was only natural that the spread of heresy in the West should have encouraged people to associate witchcraft and sorcery with heresy and, by the same token, to credit the heretic with the sort of behaviour which popular superstition ascribed to witches.

One of the earliest recorded trials in which a contemporary commentator suggests that a group of heretics was accused of witch-like activities took place at Orléans in 1022 before King Robert II of France. From the evidence, it seems that the heretics had denied the presence of Christ's body or blood in the eucharist, and had refused to believe in the efficacy either of Christian baptism or the intercession of the Saints. But in his eagerness to point up the wickedness of the wrong believers (who had eventually been pronounced guilty of heresy and burned), the chronicler Adhémar de Chabannes alleges that they attended secret meetings in the night at which they summoned up the Devil and other evil spirits; that they indulged in incestuous orgies; and that they baked the ashes of the resulting babies, who were killed eight days after birth, into a blasphemous communion bread.* Since the heretics themselves claimed to have ecstatic visions in which they were transported from one place to another, it is perhaps surprising that Adhémar did not further accuse them of flying through the night air. But for the time being invoking evil spirits, making human sacrifices and eating babies was enough.

* In his diatribe against the Manichees, St Augustine had described how some of these heretics had eaten their babies in order that their souls might be released from the burden of the flesh.

48 The devil seducing a witch.

The idea that someone might make a pact with the Devil was as old at least as the fourth century, when St Basil is reported to have released a man from such a contract. To those who were suspicious of his erudition, it had seemed that the scholar Gerbert of Aurillac must have acquired his learning by magical means, and that his elevation to the papal throne in 999 (as Pope Sylvester II) had been accomplished by means of a pact which he had made some years earlier with his tutor, the Devil. And, when in the twelfth century Satan 'in his usual and well-known shape' appeared before St Wulfric to claim the soul of a poor wretch who in his misery 'had yielded himself and done homage to the devil', the Saint was able, so Roger of Wendover tells us, to save the man by sprinkling Holy Water in Satan's face.[5] Yet, although some people clearly believed in the reality of these pacts, it does not seem to have been until the time of the growing alarm at the success of the Cathar heresy in Southern France that a group of heretics was suspected of actually worshipping the Devil by doing him obscene obeisance. Hitherto people had been accused of invoking the Devil or demons, or sometimes of having acquired their magical powers in return for a promise to serve the interests of evil. But such was the popularity of Catharism that men like the English chronicler Walter Map thought it necessary to impute to them the vilest crimes imaginable. Consequently, to the already familiar picture of the sort of orgies in which others before him had supposed heretics to indulge, Map in about 1190 added the detail of a black cat. At the meetings of the heretics in Aquitaine and Burgundy, according to Map, this animal would slide down a rope into the midst of his devotees, who, well aware that he was in fact Satan, all rushed to worship him by kissing his arse or his genitals.*

With the founding of the Inquisition and the subsequent authorisation in 1252 of torture as a means of extracting confessions from heretics, it was inevitable that such confessions should become not only more frequent but increasingly far-fetched. But it is interesting to note that in the thirteenth century the imputation of diabolism appears to have been confined mostly to the imaginations of the chroniclers or to occasions such as that when, in the 1230s, the Archbishop of Bremen decided that the best way to encompass the ruin of the people of Steding, who had defied his authority, would be to accuse them of heresy. Originally, the quarrel between the Archbishop and the Stedingers had been about hunting rights and rival claims to the tithes from certain lands. Annoyed by the Stedingers' refusal to comply with his wishes in the matter, the Archbishop had ordered an armed force into the field against them. To his fury, the force had been routed. And still worse had followed. When one day at Mass a priest had stuffed the small amount of money given him by a noblewoman of the district into her mouth, instead of the consecrated host, the woman's husband had avenged the insult by killing him. To this attack on one of his subordinates the Archbishop had promptly replied by excommunicating the man. But so rebellious had the Stedingers by then become that large numbers of them had risen up in arms and, shortly afterwards, a second military assault which the Archbishop had persuaded the neighbouring princes to lead against them had been successfully repulsed.

It was at this point, it seems, that the Archbishop determined to denounce the Stedingers to Pope Gregory IX as being the most

---

* Of the various forms which the Devil might assume, a long list is provided by Peter the Venerable, a twelfth-century Abbot of Cluny, in his *De Miraculis*. Although Satan was usually pictured as a hideously distorted and sometimes black human being, he might also appear to people in the shape of an animal, a bird, a reptile or even a spider.

thoroughgoing and dangerous sort of heretics; and, in order to provide the founder of the Inquisition with a dossier which could leave him in no doubt on this point, the Archbishop evidently ferreted out all the most lurid and disgusting details he could find either in earlier writings against heretics or in popular superstitions about witches. In response to the Archbishop's appeal for help in dealing with the 'heretics', the Pope in 1232 issued a Bull urging the Bishops of the surrounding area to preach a crusade against the people of Steding, who were guilty, among other things, of making wax images, of communicating with demons and of holding consultations with witches. At the same time Gregory appointed Konrad of Marburg first Papal Inquisitor in Germany to deal with the heretics; and it was as a result of this man's zeal, apparently, that one Lepzet confessed to performing an oblation with the help of a silver spoon which had been inserted into the anus of a man whom the heretics called their Bishop. A year later, a second Bull gave a still more detailed account of an initiation ceremony at which the heretics were alleged to require the new recruit to their sect to kiss, first a toad, either behind or in the mouth so as to exchange spittle; then a pale man who was as cold as ice, after which contact all knowledge of the Catholic faith was forgotten; and lastly the posterior of a black cat who stepped out of a statue and was twice the size of a middle-sized dog. After the candles had been snuffed and everyone had joined in an indiscriminate and bisexual orgy, there suddenly appeared a radiant being, the top half of whom lit up the whole room but whose lower half was covered with fur. To this creature, who was called 'Master', a piece of the novice's shirt was given as a token of obedience. Then, when the Master had entrusted his new servant to the care of the sect's leader, he vanished again and the meeting was over.

To Pope Gregory IX it was by now obvious that these people were devil-worshippers, and in 1234 he prevailed upon the Archbishop of Mainz to send an army of 40,000 crusaders against them. But it is significant that no sooner had the Stedingers been defeated in battle, and those who survived the fighting had promised to make good any damage done to the interests of the Archbishop of Bremen, the charges of witchcraft and devil-worship were dropped. For like King Philip IV of France in the early years of the fourteenth century, when he charged the Templars with sexual perversion, idolatry and devil-worship so as to be able to confiscate their vast wealth, the Archbishop of Bremen had clearly exaggerated, if not indeed invented, the nature of the Stedingers' heresy to serve his own purposes, in order that he might drum up the support he needed for a crusade against them and so bring them to heel.

As a backdrop to the cynicism which seems to have lain behind these charges of diabolism, it is interesting to see what Jean de Meun makes the character called Nature say about demons in the thirteenth-century *Romance of the Rose*. Very often, Nature tells Genius, people are 'given to think too much in an unregulated way when they are very melancholy or irrationally fearful', and as a result of this they tend to turn the nebulous images which appear 'inside themselves' into external realities. Some people, for instance, are by nature prone to sleep-walking but are so disturbed when they wake up somewhere other than in their beds that 'they aver . . . that devils have taken them from their houses and brought them there'. Other people, 'in their folly, think themselves sorcerers by night, wandering with Lady Abundance'. As for those who think storms, thunder, the uprooting of trees and suchlike events are caused, not by 'tempests and the winds that go in pursuit', but 'by devils with their crooks and battering-rams, their claws and hooks', their opinion, says Nature, 'is not worth two turnips'.[6]

Yet, however sceptical some medieval people may have been about the part played by evil spirits in day to day life, both St Augustine and St Thomas Aquinas had expatiated at some length on the nature of demons, and not to believe in their reality was heresy. Indeed, in the thirteenth century the schoolmen had been much exercised to decide whether incubi emitted their own sperm or, as succubi, stole sperm from one human and then, having transformed themselves back into incubi, impregnated another human. And then again, as we have seen, many illnesses were thought to be the result of possession by demons, for which the cure prescribed by the Church was the ritual of exorcism.

Given the official belief in the reality of demons, it was only to be expected that, as God gradually came to be thought of as being more accessible to the ordinary Christian, so too would the Devil and his host of demons. Yet even though some unscrupulous persons had already used charges of worshipping the Devil for political purposes, to lend weight to their cases against those whom they sought to establish as being heretics, it was not until late in the fourteenth century that such accusations began to crop up with any regularity in the lists of charges brought against witches. In the meantime, the majority of people who are recorded as having been tried for witchcraft seem to have been accused of practising various forms of low magic, sometimes with the help of invocation and

49 An exorcism; the evil spirit is here represented as a serpent.

sometimes without. In England, in 1325, Master John of Nottingham was accused before the Court of the King's Bench of having
taken a cash advance from some men of Coventry in return for his
promise to kill the King, the Earl of Winchester, his son Hugh
Despenser, the Prior of Coventry and three others by making wax
effigies of these people and sticking lead brooches into them. But
although his assistant, Robert Marshall, claimed that Master John
had proved his skill in the art of necromancy by bringing about the
death of a test victim, one Richard of Sowe, he does not appear to
have told the Court the names of any evil spirits whom the necro-
mancer may have called upon to help him in the performance of his
magic. Nor did Robert Marshall say whether his former employer
had worked from manuals of magic or any of those 'wicked books'
on subjects such as astrology and alchemy, which had become
increasingly numerous since the influx of classical learning in the
twelfth and thirteenth centuries, and the mere possession of which
was sometimes seized on by the authorities as providing proof
positive of sorcery. In the Middle Ages, any degree of learning, especially in the natural sciences, could be a very dangerous
thing.

In 1324, the year before John of Nottingham was in the end

50 An alchemist and his assistant in their laboratory.

acquitted of the charges against him in the English Court of the
King's Bench, a lady named Alice Kyteler had been accused in
Ireland of killing three husbands and reducing a fourth to a state of
near-collapse by means of unguents, powders and other bewitch-
ments. According to her enemies, this rich and well-connected
woman invoked the aid of a lesser demon called Robin Artisson to
help her in her sorcery. She and her accomplices denied Christianity, pronounced sentences of excommunication against those
whom they wished to harm and sacrificed live animals to demons,
from whom they sought advice. As for the medicaments which
these sorcerers used in working their magic, they were boiled up in
the skull of a beheaded robber and were concocted from such
ingredients as herbs, dead men's nail-parings, the clothes, hair and
brains of babies who had died unbaptised, cocks' intestines, spiders
and black worms. After a complicated legal battle between her
influential relatives and her chief adversary, the Bishop of Ossory,

when at last the Bishop succeeded in establishing his right to try the case, Alice Kyteler herself is thought to have been smuggled away to England. But, by the time a girl called Petronella de'Meath had been six times flogged, she was found to be quite ready to confess in public that the majority of the charges brought against the sorcerers were true and that she herself had witnessed obscene acts between Dame Alice and her familiar imp, Robin Artisson. Having made her confession, Petronella was burned to death, while some other associates of Alice Kyteler's were subsequently either burned as confessed sorcerers, flogged or expelled from the diocese. For his part in the affair, William Outlawe, the richest and most dearly beloved of Dame Alice's offspring, undertook to finance the weather-proofing of both the Cathedral roof to the east of the steeple and the roof of the Bishop of Ossory's chapel of the Holy Virgin, by having them covered with lead.

As with Philip IV of France and the Templars, covetousness of Alice Kyteler's and her son's riches may well have encouraged the Bishop of Ossory to accuse the Dame and her associates of sorcery. But it is nonetheless significant that the Bishop should have been appointed to the see of Ossory by mandate from Pope John XXII, a Pope whose own fear of sorcerers had in 1318 prompted him to issue the first in a series of directives urging churchmen to proceed against the practitioners of magic with the same diligence as they used against heretics. For it was the increasingly specific identification of sorcery and witchcraft with heresy which in the fourteenth century led to more and more supposed witches being interrogated under threat of torture, not only by the Inquisition, but in those parts of Western Europe where the royal or municipal courts had adopted an inquisitorial form of trial, by the secular authorities as well. And, once this began to happen, it was not long before the officials charged with examining witches were extorting a growing number of confessions in which the accused confirmed their persecutors' worst suspicions about them by admitting to having invoked evil spirits or, worse still, as a North Italian woman did in 1390, to being on intimate terms with the Devil himself.

It had in fact been six years earlier, in 1384, that Pierina de' Bugatis had first confessed to an Inquisitor at Milan that she went every Thursday evening to a meeting presided over by a woman whom she called Oriente. From Oriente those who attended these soirées received instruction in occult practices and were sometimes privileged to hear prophecies concerning the future. When asked why she had not mentioned this to the authorities, Pierina had replied that she had not realised her behaviour was either sinful or illegal. After this she had been released. But in 1390 she was again arrested and this time more thoroughly examined by an Inquisitor well versed in the habits of witches, to whom her case was referred by the Podesta. In the confession extracted from her by this Inquisitor, Pierina now admitted that she had gone on night rides with Oriente, during which she and the other participants had stolen food from the houses of the rich (those of the poor were passed by with a blessing); that it had been her custom to call on Lucifer to transport her to the meetings; and that at the age of thirty she had taken a spoonful of blood from her body and made a pact with the Devil. For confessing to these offences, Pierina de' Bugatis was sentenced to be roasted to death.

For the steady growth from now onwards in the number of cases in which sorcerers and witches were accused of devil-worship there seem to have been three main reasons. First, there was the identification of sorcery with heresy, which the Faculty of Theology at Paris University endorsed in the last decade of the fourteenth century by declaring that all magic that went beyond natural means entailed an implicit or explicit pact with the Devil, and therefore involved the practitioner in both apostasy and idolatry. Secondly there was the increasing use of torture in trials for witchcraft and sorcery. And thirdly there was the proliferation in the late fourteenth and the fifteenth centuries of theological and judicial treatises in which those concerned with the suppression of illicit magic collected together detailed descriptions of diabolical practices which either they themselves or their acquaintances had heard of as being given to their examiners by confessed sorcerers and witches.

The most comprehensive of the early fifteenth-century tracts dealing with the activities of sorcerers is the fifth book of the Dominican John Nider's *Anthill*, a work in which the author sets out to describe the various sins against religion. Although the *Anthill* was not published until about 1435, a large part of Nider's information about sorcery seems to have been related to him by a secular judge, Peter of Greyerz, who had superintended the trial of a group of Swiss sorcerers at Simmenthal some thirty-five or so years earlier. Unfortunately no original record of the trial survives. But, according to Nider's account of their behaviour, the Simmenthal witches had repudiated Christianity in favour of worshipping the Devil, whom they called 'the little master' and to whom they personally did homage on being initiated into the sect. On these occasions, the initiate was given a potion to drink, which instantly revealed to him a thorough knowledge of magic. Essential to the preparation of this miraculous beverage was the flesh of dead babies—preferably of those who had died before baptism—which the witches also sometimes ate or, alternatively, reduced by rapid boiling to a magical unguent. Altogether the witches were accused of having caused the deaths of thirteen infants, for the purpose of killing whom some of them had turned themselves into wolves. Apart from practising weather magic and love magic, the witches might cause quarrels, poor harvests and barrenness in women; they could strike people down with terrible diseases; and they could spirit away other people's property for their own use. Yet, although they had made many efforts to use their magical powers to overcome their persecutors, Peter of Greyerz had been a determined man and, so John Nider reports, numerous witches of both sexes had been burned at the stake.

No less remarkable than the supposed confessions of the Simmenthal witches are those which were apparently extracted from some of the thirty-four people who were charged with devil-worship in the town and neighbourhood of Arras in the years 1459 and 1460. If the story of a Dominican named Pierre de Broussart is to be believed, the presence of a large number of diabolists in the district of Artois had first been brought to his notice when he had heard the confession of one Robinet de Vaulx, who had been condemned to be burned to death by the Chapter General of the French Dominicans, or Jacobins, which had taken place in 1459 at Langres. According to Pierre de Broussart's version of Robinet's confession, the diabolist had included in the roll of his associates a prostitute called Demiselle, who lived in Douai, near Arras, and a painter, poet and composer of religious ditties called Jehan Levite, who was also sometimes known as 'the Abbot of little sense'. And so, on his return to Arras, where he was an official Inquisitor, Pierre de Broussart had given orders that Demiselle should be brought to Arras and there tortured before the vicars of the city's Bishop. After being tortured several times, Demiselle finally agreed that she had been at the meeting of the diabolists, or 'Vaulderie', described by Robinet in his confession, and that among the other people she had recognised there had been Jehan Levite. Lengthy enquiries eventually revealed that Levite was now living in Ponthieu, but when the Inquisitors' men arrived there to arrest him the man took such fright that he tried to cut out his tongue. On being brought to Arras in February 1460, Levite was also tortured and forced to make a written deposition in which he gave a long list of the people he remembered as having been present at the Vaulderie. Yet, although he was said to have supplied the names of many prominent merchants, nobles and ecclesiastics, the only people who were now

51 A witch pays homage to the Devil, who has assumed the guise of a goat.

seized on the strength of his evidence were poor people—three more prostitutes, the mistress of the city baths, a barber and a sergeant in the service of the City Council.

At this point the vicars of the Bishop of Arras seem to have tried to put a stop to the proceedings by suggesting that the prisoners be set free at Easter. But to this proposal the Dean of the Church of Notre Dame at Arras, Jacques Dubois, who had by then taken charge of the investigation, refused to give his consent. Instead, he sought an interview with the Count of Etampes, whom he persuaded to come to Arras and tell the Bishop's vicars that, if they would not deal with the prisoners as it was their duty to do, he himself would take charge of the case. This was a serious threat to the Bishop's privileges: so, reluctantly, the vicars allowed their colleague Jacques

Dubois to return the accused persons to the torture-chamber, where still more names were extracted from them of people who had attended the Vaulderie. Nor was a second attempt on the part of the vicars to cool Jacques Dubois's ardour any more successful than the first. When two learned theologians gave it as their opinion that, since the confessions made no mention of causing death or of abusing the consecrated host, the prisoners should not be too severely punished, Dubois retorted by claiming that he and his ally, the suffragan Bishop of Bayrut, had uncovered a plot so villainous that it might well threaten to overthrow the whole world. Indeed, so vicious were the Vauldois, said Dubois, that even those who refused to confess should, if they were accused by four or more of the admitted diabolists, be sent to the stake. Soon a letter arrived from the Count of Etampes, again urging the Bishop's vicars on in the cause of God and their duty; and, soon after this, a large scaffold was put up in the centre of Arras and the prisoners were produced before the public to hear their confessions read out by the Inquisitors.

On the night of a Vaulderie, the citizens of Arras learned from these confessions, the diabolists anointed a wooden rod and the palms of their hands with a special embrocation given them by their master, the Devil, and, when they put the rod between their legs, were whisked away to a meeting presided over by the Devil in the shape of a goat, with a human face and a monkey's tail. At these meetings, the Vauldois did homage to the Devil, first by offering him either their soul or some other part of their body, and secondly by kissing his arse. Next, they spat and jumped up and down on the Cross, profaning the name of Jesus and the Holy Trinity. Then came feasting and drinking, followed by an orgy in which the master participated both as a male and a female. Finally, to conclude the Vaulderie, the Devil made a hortatory speech reminding his subjects that they must on no account take part in any of the rites of the Catholic Church.

After the reading of the confessions, the prisoners were asked if they admitted doing these things; a question to which they all replied loudly and clearly in the affirmative, before being taken away to the town hall. But when they learned that their inheritances had been declared forfeit to the Count and their goods to the Bishop, and that they themselves were sentenced to death, they all at once started to swear that they were innocent, saying that Jacques Dubois had promised them their lives would be saved if they confessed to having done the extraordinary things which he had suggested to them. Yet, even though many of the townspeople seem to have been convinced that the charges against them were fabrications, the prisoners had confessed in public to being devil-worshippers and it was too late for the Court's decision to be reversed. First to be burned was the aged song-writer, Jehan Levite; while Demiselle was returned to Douai for execution of sentence, so that the people there too should be warned against the wickedness of the Vauldois.

So far, although it was rumoured that more important people had been denounced as Vauldois, those actually arrested had all been people of little social consequence, whose goods and whose inheritances can hardly have been worth a great deal. But, now that the first witnesses were safely out of the way, Jacques Dubois was free to use their confessions as a basis for bringing similar charges against more substantial citizens and even nobles. The second series of arrests began on the night of July 16, 1460, and among those subsequently thrown into the Bishop's prison were several rich aldermen, the City Serjeant and a nobleman called the Chevalier Payen de Beaufort. Of the many wealthy people who fled the city, some were pursued by the Count of Etampes' men as far even as Paris, and brought back to Arras. Meanwhile, tension in the town continued to mount, until it seems that the Duke of Burgundy sent word from Brussels to say that no more arrests were to be made before some at least of the accused had stood trial.

In the autumn of 1460, on October 12, the five most important prisoners were produced before the public, and a concourse of the citizens of Arras was astonished to hear the Chevalier Payen de Beaufort solemnly declare that he had known the prostitutes who had been burned to death; that these ladies had given him some of their special unguent, which he had smeared on himself and on a stick; and that, after doing this, he had been transported through the air to a meeting at which he had done homage to the Devil, who on this occasion had appeared in the form of an ape, by kissing his paw. He had been led astray by the prostitutes, he said: and even though the repeated application of torture had failed to elicit confessions from any of the other prisoners, the Chevalier de Beaufort's rank and reputation were sufficient to persuade the Court that all those who stood accused must be guilty. But this time nobody was put to death; instead, the condemned were given prison sentences of varying length—the Chevalier de Beaufort got ten years–and were ordered to pay heavy fines, the greater part of which went into the Bishop's coffers or to the Inquisitors.

When, early in 1461, Jacques Dubois collapsed in a paralytic fit and soon afterwards died, there were those who maintained that his death had been magically caused by the Vauldois. To others, however, it seemed that the sudden demise of the Dean of Notre Dame had been an act of divine retribution; and added weight was given to the latter view when, in June 1461, the Court of Parlement at Paris accepted an appeal pleaded before it by counsel for the Chevalier de Beaufort, who claimed that Jacques Dubois had blackmailed his client into confessing by telling him it was the only way in which he could avoid being condemned to be burned as a Vauldois and so forfeiting all his property, which would otherwise have gone to his widow and his children. Having acquitted the Chevalier de Beaufort, the Court ordered the other people who had been found guilty of Vaulderie to be brought to Paris, where, after each of them had been separately examined, they too were all in the end pronounced innocent and had their sentences quashed.

Whatever the findings of the French Parlement in the affair of the Vaulderie, the crimes with which the Vauldois had been charged are fairly typical of the behaviour which fifteenth-century witch-hunters were inclined to impute to their quarry. For, although there continued to be a large number of cases in which people were accused of no more than simple sorcery, it was in the fifteenth century that men seem to have become really frightened by the idea of a satanic sect, whose members attended what were increasingly often referred to as 'sabbats', where, like the Jews, as it was popularly believed, they did homage to the Devil. And, as the terror of this sect became more and more hysterical, so did more and more Christians begin to bring charges of witchcraft and sorcery against apparently Christian neighbours, who, unlike the few Jews who still remained in Western Europe, bore no outward sign of their perfidy and were, in consequence, still more to be feared.

Particularly pronounced was an outbreak of witch-hysteria on the borders of Germany and Italy which, in 1484, caused Pope Innocent VIII to send a special team of Inquisitors to the area. At Bormio alone, in 1485, at least forty witches were sentenced to death by these Inquisitors, among whom were Jacob Sprenger and a man known as Henricus Institor, who compiled an account of their fight against witchcraft under the title of *Malleus Maleficarum* or *The Hammer of the Witches*. According to this influential work, witchcraft was the most abominable of all heresies and involved renunciation of Christianity, the devotion of the body and the soul to the pursuit of evil, the sacrificing of animals and unbaptised babies, and sexual relationships with incubi. Because of the well-known frailty of women and their susceptibility to the kind of suggestions made to them by demons or incubi, there was a tendency for witches to be more often female than male.* As to the claims of witches of either sex to fly through the air (a sensation which might very possibly have been induced by the taking of drugs such as belladonna), although some of these journeys may have been imaginary, such flight was certainly possible and was most commonly accomplished by using an ointment made from dead men's bones and unbaptised infants. No less real either was the power of witches to appear to ordinary people in assumed forms: several witnesses had seen a man called Stauff turn himself into a mouse and so avoid being captured by the officers who had been sent to arrest him.

On the whole, in the fifteenth century, as before, most accusations of sorcery and witchcraft seem to have been made as a result either of personal quarrels or actual attempts to work magic, sometimes for maleficent purposes and sometimes for purposes, like curing illnesses or turning base metals into gold, which would not today be considered in any way reprehensible. But, whereas in earlier centuries there had been a good deal of diversity in the charges brought against individual witches and sorcerers, the authors of the *Malleus Maleficarum* had presented the fifteenth century with a composite picture of the witch as a person endowed with a collection of characteristics which had previously been ascribed variously to sorcerers, striga and heretics by classical writers and lawyers, by folkloric traditions and by orthodox Catholicism. In doing this, of course, Jacob Sprenger and Henricus Institor were doing no more than taking the next step which must logically be taken in a process that had begun many hundred years earlier; but in the following three or four generations the *Malleus Maleficarum* was to be frequently reprinted; and it was on the stereotype of the witch suggested by the *Malleus* that the leaders of the great witch-hunts of the sixteenth and seventeenth centuries were to base their picture of the witch as the diabolical opponent of everything that Christendom held to be most sacred.

---

* In those instances where medieval women admit to having had sexual intercourse with the Devil himself, the experience seldom seems to have been a pleasant one. The Devil's member is usually described as being icy cold, unpleasantly hard and cruelly big—all of them attributes which might equally well apply to a large metal dildo.

10

Jews

WITHIN ONLY a few decades of the Crucifixion, many converts to Christianity had already chosen to forget that the four evangelists, the twelve apostles and even Christ himself had been devout and practising Jews; and, when the gentile faction triumphed in the early Church dispute as to whether or not strict observance of the Mosaic law should be incumbent upon Christians, the matter was settled. The revelations of the New Testament, the victorious party proclaimed, had superseded the Mosaic law. Henceforth a Christian was a Christian and a Jew was a Jew. Each had his own law.

The Judaeo-Christian link had been neatly snapped. And, since Christianity was struggling to make its way in a Roman world, Pontius Pilate's role in condemning the Son of God to a Roman cross on Calvary was played down.* The blame for the crime of crimes was laid, instead, unfairly but squarely, on the shoulders of the Christians' new enemies, the Jews: for the enormity of their failure to recognise the divinity of their own Messiah, the entire Jewish people was branded a race of deicides, wilful and unregenerate, who had fulfilled the Christian interpretation of the Old Testament prophecies by their responsibility for the ignominious death of the Saviour.

All that was well done in the Old Testament or that might be interpreted as proof of the Messianic authority, the Christians claimed for themselves; the failures and the denunciations they allotted to the Jews. Seeing their sacred texts so plundered and

* For a full discussion of the part played by the Jews in the crucifixion drama see *On The Trial of Jesus*, Paul Winter, Berlin, 1961.

perverted, the Jews responded by compiling the so-called *Book of the Generations of Jesus*—an alternative and, in Christian eyes, a highly blasphemous life of the false prophet, Jesus. Christian writers retaliated with hideous accounts of Jewish depravity.

It is here, in the rantings of the early Church Fathers against the Jews, that the first fertile seeds lie buried of the hysterical anti-semitism that was to become so rampant in the Middle Ages. For what had started as a politically motivated smear-campaign was gradually to engender a religious fanaticism of such intensity that in the course of a thousand years the Jew, from being a Roman citizen, was to be transformed into a social outcast, the pawnable private property of Baron or Prince, marked out from his fellow men by a ridiculous hat or some other distinguishing garment or emblem, forced to live apart in segregated quarters, ceremonially insulted on Christian Holy Days, taxed at will, pillaged or deported by a society which allowed him no right beyond that of bearing witness, by his pitiful existence, to the glorious veracity of the Christian religion.*

For as long as the Roman Empire remained pagan, the Jew was a man like any other. Even though a good deal of violent anti-Jewish literature was written in this earlier period, there does not seem to have been any serious worsening in relations between the Jews and devotees of other religions—all of which, except occasionally Christianity, the polytheistic Empire allowed its citizens to practise. But, upon the conversion of the Emperors to Christianity, the situation changed. Starting with the first Christian Emperor, Con-stantine, in the early fourth century, theological diatribes against the Jews began to make their mark on Imperial legislation. By the time of Theodosius II, whose Code of 438, together with that of Justinian, in the sixth century, was the authority on Roman law to which subsequent legislators referred, the Jews had been excluded (since it was unthinkable that a member of that race which had brought about the death of the Redeemer should exercise any authority over those for whom the Redeemer had shed his blood) from all political or military functions. A Jew was forbidden to own Christian slaves. A Christian who converted to Judaism forfeited his property and the right to make a will. The marriage of a Chris-tian to a Jew or a Jewess was equated with adultery.

* 'It is in order to give this testimony, which, in spite of themselves, they [the Jews] supply for our benefit by their possession of those [Old Testament] books, that they themselves are dispersed among all nations in whatever direction the Christian Church spreads.' St Augustine, *City of God,* Book XVIII, Chapter 46. The theological basis for Augustine's attitude is to be found in the exegesis to Psalms 59.11: 'slay them not, lest my people forget.'

Apart from these limitations and some malevolent restrictions on the adorning of synagogues and the use of honorific titles, the Jew was still under Theodosius a Roman citizen assured by law of protection in the basic rights that his citizenship implied. Between Theodosius's legislation and Justinian's, however, there was a significant difference. 'It is established,' Theodosius had stated, 'that there are no laws by which the sect of the Jews is forbidden to exist:'[1] Justinian's Code contained no such declaration; nor did the later shortened versions, known as breviaries, of the Theodosian. As the Western Empire disintegrated and the new barbarian rulers of Europe converted to Catholicism, the fundamental concept of Jewish citizenship came to be overlooked while the limitations of their rights prescribed by the breviaries, on which the Catholic barbarians relied as a guide to Roman law, were zealously retained.

The earliest and, for the speed with which it reached its inevitable conclusion, the most striking illustration of this process is offered by the Visigothic kingdom of Spain, whose first rulers seem in general to have followed the usual barbarian practice of allowing their conquered Roman populations to use Roman law in settling at least some categories of disputes amongst themselves. As to the precise way in which the various systems of law operated in Visigothic Spain, there is a certain amount of historical disagreement; yet it would still appear that under the Arian Kings the Jews of Spain, as Roman citizens and subject only to those disabilities decreed against them by Roman law, enjoyed religious toleration and the right to regulate their own affairs according to Talmudic law. But to this relatively satisfactory situation the conversion of King Recared (589) and his successors to Catholicism soon put a stop. From the moment the voice of Catholic orthodoxy gained the royal ear, from Recared's conversion at the Third Council of Toledo onwards and throughout the seventh century, a series of Church canons and royal enactments complemented one another in a rising crescendo of anti-Jewish measures that was to culminate, at the end of the same century, in the total destruction of Spanish Jewry.

The part that religious feeling played in inspiring this legislation is emphasised by the fact that the Kings whose elections had not been supported by the Church party either ignored or even reversed the more savage anti-Jewish enactments of those monarchs who owed their crowns to the Church. King Sisebut, who ascended the throne in 612, with clerical backing, was quick to show his gratitude. In 613, moved by a fervour that swept aside any concern for legality, he ordered all Jews in his territories to convert to Christianity or forfeit their property and remove themselves from

Spain. This comprehensive measure points to another impulse that was to have an increasing influence on both popular and princely relations with the Jews: namely, greed. For, at a time when in Northern Europe the Jewish settlements were still scattered and in some cases so small as to consist only of a single family, in Spain the communities were numerous and some of their leading inhabitants already appetisingly rich. If King Sisebut was anxious to prove himself a good Catholic, his desire to fill his royal coffers was equally evident. So radical, indeed, were the steps that he had taken against the serpent nestling in the Catholic bosom that the Church of Spain found herself in a quandary: on the one hand forced conversions were frowned upon by official Church policy as being demeaning of the obvious truths of Christianity and yet, on the other, it seemed to any decent Christian unthinkable that a Jew who had once accepted those truths, no matter how he had come to do so, should be permitted 'to return, like a dog, to his own vomit'.*
It was left to King Sisebut and the fourth Church Council of Toledo in 633, to effect an inconsistent and a typical compromise; forced baptism was abolished but those Jews who had already been compelled to convert and who had relapsed were to be made to return to Catholicism.

Of subsequent Spanish Visigothic Kings, some favoured forced baptism and others did not. In 654, King Receswinth, who had scruples, took care to repeat the ban on compulsory baptisms before going on, in the same legislation, to render it virtually meaningless by forbidding the Jews to practise circumcision, observe the Sabbath or celebrate any of their holy days. A Jew who was unable to produce a priest prepared to swear to his Catholic orthodoxy was deprived of the civil privileges of his Christian compatriots. King Erwig had no time for such niceties; he was a King who called a Jew a Jew. In 681, with the support of the twelfth Church Council of Toledo, he ordered all Jews to take an oath abjuring their own religion and swearing fidelity to Christianity. The signed oaths were to be preserved in the archives of each parish and violations punished by one hundred blows of the lash, decalvatio,† confiscation of the recalcitrant's property and exile.

Many Jews must by now have been ruined. But, for those who had not been beggared by the laws, it was still possible to get round

---

* One of the most emphatic opponents of forced baptism, as indeed of any other infringements of the legal rights of the Jews, was Pope Gregory the Great, some twenty of whose collected letters are concerned with matters to do with the Jews.

† From a Latin word meaning, literally, to make bald, which here might presumably indicate anything from a severe haircut to the removal of the scalp.

them. It was this Jewish aptitude for evading the regulations, together with the government's inefficiency in applying them, that had been responsible both for their repetition and their mounting ferocity. Not only might a bribe persuade a priest to perjure himself on a Jew's behalf; magistrates, who were similarly charged with seeing that Jews did not revert to their old religious habits, could also be bought, while a powerful noble might, for a consideration, guarantee protection to whole communities. King Egica grasped the root of the problem; and struck at it. With forced baptism he did not bother. All civil disabilities were removed from converted Jews who promised to remain good Christians. All non-baptised Jews, however, and any baptised Jews whose enthusiasm for their new religion was considered deficient, were required in 693 to sell at a fixed price to the royal treasury any slaves, buildings, vineyards or other property they had ever bought from Christians. Commerce with Christians was henceforth forbidden them, together with overseas trading. Having thus made sure that the Jews had no means of paying their taxes, he increased them.

So effective did King Egica's legislation prove that when, within a year of its promulgation, the Spanish Jews were accused of plotting with their African co-religionists to deliver Spain into the hands of the Moors, the communities were quite unable to produce the funds that might have purchased their exoneration. No assets meant no protection. The end had come. For his implication in an act of 'treachery' that any sane Jew must at least have contemplated, the seventeenth Church Council of Toledo bound over every Spanish Jew, except the Jews of Septimania and, of course, those fugitive Jews who had managed to escape into the territories of a noble prepared to hide them, into perpetual slavery. Whatever their intentions in 694, there can have been few Jewish slaves who regretted the annihilation in 711 of the Visigothic kingdom at the hands of the Moors, under whom the subject peoples, both Christians and Jews, were permitted to practise their own religions in a more tolerant atmosphere of cultural exchange—an atmosphere that was to linger on even into the Spain of the Christian reconquest and so, through Jewish scholars such as Maimonides, transmit to Christian European scholars much of ancient and Arab learning that had been lost or unknown to them.

The Visigothic Kings of Spain were ahead of their time. But already, in Frankish Gaul, there had been rumblings. In 555 Bishop Ferreolus of Uzès was banished to Paris for inviting Jews to his dinner table and there trying amicably to convert them. On his return to Uzès in 558 he was forced to hold a synod which drove all

Jews who refused to convert from his diocese. Gregory of Tours writes scathingly of Bishop Cautinus of Clermont, who was 'on familiar terms with the Jews, to whose influence he submitted', not, as should have been the case, with a view to their conversion but rather to buy from them precious objects 'at a greater value', Gregory reckons, 'than they were worth'.[2] A subsequent Bishop of Clermont, however, receives Gregory's praise: in 572 a Jewish convert was walking, clothed in white baptismal robes, in the Easter procession when, as he passed beneath the city gate, a pious Jew poured rancid oil over him. Bishop Avitus managed to prevent the indignant crowd from stoning the culprit but some days later the populace achieved its revenge by levelling the synagogue 'flat with the ground'. In the aftermath of the affair—and it is this Gregory admires—Avitus managed to make five hundred converts before packing the rest of the community off to Marseilles. Since there is virtually no evidence of Jews living in France for rather more than a century from 629 onwards, it is thought that King Dagobert may in that year have responded to an appeal from the Emperor Heraclius, whose astrologers had foretold the destruction of his Empire at the hands of 'a circumcised people', and ordered the expulsion of all Jews who refused to convert from the Frankish domains.*

Gradually, the idea of the Jew as a citizen with his own particular limited rights was forgotten. The remnants of the Roman scheme of society became absorbed into the tribal world of the barbarians, and the Jews came to be considered as strangers and therefore legally without any rights at all. For, in Germano-Christian law, there was no place for the stranger; any rights he might be granted were special concessions, dependent on the policy and generosity of the ruler in whose territory he resided. These concessions to strangers, whether foreign merchants or Jews, were, in Carolingian Gaul, sometimes made by charter to individuals or groups and sometimes contained in royal capitularies. There are extant a few such charters, granted by Charlemagne's successor, the Emperor Louis the Pious, in or around the year 825. In return for a tax paid to the Emperor, the Jews were put under royal protection and allowed to order matters amongst themselves according to their own laws. As the stranger had no 'wergild', a payment of ten pounds in gold was extracted from anyone who killed a Jew; significantly, though, this payment was to be made to the treasury and not—which was the normal Teutonic practice—to the relatives of the victim. It was but a natural

---

* In fact the 'circumcised people' referred to would almost certainly have been the Moslems, whose invasion and conquest of the Holy Land offered a very much more real threat to the Eastern Emperors than the Jews could ever do.

development from these Imperial grants of protection to Jews that this authority should be transferred to others and that the concept would develop of the Jew as the private property of the ruler whose protection he sought. Already by 920, when the Emperor Louis of Bavaria wrote to confirm the Archbishop of Arles' possession of his city, he included also confirmation of the Archbishop's possession of the city's Jews.

The few surviving charters of Louis the Pious are, however, the only surviving documents dealing with details of Jewish residence for a period of nearly two centuries. That there are so few of them would seem to suggest that there was little need of such special letters of protection and that most Jews, although distinguishable by their religion, must have lived quite peaceably side by side with their neighbours whether in the country or, as was more often the case, in those small settlements which were later to become the medieval towns. With the conversion, in the seventh century, of much of the Arab world to Islam, the Jews had soon replaced the Syrians as the long-distance merchants of Western Europe and by the time of Louis the Pious the words 'merchant' and 'Jew' are often synonymous. The first Christians to turn their minds to commerce found they had much to learn from this longer Jewish experience of trade while Kings and Emperors were quick to see that the Jews, besides making better physicians than their Christian counterparts, were a useful source both of financial advice and of revenue.

The Church was less friendly. True, one of Charlemagne's monkish biographers tells how that Emperor used a Jew to expose Richulf, Bishop of Mainz, who was 'vainglorious and greatly occupied with all manner of stupid things'. In the pretence that it was an object of great rarity, the Jew, who was known to travel regularly to the Holy Land in search of costly and wonderful merchandise, tricked the Bishop into parting with a huge sum of silver to buy 'an ordinary house mouse', whose inside the Jew had stuffed with various aromatic spices and whose outside he had brightly painted. The silver was handed over to Charlemagne, who called together the Bishops and chief men of the province and showed them how one of their number, whose duty it was to minister to the poor, had been squandering his substance.[3] Notker the Stammerer records the performance of the Jew in thus duping a Christian dignitary with approval, but the general reaction of the Church towards Imperial patronage of Jews was far less favourable. Archbishop Agobard of Lyon complained loudly and often about the number of Jews at the court of Louis the Pious.

The Church's attitude to the Jews was, as we have seen, governed by two main concerns: first, that no Jew should occupy a position of authority or influence over a Christian and, secondly, that all Jews should be maintained in that condition of social inferiority to which they had condemned themselves by their responsibility for the crucifixion of the Christian Saviour. When, therefore, Louis the Pious, in defiance of previous legislation on the subject, declared that Jewish slave owners might refuse permission to convert to those of their slaves who wished to become Christians, Archbishop Agobard was understandably outraged. He tried to remonstrate with the Emperor; but without success. Deeply disappointed by his failure, he returned to Lyon and there devoted himself to composing and circulating venomous anti-Jewish propaganda, including a catalogue of supposed Jewish iniquities, amongst which he listed cases of Jews stealing Christian children in France and selling them to the Spanish Moors.

At a time when the Church was taking the lead in questioning the morality of slave-ownership in a Christian world, the predominance of Jews, as long-distance merchants, in the operation of the slave traffic was inauspicious. Misguided and illegal concessions from the Emperor did little to help, nor did the remarkable conversion to Judaism of Bodo, a priest, at Louis's court. With the collapse of centralised power in the Carolingian Empire that followed the division of the Empire between the three sons of Louis the Pious at the Treaty of Verdun in 843 and the subsequent splitting up of Western Europe into the still smaller units of feudalism, a new age of lawlessness began. The Jews, who could not rely on the protection of an Emperor with little more than nominal authority, were forced to seek the patronage of the local feudal magnates, were they lay or ecclesiastical.

Christian Europe was, meanwhile, attacked from all sides by the Infidel. Fear of the Infidel without focused attention on the unseemly presence within Christian society of the deicide race. At Toulouse, in alleged memory of the Jews having at some point betrayed the town to the Saracens, the practice grew up of requiring a Jew to stand up once a year before the church of St Stephen and be struck in the face. On one occasion, we are told by Adhémar de Chabannes, Hugh, the chaplain of Aimery, Viscount of Rochechouart, administered the ritual blow with such vigour as to smite 'the brain and eyes from the faithless fellow's head', scattering them upon the earth and killing the wretched Jew outright.*[4] At Châlons, on Palm Sunday, the Jews were, for having 'stoned Jesus', them-

* This feat is attributed by other chroniclers to the Viscount himself and not to the cleric.

selves stoned by the clergy and populace; at Béziers, after the Bishop had preached a sermon in the cathedral exhorting his congregation to 'atone manfully for the evil done to Our Lord', the people were permitted by the governor's licence to bombard, though with no other ammunition than stones, both Jews and their property throughout the whole of Holy Week.[5]

The growth of popular violence was matched by a new spate of theological abuse. The warnings of the Church Fathers were remembered; stories of Jewish atrocities circulated afresh. Jerome had called the Jewish house of prayer 'a synagogue of Satan', and Isidore of Seville, an opponent of the Visigothic forced baptisms, had referred to 'sorcerers and Jews'. In the tenth century Adso of Montiérender, who was later to become a much-quoted authority, embroidered upon the traditional belief that Antichrist would be a Jew of the tribe of Dan by adding that he would be the offspring of a worthless wretch and a harlot, into whose womb the Devil would also enter at the moment of conception to ensure that the child should be the very incarnation of all evil, and that he would be brought up in Palestine by Jewish sorcerers and magicians who would educate him thoroughly in the black arts and all that was iniquitous.

According to reports of twenty and forty years later, the Jews of Orleans were accused in 1010 of having sent a beggar with a letter concealed in a baton to the Caliph Hakim at Jerusalem, which alerted him to the danger of a proposed Christian expedition against him and had prompted him to destroy the most sacred of Christian shrines in Judaea, the Church of the Holy Sepulchre. At Orleans there were massacres in reprisal and, under the same year, which is known to have been one of famine, pestilence and floods, there are also reports from elsewhere of Jewish massacres, forced conversions and expulsions. Similarly, when, on Good Friday 1020, the city of Rome was 'imperilled by an earthquake and an exceeding great whirlwind, . . . forthwith a certain Jew brought word to the lord Pope that at that hour the Jews in their synagogue were wont to make a mock of the image of the crucified Lord'. The 'certain Jew' would very likely have been, as were so many of the informants who denounced these secret Jewish rituals, a recent convert to Christianity; Benedict VIII at any rate took the precaution of checking the story but on 'finding it to be true, he presently condemned the authors of that crime to death. And no sooner had they been beheaded,' says Adhémar de Chabannes, 'than the fury of the winds ceased'.[6]

In 1063 an army of Christian knights marched through Southern

France against the Saracens on the Spanish border, slaughtering as it went, in the name of Christ, any Jews it found in its path. Alexander II wrote at once expressing papal horror at the tacit approval with which the Archbishop of Narbonne had regarded these massacres; at the same time he wrote to commend the Viscount of Narbonne and the Spanish clergy, who had done their best to protect the Jews, and to condemn the stupidity of the soldiers, who had sought to exterminate that race which St Paul himself had declared would in the last days be gathered in. But the enhanced stature of the reformed Papacy was to prove as powerless to stem the rising tide of popular antisemitism as had the protests of earlier Popes against compulsory baptism.

The preaching of the First Crusade against the Saracen Infidel who had desecrated the Holy Places provoked a surge of religious fanaticism that was further exacerbated by Christian envy of the wealth that some Jewish merchants had managed to accumulate. To many crusaders, and most particularly to the riff-raff of poorer people whose souls were stirred by the summons to the Holy War, it seemed only right that before setting out on the long and perilous journey eastwards they should first settle the more immediate question of the Infidel resident in their midst. And so, along the crusading routes, there were massacres. The Jews of Rouen were set upon by the Norman contingent, those of Prague by the motley army marching under the priest Volkmar; Count Emicho of Leiningen urged his followers on against the Jews of Speyer, Würms and Mainz, and a Flemish band of crusaders fell upon the Jews of Cologne. In some cases the Jews were able to use the superior system of communications, which as long-distance traders they had evolved, to warn their co-religionists in other towns. Where this happened the communities either dispersed until the danger had passed or sent large sums of money in advance to buy the crusaders off; but in those towns where the Jews had not been forewarned, the authorities, in whose interest it lay to protect their Jews, mostly found themselves incapable of doing so. 'Convert or die' was the zealous cry of the masses. The palace of the Archbishop of Mainz, who had tried to shelter the Jews, was stormed by a furious mob and the Archbishop forced to flee the city.*

---

* Once they were settled in the Holy Land, the anti-Jewish fulminations of churchmen such as William of Tyre notwithstanding, the crusaders seem soon to have overcome their religious prejudices. Although, as an act of piety, Jews and Moslems were forbidden to live in the sacred city of Jerusalem, it was not long before the Jews were allowed to found new communities in the cities of the Latin Kingdom whose infidel populations, both Moslem and Jewish, had been

It was the same story with later crusades. In 1146, at the outset of the Second Crusade, even so respected a figure as St Bernard was nearly lynched when he arrived in Mainz to order a fanatical monk, Rudolph of Hainault, who was preaching popular violence against the Jews, back to his monastery. Roger of Hoveden describes the activities of an English band of crusaders, some of them 'evil-doers and vicious persons', who disembarked at Lisbon in 1190 en route for the Holy Land: having gone about the city 'giving themselves airs' and assaulting the wives and daughters of the citizens, 'they also drove away the pagans and Jews, servants of the king, who dwelt in the city and plundered their property and possessions, and burned their houses; and they then stripped their vineyards, not leaving them so much as a grape or a cluster!'[17] In 1189 and 1190, in England itself, there were massacres at London, Thetford, Norwich, Colchester, Stamford, Dunstable, Lynn, Ospringe, Bury St Edmunds and York, where one hundred and fifty Jews preferred to immolate themselves rather than be baptised.

To the massacres that accompanied the First Crusade the reaction of the Church was, as usual, schizophrenic. At Rome, the head of Christendom found himself in a dilemma; for although traditionally the Papacy had always been against both violence to the Jews and their forced baptism, it was Pope Urban II whose preaching had set the whole machinery of the Crusade in motion: not knowing what to say about the atrocities his preaching had indirectly inspired, Pope Urban said nothing. At Mainz, meanwhile, there were insinuations that the Archbishop had turned a blind eye to the behaviour of some of his relatives who had done rather well out of the looting, but on the whole the higher clergy, whose lay role as great property owners may have added force to any spiritual duty they felt to protect their Jews, seem to have done what they could to prevent the massacres. The record of the lower clergy is not so good: while some priests pronounced excommunication on those who sought forcibly to convert the Jews, there were others who shared or even devoted their energies to inflaming the popular animus against them. It was no mere coincidence that of the crusading bands who fell on the Jews in 1096 three had priests as their leaders.

exterminated by the onslaught of the First Crusade. Acre became the most important Jewish centre and the Jews were in general treated like all other non-Franks 'because', in the words of a crusader law treatise quoted by Professor Prawer in his *Latin Kingdom of Jerusalem* (p. 237), 'whatever they be . . . they are still men like the Franks'. Professor Prawer also points out that under Frankish rule the number of Jewish pilgrims to the Holy Land actually increased.

If the higher clergy were in the main sympathetic, this sympathy counted for little once they had shown themselves to be incapable of curbing the religious fervour of the more rabid element in their spiritual charge. It counted for still less when, after the event, official Church doctrine forbade those Jews who had preferred baptism to suicide or murder to return again to their own faith. The horrors of 1096, and the Church's refusal to permit a forced convert to revert to Judaism, induced in many Jews a renewed solidarity in their own religion and a corresponding distrust and even loathing of Christianity, which only served to set them more emphatically apart from the Christians.

Despairing of assistance from the Church, the German Jews appealed to the Emperor Henry IV, who, on his return after the massacres from Northern Italy, scandalised the ecclesiastical establishment from Pope Urban downwards by declaring that all Jews who had been compelled to convert to Christianity might, if they so wished, return to Judaism. Next, the Emperor attempted to impose fines—payable to the royal treasury rather than to the surviving Jews—on anyone who had taken part in the mayhem; but, since the crusading armies had by now passed on and there were few townsmen prepared to denounce their neighbours for having joined in the riots, this measure was largely ineffectual. More important, and with far-reaching effects for the Jews, was their inclusion in the special protection clause of the Imperial Landpeace of 1103, which announced that 'on all days and at all times priests and clerics, girls and women and Jews shall have peace for their possessions and their persons'; offences against the lives and possessions of any of these groups were to be punished from now on by beheading instead of fines.[7A]

There can be no doubt that the extension of special protection to cover the Jews was originally a move in their favour but it was nonetheless unfortunate that it should have involved their being lumped together with women and clerics, for whom it was considered improper to carry arms. By the time of the Sachsenspiegel, a review of customary law compiled by Eike von Repgow in 1221–4 which contains the earliest surviving text of the often-repeated 1103 Landpeace, the Jews too had, as a corollary to their inclusion in the Landpeace, been forbidden to bear arms—a ban which not only excluded them from the right of feud but also implied considerable diminution of status in a society which forbad arms otherwise only to serfs and the unfree. A century later, Johann von Busch managed to distort the original intention still further. 'Note here,' he wrote in his gloss on the Sachsenspiegel, 'a great difference:

weapons are forbidden to priests and clerics for their own honour; and forbidden to Jews for their ignominy.'[8]

From the time of the First Crusade onwards the lives of Jews in Western Europe became increasingly precarious. Lack of effective protection drove most of those Jews who still followed rustic occupations into the towns where they could rely at least on the mutual support of their co-religionists and where, by now, it was becoming the practice in Germany for the overlord of the town to regulate conditions of Jewish residence by granting charters of specific rights and obligations. In some cases the Jews were actually invited to settle in a city by a Bishop or a Prince who was anxious to benefit from their financial services and would offer them special terms. The first such charter of which we have any account was granted in 1084 by Bishop Rüdiger of Speyer to a group of Jews whose establishment in Speyer he considered would 'amplify a thousand times the dignity' of the town he was trying to build up to be a busy merchant city.

Although his charter predates the First Crusade by twelve years, it is interesting to see that Bishop Rüdiger already thought it prudent to offer the Jews, amongst other advantages, a quarter of their own, walled off, so that they might be safe from possible outbreaks of violence against them. In return for an annual rent, the Jews were also guaranteed various rights at law and trading concessions, together with permission to change money, own Christian servants and sell meat unfit for their own use to Christians.

In the text of the Speyer charter there is no hint that the Bishop might consider the Jews to be his private property, but in a charter of six years later, this time from the Emperor Henry IV, to the same community at Speyer, there is a crucial addition: the Emperor's charter stipulates that, if a Jew converts to Christianity, all his property shall be forfeit. The Emperor does not say to whom the property is forfeit, but in the light of later practice it seems reasonable to assume that it must have been either to himself or to the Bishop. The implication is in any case clear. By the end of the twelfth century the idea of the Jews as the personal property of their overlord—whether Baron, Bishop, Emperor or King—was firmly established; and since, if he converted, the Jew deprived his owner of a valuable asset, it was considered only natural that the new Christian's Jewish property should pass in compensation to the owner whose patronage had made possible its accumulation. St Thomas Aquinas gives the principle theological backing in his *Summa Theologica* when, reiterating the views of St Bernard, he declares that 'since the Jews are the slaves of the Church, she can

dispose of their possessions', and again, here endorsing the trans-
formation of what had initially been envisaged as a purely spiritual
servitude into a condition of absolute bondage, 'the Jews are the
serfs of the Christian princes'. More succinct still is the lay theory of
the matter given by the mid-thirteenth-century English jurist
Bracton. 'A Jew cannot have anything of his own,' he writes some
time before 1256, 'because whatever he acquires, he acquires not for
himself but for the king, because they do not live for themselves but
for others and so they acquire for others and not for themselves.'

While mob violence, induced by religious fervour, had forced the
Jews to seek the protection of authorities who gradually came to see
them as their own property—or 'servi camere nostre' as the
Emperor Frederick II was to describe them in a letter of 1236 to Pope
Gregory IX—resentment of the advantageous trading terms often
granted to the Jews and their employment in invidious tasks such as
tax-gathering, which in return for their special protection they were
frequently required to undertake, added greatly to the general
animosity towards them. This popular jealousy was further
aggravated by popular superstition, and in 1140, in England, there
occurred the first accusation of ritual murder.

According to William of Malmesbury—and certainly there is no
record of Jewish settlement in England before 1066—it was William
the Conqueror who imported Jews to England from Rouen, where
already they had been compelled for some time to act as financial
agents for the Crown. Once arrived in England, the Jews took up
residence in those of the larger towns that were also centres of the
royal administration. Such a centre was Norwich where, on Good
Friday, March 24, 1144, the body 'dressed in his jacket and shoes
with his head shaved and punctured with countless stabs'⁹ of a boy
aged eleven or twelve was discovered in Thorpe Wood, a little way
east of the city.

So far as the facts of the case go, it appears that the woodman who
found the body did not bury it until the following Monday, by
which time some people who had ridden out from the city to inspect
the corpse had noted, amongst other things, that ravens had been
pecking at it. Later the same Monday the body was exhumed and
identified by a priest as his wife's nephew William, who had at the
age of eight been apprenticed to a skinner in Norwich and was said
to have been regarded by the Jews, with whom he had had dealings
in the course of his trade, 'with special favour'. Both the priest and a
man named Wulward, with whom the boy lived, had thought it
necessary to warn William against this association, but it was the
boy's aunt, Livinia, the priest's wife, who became worried when on

52 *An imaginative illustration of the sort of atrocities allegedly perpetrated by the Jews: the crucifixion of a Christian child.*

Tuesday, March 21 a man purporting to be the cook of William, Archdeacon of Norwich, brought her nephew to see her. Although her sister, William's mother, had the day before been persuaded by a payment of three shillings to allow the boy to abandon his apprenticeship in favour of a position in the Archdeacon's kitchen, Livinia evidently had misgivings about this 'cook' who was so anxious to employ her nephew and, after they had left her house, told her daughter to follow them. The daughter in due course reported back that she had shadowed the pair as far as a Jewish house, into which they had both gone, and William's relatives heard or saw no more of him until six days later when Livinia's husband exhumed his punctured remains.

On being told the manner of her son's disappearance and death, William's mother, a farmer's wife, seems immediately to have been convinced that the Jews were responsible for, no sooner did she hear the news, than she hastened into the city and there cried aloud in the streets that the Jews had foully slaughtered her little boy. A few days later, at a synod of the clergy of the diocese, Livinia's husband, the priest, formally accused the Jews of the murder. At this point, the Jews were able to use their position as royal chattels to advantage: they appealed against the summons to the King's local representative, the Sheriff, and the Sheriff reminded the Bishop on the Jews' behalf that as they were the King's own property the Bishop had no right to require their presence in his court. Instead of complying with the Sheriff's instructions, however, the Bishop issued two further summonses and, when these remained unanswered, threatened the Jews with peremptory sentence to be passed on them in their absence, as well as probable extermination at the hands of the infuriated citizens. Once again the Jews appealed to the Sheriff, who was outraged by the Bishop's behaviour and agreed to accompany the Jews to the synod where he advised them to deny the charges against them. This the Jews did but, on being asked by the synod to submit to the ordeal, which was administered by the Church and would almost certainly have convicted them, the Jews refused and another quarrel broke out between the Bishop and the Sheriff. Neither party would give ground and in the end the Sheriff took the Jews back into custody in Norwich Castle, where they stayed until the clamour against them died down and it was considered safe for them to return to their homes.

For the construction put upon these events—and in particular on the actual murder of the boy, which might seem to suggest a child sex-murder rather than a martyrdom—we are indebted to the account of them given by Thomas of Monmouth, a monk, whose agitation, stimulated by a series of 'visions' some six years later, was primarily responsible for establishing the cult of 'St William'. Since the Church maintained that it was not the suffering itself but the cause of the suffering that made the Martyr, it was vital for Thomas to prove that William had been a ritual murder victim of the Jews and that he had therefore died for his faith. In his efforts to achieve this, Thomas resorts to such evidence as a dream warning her against the Jews which the shock of her nephew's murder suddenly reminded William's aunt Livinia she had had the night before the boy's disappearance. He also records that on April 24 (a month after the murder) some significant marks were found on the body and goes on to cite the much later claim of a maid in a Jewish household to have discovered a knife in the room through whose keyhole she had caught a glimpse of William tied to a post. Finally, there is the even more dubious allegation of a converted Jew that William's body had been taken to Thorpe Wood on Good Friday (a day when

Jews rarely ventured out for fear of mob violence) by the chief Jew of
Norwich and another Jew, but that the two of them had been
surprised there and had therefore abandoned it where the woodman had found it. As if to reinforce this evidence of Jewish guilt,
Thomas quotes stories of how, when the priest began to exhume
the corpse, William 'seemed to rise towards them' and an odour of
sanctity 'was noticed'.

In 1144 the Prior of St Pancras at Lewes, who was visiting
Norwich, had already seen the possibilities of William as a Martyr
and had tried to secure the body for his own establishment; but the
ecclesiastical authorities of the diocese, which suffered from a
similar lack of a local Saint, had shrewdly refused to part with this
potential object of money-spinning veneration. In 1150 the remains
were translated and, despite the scepticism of Prior Elias and the
higher clergy of the diocese, Thomas of Monmouth succeeded, by
adding the weight of his own 'visions' to the multiplicity of superstitious allegations against the Jews, in establishing William as a
local Martyr. In his version of the 'Martyrdom' he suggests that,
after their service on March 22, in celebration of the second day of
Passover, the Jews gagged and bound William to a cross, where
they performed upon his body a ceremonial parody of the Crucifixion, which reached its dramatic conclusion with the boy's left
side being pierced to the heart. The wounds were, according to
Thomas, then stanched with boiling water and the body disposed
of two days later in the fashion described by the Jewish convert.

Although the Jews of Norwich were lucky enough to escape
unscathed, at any rate physically, from the accusations against
them, Thomas's account of St William's martyrdom is important in
that it relies on many of the devices that were to be used so often in
the later manufacture of these pictures of Jewish depravity. Similar
accusations were made in Gloucester in 1168, at Bury St Edmunds
in 1181 and at Bristol in 1183, but, apart from the injurious effect
they must have had on the general idea of Jewish habits, with no
graver consequences for the Jews than had followed the Norwich
accusation of 1144.

More serious were the results of a ritual murder charge made
against the Jews at Lincoln in 1255, when the body of an eight-year-
old Christian child named Hugh was found in a well. The Jews were
on this occasion accused of having fattened the 'little saint' up, on
'milk and other childish nourishment,' Matthew Paris tells us,[10]
before crucifying him and drinking his blood. A Jew of Lincoln
known as Copin, in whose house these atrocities were supposed to
have taken place, was soon afterwards snatched from his house by

armed men, dragged about the town, tied to the tail of a horse until
he was half dead and then hanged. On hearing of Copin's fate, the
Jews of the district fled but were pursued by a royal order commanding that any Jew suspected of even indirect complicity in the
crime should be arrested. Within a few months eighteen Jews had
been executed on this vague suspicion and a further seventy-one
were saved only by the intercession of the King's brother, Richard
of Cornwall, to whom Henry III had pawned the English Jews for a
loan of five thousand silver marks. In 1171 at Blois, in France, there
had been executions following a ritual murder charge; while the first
recorded case in Germany is from Fulda in 1235. From this time
onwards such accusations became not only more widespread and
more frequent but also more hideous in both their alleged details
and their consequences.

Popular credulity with regard to the Jews was by now so developed as to hold them capable of practically anything from the truly
horrific to the ludicrous. The widowed Knight de la Tour Landry, for
instance, in his instructions to his daughters, so far loses sight of
chronology as to tell his girls how the Old Testament villainess
Jezebel 'hated hermits, men of Holy Church and all them that
taught the Christian faith, and made them to be robbed and beaten
so that it behoved them to flee out of the realm', while Matthew
Paris does not hesitate to include in his chronicle an account of a Jew
whose respect for the Sabbath was so great that, when on a Saturday at Tewkesbury he fell into a privy, he 'would not allow himself
to be extricated until the following day, which was Sunday; and in
consequence he died, being suffocated by the foul stench.'[11] If
such a story could be taken seriously, it is scarcely surprising that
many people in the later Middle Ages believed that Jews had tails
and that they were distinguished from other people by a bloody flux
and a disagreeable smell which vanished immediately upon the
administration of the Christian baptismal waters. So monstrous,
indeed, was the Jewish race credited with being that if any
abnormal event or a disaster such as a plague occurred it became
common practice for the Christians to blame the Jews for it. (In
1348-9, for example, the Jews were accused of poisoning wells to
spread the Black Death.)

The association of the Jews with sorcery was at the same time
strengthened by general ignorance of the context in which that
body of Jewish mystical thought known as the Kabbalah had
evolved and by the eagerness of some Christian would-be sorcerers
to master its magical prescriptions without any consideration of the
Judaic abhorrence of what we would now call 'black magic' or the

contemplative ends to which the Jewish mystics themselves used these formulae. The Christian version of the Jewish role in the Crucifixion drama, and the Christian view of magic as relying on the assistance of those evil powers who opposed God, combined to produce the particularly Christian variety of blasphemy that the popular imagination ascribed to the Jews: apart from the accusations of ritual murder and the lapping of Christian blood, the Jews were also supposed to perform strange ceremonies on the Communion host, which, in some cases, on being stabbed by profane Jewish knives, was reported to have turned into a piece of bleeding flesh, or even a mutilated child, and to have screamed out with pain.*

It was in the thirteenth century too that a meeting of witches was first referred to as a 'sabbat'. As the number of heretics multiplied and the battle against the Supreme Enemy of Christ intensified, so did the Church become increasingly alarmed at the influence that the Jews, who were as a rule better instructed in their religion, might have on the less educated Christians or even the lower ranks of the clergy. While the Papacy discounted both the accusations of poisoning wells to spread plague and of ceremonial cannibalism (charges of ritual murder were expressly forbidden by Papal Bull in 1247) it nevertheless took the lead in initiating, at the Fourth Lateran Council of 1215, a series of regulations designed to avert contagion by limiting the number of occasions on which Jews and Christians might come into close contact with one another.

In the preamble to this legislation, the Council expressed alarm that in some Church provinces there was no difference in dress to distinguish Jews, or Saracens either, from Christians, 'and thus it happens at times through error that Christians have relations with Jews or Saracen women and Jews and Saracens with Christian women . . .' 'That they may not, under pretext of this sort, take recourse to excusing themselves in the future for the excesses of such accursed intercourse,' the Council decreed that 'such [Jews and Saracens] of both sexes in every Christian province and at all times shall be marked off in the eyes of the public from other peoples through the character of their dress'.[12] As punishment of 'such accursed intercourse' the Council substituted the death penalty for the earlier fines and henceforth the Jews of Europe were required, with occasional local exemptions, to wear a variety of

---

* It is because of charges of drinking human blood, which were to be revived by the Nazis and which a group of Syrian Jews were accused of doing as recently as 1974, that some Jews today still drink white wine rather than red at their Passover celebrations.

distinctive paraphernalia ranging from ribbons or yellow badges to veils and cloaks 'with head windows' for German Jewesses and tall 'horned hats' for their menfolk.

Besides reiterating the bans on Jews employing Christian servants, holding public office, erecting new synagogues, committing blasphemy or appearing on Good Friday in public, the Fourth Lateran Council also speeded up the process which was to culminate in the official enactment of the ghetto at the Church Council of Basel in 1434. For, whereas in 1076 the Bishop of Speyer had offered the Jews a walled district of their own that they might be safe from outbreaks of violence against them, by the time of a Provincial Council of Breslau, held in 1267, it is clear that the original intention of protecting the Jews had been superseded by the new papal purpose of establishing these segregated quarters as a means of further isolating the Jews from the Christians. 'Since, declares the resolution of the Breslau Council, which was to cover conditions of Jewish residence throughout the archdiocese of Gnesen, 'the Polish country is still a young plantation in the body of Christendom, in order that the Christian populace be not the more easily infected by the superstitions and the depraved mores of the Jews dwelling among them . . . the Jews . . . shall have their houses either contiguous or adjoining in some segregated location of a city or village, in such manner that the quarter of the Jews be separated from the dwellings of the Christians by a fence, a wall or a moat.'[13]

Having sought thus to prevent contamination of the Christian flock by the Jews, the Fourth Lateran Council went on to recommend, that conversional sermons should be preached to the Jews by the newly recognised Orders of Friars Minor—a seemingly harmless development which was, by directing the friar's attention to the Jews, to have terrible consequences. For no sooner was the Inquisition set up to stamp out heresy than the friars who manned it began to see the lapsed convert from Judaism as just another form of heretic. In 1267 the Bull *Turbato Corde* of Clement VI expressly declared him so, and from then onwards any Jewish convert, forced or otherwise, who might be suspected of returning to the Judaic rites, was placed within the remorseless and often arbitrary jurisdiction of the Inquisition.

Not only as officers of the Inquisition but in the ordinary performance of their brotherly duties, the attitude of the friars towards the Jews appears to have been in general antipathetic. In England, in 1235, when some Dominicans intervened to try and protect the Jews from the persecutions that followed the murder of 'little St

53 *Jews are cast into a pit and burned.*

Hugh', the astonishment of the populace was such that it was assumed that the friars must have been corrupted by Jewish money. While there are, of course, other instances of friars seeking to protect the Jews, far more usual are reports of their zeal in enforcing the humiliating laws by which the Jews were supposed to be kept apart from the Christians. It was the friars who were chiefly responsible for the public burning of Jewish books, and there are even cases of friars so abusing their authority to preach conversional sermons as to arrive in the Jewish quarter at the head of a rabble intent only upon beating up the prospective audience.*

If the Church, though, in its struggle to maintain Catholic orthodoxy, was concerned to ensure that the Jews be preserved as a cringing monument to their crime, the secular owners of the Jewish communities had more practical considerations in mind. The

* More subtle was the ploy of the Knights of St John who, wishing to provoke Jewish riots in Valentia, hacked a passage through the wall of the Jewish quarter in order to litter its streets with crucifixes and other Christian religious objects. (c.f.J. Regné, *Catalogue des Actes de Jaime 1er, Pedro III et Alfonso III, rois d' Aragon, concernant les Juifs (1213–91), Revue des Etudes Juives,* No. 1715; LXVIII p. 200. 1918.)

Princes and those Barons who owned Jews were interested in making money out of them and, for as long as their Jews were able to provide them with a decent income, they continued to do what they could to protect them from both mob violence and religious interference.

The deterioration of the Jewish position after the First Crusade, however, and the growth of the idea of the Jew as being without any basic rights whatsoever, radically altered the economic character of Jewish life in Western Europe. While popular hostility made the trade routes dangerous for the Jew to travel, the religious framework within which the increasingly powerful and monopolistic Christian guilds developed necessarily excluded him from membership. Since feudal land tenure involved the concept of honour and the obligations of knight service, the bans on Jews bearing arms were soon followed by legislation forbidding them to own land. With any property they could be seen to have retained liable to heavy taxation or looting by the mob, those Jews who had any assets left preferred to keep them in coin or jewels, which could be more easily hidden away .

But how, once the facilities of trade were no longer available to him, was the medieval Jew to earn a living from his capital?

Imputations of a religious or superstitious nature apart, the most common charge made against the Jews was that they were usurers. As early as the sixth century Gregory of Tours tells the story of Armentarius, a Jew who, some time before 584, advanced enough money to Injuriosus, an ex-vicar, and Eunomius, an ex-count, to prompt the two ex-dignitaries to invite him to dine with them and there have him murdered by their servants.[14] But, although their activities as merchants must have involved some Jews from time to time in credit and loan situations, the Jews were in fact forbidden to practise usury by those self-same passages of the Old Testament (Exodus XXII 25, Deuteronomy XXIII, 19–20 and Leviticus XXV, 35–37), upon which, some hundreds or even thousands of years later, the Christian theologians based the Christian prohibition of usury.

For the Jew in the earlier Middle Ages, as for the Christian, to lend money at interest was a sin; and, with the expansion in the twelfth century of commerce and the increasing circulation of money and bonds, the problem loomed suddenly large in the minds of both the Christian and the Jewish religious authorities. Although, as the capitalists of the earlier Middle Ages, the clergy had, with the tax-gatherers and merchants, supplied what little demand there had been for moneylenders, the Church had always disapproved of the practice and now came out even more strongly against it. The Parable of the Talents, in which the servant is rebuked for not investing his master's money in order to earn him interest, was ignored and the Third Lateran Council of 1179 pronounced those Christians who lent out money at interest to be unfit for Christian burial.

But for Kings to raise armies, for Christian merchants to embark on trading enterprises, even for the more idle Abbots and Bishops to keep themselves in their luxurious ways, it became more and more necessary to borrow money. And yet there was a great dearth of people prepared to lend it without interest. The tightening up of Canon law against usury and the changing circumstances of both Christian and Jewish life in the twelfth century forced the rabbis to recognise that moneylending was often the only means by which a Jew could now hope to support himself and so to abandon the strict application of the Talmudic ban in favour of a new interpretation of the sacred texts which followed, in the words of the twelfth-century Rabbi Eliezer b. Nathan of Mainz, that 'where Jews own no fields or vineyards whereby they can live, lending money to non-Jews for their livelihood is necessary and therefore permitted'.[15] If a Jew could find alternative employment he was to take it, the rabbis insisted, but if he could not, the unwelcome evil would in future be tolerated.

The emergence of the already unpopular Jews as the money-lenders of twelfth- and early thirteenth-century Europe only added to the animosity against them while, as more and more property came to be pledged to them, Christian debtors who either could not or would not repay their debts seized on the unpopularity of the Jews as a convenient means of extricating themselves from their predicament. A riot or a massacre, in which, with luck, the records of the transaction would be destroyed and so preclude the King, as the Jews' owner, from claiming retribution, was a neat way of cancelling an obligation. But, if the prevalence of the Jews as moneylenders was generally harmful to them, far more so was the appearance and rapid spread in the thirteenth century of the Caorsini, or papal money-changers, who were within a few generations to oust the Jews even from the hated profession of usury. For although Church Councils continued to legislate against both Jewish and Christian moneylending—in 1311 the Council of Vienne went so far as to equate the lending of money at interest with heresy*—the gradual development, in Italy especially, of

* The theologians denounced Jewish and Christian usury alike, but the more popular theory of the matter held that Deuteronomy XXIII 19.20, which stated that

banking necessarily softened the practical application of these laws until, in the late fourteenth century, the theorist Peter of Ancharano managed to slip round the prohibition altogether by saying that 'reasonable interest' was in keeping with Canon law because of the loss of profit that the lender might have made during the time that elapsed before repayment of the loan. And, since trade could not have flourished as it did without the facilities provided by the banks, in the early fifteenth century we find the Church Council of Constance itself tacitly accepting what had long since become common practice by trying to regulate the abuse and declaring that 'reasonable interest' should be fixed at eleven per cent.

Against this respectable new variety of Christian usury—of which in 1493 Sebastian Brand in his *Ship of Fools* writes:

> 'Really tolerable was what the Jews had asked;
> The Christian-Jews drove them out.
> They practise the art of the Jewish cutthroat
> And all justice and laws are silent about it'—

the Jews stood little chance of successful competition. Even before the introduction of the Caorsini or Lombards, as the Christian moneylenders were sometimes called, feudal lords had grown impatient and, on the pretext that their Jews were cheating them, resorted to holding them to ransom on charges of clipping the coinage or otherwise defrauding their treasuries. Thus in England, where in the twelfth century the King had been content to wait until the enormously rich Aaron of Lincoln died in order to inherit, as the Jew's owner, a property extensive enough to require that a separate department of the Exchequer be set up to deal with it, in 1210 King John found it simpler to arrest all the Jews in his kingdom and insist that they purchase their freedom. A Jew of Bristol who challenged the official assessment of his wealth had a tooth torn out of his gums every day until he agreed to save the last few by paying up the full ten thousand marks expected of him.

Life by bribery had for long been a normal condition of Jewish existence but, with the repeated extortion of arbitrary taxes and the increasing number of occasions on which the Jews were obliged to produce large sums of money to clear themselves of the various fiscal or superstitious charges brought against them, the communi-

Continued from previous page.
'unto a stranger thou mayest lend upon usury', was to be interpreted as meaning that for a Jew to lend money to a Christian at interest was permitted, whereas for the Christian to do so was not.

ties were soon reduced to a state of such poverty that they were unable to scrape together the money required of them. Thus, again in England, whereas King John's tax of 1210 had succeeded in extracting sixty-six thousand marks from the Jews, by the mid-thirteenth century, when Henry III pawned the whole of English Jewry to his brother, it was, as we have seen, for a paltry five thousand marks in toto. Only forty years later, it was not even worth Edward I's while to keep any Jews in the country. So useless had they become to him that in 1290, having confiscated those few assets that they had managed to preserve, he ordered the expulsion of the three thousand Jews still remaining and no Jew, who did not pretend at least to convert to Christianity, was allowed into England again until the time of Oliver Cromwell.*

Throughout Western Europe, although in some countries later than others, the general pattern was the same. The springtime of Christian usury and the pillaging, burning and looting of Jewish property at the hands of the mob meant diminishing returns for the Jews' owners, who therefore preferred to extract what money they could from their Jews and then expel them. In France, from 1198 when some of the Barons expelled their Jews until the last royal expulsion of 1394, the Jews were alternately expelled and re-admitted, the cycles often coinciding with temporary expulsions of the Caorsini or Lombards. In Germany, likewise, most of those cities and principalities whose Jewish communities had not been obliterated by outbreaks of mob violence followed a similar course of banishing and then recalling their Jews before, in the late four-teenth century and the fifteenth, expelling them for good. And from Spain and Portugal too, where Jewish prosperity lasted longer than in the North, all Jews who refused to convert to Christianity were finally driven out in the last decade of the fifteenth century;†so that by the end of the medieval period, although practising Jews still lived openly as such in Italy and in some German towns, the main bulk of the European Jewish population had been pushed

---

* It is remarkable that Shakespeare, whose Shylock is generally regarded as a masterly portrait of a Jew, can never, if this ban was strictly enforced, have met one.

† In the early years of the 1460s Alonso de Espina had advocated expulsion of the Jews from Spain in his book *Fortalicium Fidei*. But, although there had been local expulsions—such as that from Andalusia in 1483—it was not until 1492, the year of Columbus's voyage across the Atlantic to 'discover' America, that King Ferdi-nand could be persuaded to withdraw his protection from the Jews and order their general expulsion. In Portugal, the final order was given in 1496; and followed, in 1497, by a spate of particularly cruel mass forced conversions.

eastwards into Poland and the European provinces along the
Russian border.

Through the enveloping gloom that had gradually settled over
later medieval Jewish life there flickered now only one bright light,
and that in Eastern Europe, where, in the year 1244, Duke Frederick
of Austria had granted the Jews of his duchy a charter, in which he
had given as the basis for the rights granted his desire to promote
the welfare of all his subjects and not, as was by then the familiar
formula, the claim that the Jews were the private property of their
owners. Upon this untypical and altogether more liberal charter a
whole series of subsequent Eastern European charters had come to
be modelled; and its moderating influence was to extend into the
sixteenth century when it helped to shape the toleration laws of
Ferdinand I and Maximilian II, which were in their turn to serve as
models for other sixteenth-century legislation dealing with Jews.

Wherever else in Europe the ghettoes were permitted to remain
after the fourteenth- and fifteenth-century expulsions, the lot of the
Jew was a grim one: abandoned, as he was, by the Papacy and the
ecclesiastical authorities who had proved unequal to the task of
protecting those whom they had pronounced fit only for popular
contempt, driven out by Kings and Princes who no longer had any
use for him, and loathed by a populace which not only imputed to
him the most ghastly of crimes but was all too often ready to execute
its own rough justice on him, he presumably derived what comfort
he could from the Jewish belief that all the sufferings of the
Diaspora were a necessary penance that must precede the eventual
return to the Promised Land. But, however strong his religious
convictions, there can have been small chance of his long forgetting
that he was a fundamentally rightless person, who was, as such, a
prey to virtually any whim that might take his owner's fancy. So it
was, for instance, that in some German provinces, over and above
the curfews and other restrictions on both his movements and the
activities in which he was permitted to engage, when a Jew was
convicted of a capital offence, he was hanged upside down between
two vicious dogs. In other German provinces, where court procedure demanded that the Jew take an oath, he was made to amuse
the court by ridiculing his religion. Even at Venice, a city much
criticised for her toleration of the Jews, the fattest citizens of the
ghetto were once a year compelled to strip naked and entertain the
citizens of the Serene Republic by running a race.

11

Hell

O F ALL MEDIEVAL VISIONS of the afterlife, none is more sophisticated, yet at the same time representative of its period, than
that offered by Dante Alighieri in his early fourteenth-
century *Divine Comedy*. So, since the mortal life of the medieval
Christian was reckoned to be no more than a brief interlude in his or
her progress towards the Life Everlasting, it seems appropriate, by
way of an epilogue, to look briefly at what Dante thought eternity
might hold in store for those denizens of the earthly underworld
who died either unrepentant or unconfessed, or whose souls'
sufferings in Purgatory were to be deemed insufficient, on Judgement Day, to save them from being set apart for ever from the
Supreme Good.

As in nearly all medieval descriptions and pictures of Heaven and
Hell, Dante's Heaven was a place of peace, lightness and bright-
ness, whereas Hell was a place of conflict, darkness, fire and ice—
in Dante's scheme a series of ten descending circles, in which those
who had chosen the Evil Way could expect to be punished in a
manner that reflected the essential nature of the particular perversion of the Truth which had sent them there. In this Hell,
through which Dante imagined himself as being guided steadily
downwards by 'The Enchanter' Virgil, the first inhabitants of our
earthly underworld to be met with by the two poets were a multitude of prostitutes, who, together with adulterers and other lustful
people, were perpetually hurled backwards and forwards, in a
swirling vortex, in which there was not the faintest flicker of light,
by a black, howling wind. The screaming turbulence and the darkness were the eternal reward of the incontinent and the self-

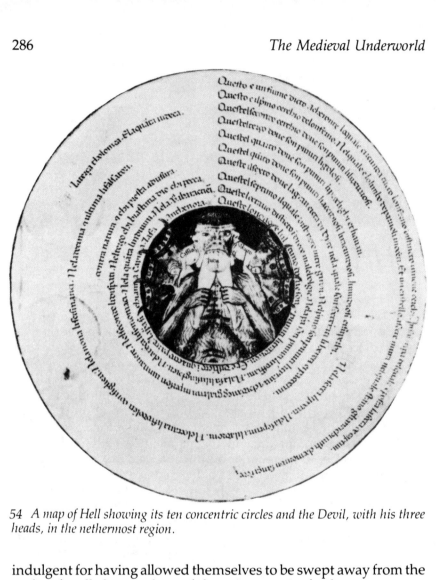

54 *A map of Hell showing its ten concentric circles and the Devil, with his three heads, in the nethermost region.*

indulgent for having allowed themselves to be swept away from the paths of godly love and moral duty, in pursuit of voluptuousness.

No less fitting were the other punishments meted out to the damned in Dante's Hell. From innumerable sepulchres, situated on a white-hot plain, came forth flames and the shrieks of the heretics, whose pride had led them stubbornly to resist all earthly efforts to cleanse them of their wrong belief. Immersed in a bubbling river of boiling blood were those who had done violence to their neighbours, bandits, freebooters and outlaws, along with tyrants and murderers. And running hither and thither, fruitlessly, in a burning desert, under a fire of rain, were homosexuals and all those who, like them, had committed crimes against nature.

Having made their way through the three rings of violence which made up the seventh circle of Hell, Virgil and Dante descended still lower into the eighth circle, which was the circle of the fraudulent and was divided into ten concentric trenches, from which it took the name of Malbowges. Here, in the outermost trench of Malbowges, were panders and all other 'seducers' who had exploited the appetites or passions of their fellows. These were set endlessly hopping and skipping by horned demons, who whipped them with scourges. In the fourth trench of Malbowges sorcerers and witches, who had sought to twist nature by their magic, were themselves now so twisted about that their heads faced backwards and their tears spilled down over their buttocks. Crawling about in the seventh pit were horrible reptiles, and among them the earthly thieves and robbers, who, in return for having robbed people of their property, were now robbed of their own personalities in one of two ways: either they were reduced to ashes by the sting of a serpent and then reassembled for the process to be endlessly repeated, or they were made to melt like wax, mingling and coalescing into one another, so that they were no more able to know who they were than they had in their earthly lives been ready to distinguish between what was their own and what was other people's.

Further on again and nearer still to the centre of Malbowges, in the ninth trench, there were to be found the sowers of discord, those who had prompted religious schism, blood feuds and civil strife. For the discord they had caused in their mortal lives, these people were continually split apart by a demon with a sword. And finally, in the tenth pit of Malbowges, there were the falsifiers— alchemists, alloyers of coinage, men and women who had passed off sub-standard goods or worthless medicines as being what they were not, tricksters and cheats—all of whom were here afflicted with hideous, suppurating sores, in a stinking valley of corruption that reflected the corruption of their dealings as mortals.

By the time the two poets had reached the centre of the eighth circle they had then encountered all the different sorts of inhabitants of our mortal underworld, save only the Jews, who were of course omitted by Dante because of the Catholic tradition that in the Last Days the Jews were to be converted to Christianity and so would no longer be eligible for eternal punishment on grounds of their Jewishness. But in the popular mind, as we have seen, the Jews would always remain the betrayers and murderers of Christ, a nation of Judas Iscariots. So, while Dante may have spared the Jews on grounds of orthodox doctrine, many of his audience would undoubtedly have thought the whole race was receiving the reward it deserved in the symbolic personage of Judas, a man for whom the poet had reserved the most ghastly torment of all: along with the two other arch-traitors, Brutus and Cassius, Judas was condemned to be forever mangled in one of the three mouths of Satan, a three-headed and six-winged monster, whose shaggy lower half was anchored in freezing ice, at the very bottom of the funnel-shaped Pit of Eternal Damnation.

Notes

Chapter 2

1 Einhard, *The Life of Charlemagne*, trans. Lewis Thorpe in *Two Lives of Charlemagne*, p. 79

2 Tertullian, *De Penitentia*, cap. IX

3 *Registrum Palatinum Dunelmense*, ed. Sir T. Hardy, vol. I, p. 315, A.D. 1313

4 John T. McNeill and Helen M. Gamer, *Medieval Handbooks of Penance*, p. 226

5 *Ibid.*, p. 107

6 *Ibid.*, p. 173

7 *Ibid.*, p. 46

8 *Ibid.*, p. 32

9 Quoted by Sidney Heath in *Pilgrim Life in the Middle Ages*, p. 34

10 Roger of Hoveden, *Annals*, trans. Henry T. Riley, vol. II, pp. 140–1

11 Berthold of Ratisbon, *Sermons*, ed. Franz Pfeiffer, Pred. I, 393; trans. G. G. Coulton, *A Medieval Garner*, Extract No. 168, p. 355

12 Geoffrey Chaucer, *Canterbury Tales*, Prologue, lines 703–4

13 Jean de Venette, *Chronicle*, trans. J. Birdsall, pp. 53–4

14 Quoted by V. H. H. Green in *Medieval Civilization in Western Europe*, footnote to p. 115

Chapter 3

1 Quoted by E. N. van Kleffens in *Hispanic Law until the End of the Middle Ages*, p. 78

2 Don Ramon Muntaner, *Chronicle*, trans. Lady Goodenough, vol. II, p. 731

3 *Legges Villae de Arkes* § xxviii; quoted by H. C. Lea in *Superstition and Force*, p. 13

4 Quoted by Paul Lacroix in *Moeurs, Usages et Costumes au Moyen Age et à l'Epoque de la Renaissance*, p. 372

5 St John Chrysostom, *In Epistolam ad Romanos*, homil, 23; in *Patrologia Graeca*, ed. J–P. Migne (Paris 1857–66), Vol. I, p. 615

6 *Legges Henrici I*, lxvi 9

7 Albertus Magnus, *De Miraculis Mundi*; quoted by H. C. Lea, *op. cit.*, p. 408

8 'William Gregory's Chronicle', ed. James Gairdner, pp. 199–202

9 Bracton, *De Legibus et Consuetudinibus Angliae*, lib. III, tract ii, cap. 24, § 4

10 *Calendar of Patent Rolls, 1381–1385*, p. 373

11 Villehardouin, *The Conquest of Constantinople*, trans. M. R. B. Shaw in *Chronicles of the Crusades*, pp. 108–9

12 Joinville, *The Life of St Louis*, trans. M. R. B. Shaw in *Chronicles of the Crusades*, p. 336

13 *Anglo-Saxon Chronicle*, trans. G. N. Garmonsway, p. 255

14 *Borough Customs*, ed. M. Bateson (Selden Society, 18, 1904) p.77

15 *Earliest Lincolnshire Assize Rolls (1202)*, ed. D. M. Stenton, Lincoln Record Society, 1926; discussed by A. L. Poole in *Obligations of Society in the XII and XIII Centuries*, pp. 82–4

16 *Select Cases from the Coroners' Rolls*, ed. C. Gross, (Selden Society, 9, 1896) pp. 79–81.

17 Iris Origo, *The World of San Bernardino*, p. 113

18 Roger of Hoveden, *op. cit.* trans. Henry T. Riley, vol. II, pp. 112–3

Chapter 4

1 Gregory of Tours, *History of the Franks*, trans. O. M. Dalton, vol. II, pp. 458–9

2 *Ibid.*, p. 459

3 *Ibid.*, pp. 409–22, 446–454, 458

4 William of Malmesbury, *Chronicle of the Kings of England*, trans. J. A. Giles, pp. 223–4

5 William of Malmesbury, *Historia Novella*, trans. K. R. Potter, pp. 40–1

6 Guibert of Nogent, *Autobiography*, trans. C. C. Swinton Bland, pp. 173–4

7 Roger of Hoveden, *op. cit.*, trans. Henry T. Riley, vol. I, pp. 502–3

8 Fr. Funck-Brentano, *Les Brigands*, p. 15

9 *Ibid.*, p. 18

10 Matthew Paris, *English History*, trans. J. A. Giles, vol. II, pp. 294–8

11 See *The Tale of Gamelyn*, with notes etc. by W. W. Skeat

12 *Select Pleas of the Forest*, ed. G. A. Turner (Selden Society, 13, 1899) pp. 38–9.

13 *Year Books, 14–15 Edward III*, ed. L. O. Pike (Rolls Series, 1889), pp. 258–62

14 E. L. G. Stones, *The Folvilles of Ashby-Folville, Leicestershire, and their*

associates in crime, 1326–1347, in *Royal Historical Society Transactions*, 5th Series, vol. 7, 1957, p. 128

15 *Select Cases in the Court of the King's Bench, Edward III*, ed. G. O. Sayles (Selden Society, 76, 1957) p. 93

16 *Calendar of Patent Rolls, 1330–1334*, p. 388

17 Statute 2 Richard II, stat. I, cap. 6, A. D. 1378. *Statutes of the Realm*, vol. II, pp. 9–10

18 Statute I° Henry VII, cap. 7, *Statutes of the Realm*, vol. II, p. 505

19 Middleton MS. (in Nottingham University Library) 6/179/Im. 5

20 *Rotuli Parliamentorum*, vol. II, p. 201; (22 E. III, 1348)

21 Quoted by G. R. Owst in *Literature and Pulpit in Medieval England*, p. 325

22 *Calendar of Patent Rolls, 1334–1338*, p. 577

23 Quoted by Maurice Keen in *The Outlaws of Medieval Legend*, p. 204

24 Jean Froissart, *Chronicles*, trans. Geoffrey Brereton, pp. 76–7

25 *Ibid.*, p. 93

26 *Ibid.*, pp. 74–5

27 *Ibid.*, pp. 151–5

28 *Ibid.*, pp. 280–90

29 *Ibid.*, p. 148

30 Jean de Venette, *op. cit.*, trans. J. Birdsall, p. 94

31 Fr. Funck-Brentano, *op. cit.*, pp. 24–5

32 *Ibid.*, pp. 32–3

33 Philippe de Commynes, *Mémoires*, trans. Michael Jones, p. 344

Chapter 5

1 Luke I, 19–23

2 From a list of the names of churches in the City of London, British Museum MS. Egerton 1995, fols. 82–86

3 From a *Commission for Enquiring Concerning Charities*, quoted by R. M. Clay in *The Medieval Hospitals of England*, p. 33

4 Quoted by R. M. Clay in *The Medieval Hospital of England*, p. 104

5 *Memorials of London and London Life in the Thirteenth, Fourteenth and Fifteenth Centuries*, ed. H. T. Riley, p. 230

6 From Bartholomew's *De Proprietatibus Rerum* (*c*. 1360); quoted by R. M. Clay, *op. cit.*, p. 65

7 *Autobiography* of Usama ibn Munquidh, amir of Shaizir, trans. Francesco Gabrielli, and trans. from the Italian by E. J. Costello, in *Arab Historians of the Crusades*, pp. 76–7

8 See. J. J. Jusserand, *English Wayfaring Life in the Middle Ages*, pp. 186–7

9 See G. G. Coulton, *Medieval Panorama*, vol. II, p. 74

10 *Diz de l'erberie*, in *Oeuvres Complètes de Rutebeuf*, ed. Jubinal (1874), vol. II, p. 58

11 *Ibid.*, vol. II, p. 58

12 Isambert, *Receuil Général des anciennes lois Françaises*, vol. III, p. 16.

13 *Rotuli Parliamentorum*, vol. IV, p. 130. (9 Hen. V.)

14 Matthew Paris, *op. cit.*, vol. I, pp. 512–3

15 Quoted by G. G. Coulton in *Five Centuries of Religion*, vol. II, pp. 101–2

16 15 Richard II, cap. 6. *Statutes of the Realm*, vol. II, p. 80

17 Rufinus, *Die Summa Decretorum des Magister Rufinius*, ed. H. Singer (Paderborn 1902), pp. 100–1

18 Guillaume de Loris and Jean de Meun, *The Romance of the Rose*, trans. Charles Dahlberg, p. 199

19 Berthold of Ratisbon, *op. cit.*, ed. Franz Pfeiffer, Pred. I, 393; trans. G. G. Coulton, *A Medieval Garner*, Extract No. 168, pp. 354–5

20 *Ibid.*, Pred. I, 146, 285, 478; trans. G. G. Coulton, *A Medieval Garner*, Extract No. 167, pp. 348–354

21 John Gower, *Mirour de l'Omme*, ed. G. C. Macaulay (London 1899), p. 279; trans. G. G. Coulton, *A Medieval Garner*, Extract No. 268, p. 576

22 Guibert of Nogent, *op. cit.*, trans. C. C. Swinton Bland, p. 153

23 *Statutes for the City of London, 13 Ed. I,* *Statutes of the Realm,* vol. I, p. 102, A.D. 1285

24 *Calendar of Plea and Memoranda Rolls of the City of London*, ed. A. H. Thomas, vol. I, p. 125

25 *Ibid.*, vol. II, pp. 138 and 154

26 Joinville, *op. cit.*, trans. M. R. B. Shaw in *Chronicles of the Crusades*, pp. 337–341

27 Johannis Wycliffe, *Tractatus de civili dominio*, liber primus, cap. XIV, ed. R. L. Poole (London 1885), p. 96

28 Jean Froissart, *op. cit.*, trans. Geoffrey Brereton, p. 212

29 Quoted by F. von Bezold in *Die 'armen Leute' unde die deutsche Literatur des späteren Mittelalters*, reprinted in *Aus Mittelalter und Renaissance* (Munich and Berlin 1918), p. 60

30 From a fourteenth-century MS. printed by F. Novati in *Giornale storica della Letteratura Italiana*, vol. II, p. 138ff; trans. by G. G. Coulton, *A Medieval Garner*, Extract No. 230, pp. 488–9

31 Archives of the French Parlement X^{2a} 25 (June 4–14, 1453)

32 University of Paris, *Archives Nationales*, 180, No.9 (Fonds du Collège de Navarre)

33 Archives of the Justiciary of Dijon (Departmental Archives of the Côte d'Or,B 360, vi). The translation of Jehan Rabustel's evidence is taken from D. B. Wyndham-Lewis's *François Villon*, footnotes to pp. 108–9

34 See Paul Lacroix, *op. cit.*, p. 510

35 *Memorials of London and London Life in the Thirteenth, Fourteenth and Fifteenth Centuries*, ed. H. T. Riley, p. 445

Chapter 6

1 St Augustine, *City of God*, Book XIV, cap. 16, trans. Henry Bettenson, p. 577

2 St Thomas Aquinas, *Summa Theologica*, II—II, x, ii

3 Boniface and Lullus, *Briefe*, ed. M. Tangl, p. 169. (*Monumenta*

Germaniae Historica; Epistolae selectae in usum scholarum, I, Berlin 1916)

4 William of Malmesbury, *Chronicle of the Kings of England*, trans. J. A. Giles, p. 279

5 Bodleian Library MS. e MUS 229, Oxford

6 Roger of Hoveden, *op. cit.* trans. Henry T. Riley, Vol II, p. 81

7 'Imad ad-Din, in *Arab Historians of the Crusades*, trans. Francesco Gabrielli, and trans. from the Italian by E. J. Costello, pp. 204–6

8 Letter Book I, fol. 193, Guildhall London

9 Joinville, *op. cit.*, trans. M.R.B. Shaw in *Chronicles of the Crusades*, p. 343

10 *Liber Albus: The White Book of the City of London*, trans. H. T. Riley, p. 242

11 *Ordinance against Harbouring Vicious Persons (1417)*, Letter Book I, p. 649

12 François Villon, *Ballade of Fat Margot*, lines 6–7

13 Joinville, *op. cit.*, trans. M. R. B. Shaw in *Chronicles of the Crusades*, p. 292

14 Quoted by J. Huizinga in *The Waning of the Middle Ages*, p. 290

15 See *Alexander VI und sein Hof, nach dem Tagebuch seines Zeremonienmeisters Buccardus, heraus gegeben von Ludwig Geiger* (Stuttgart 1912), p. 315

Chapter 7

1 St Augustine, *Confessions*, Book 3, VII, trans. F. J. Sheed, p. 39

2 W. K. L. Clarke, *The Ascetic Works of St Basil*, p. 66

3 John T. McNeill and Helen M. Gamer, *op. cit.*, pp. 112–3

4 *Ibid.*, p. 185

5 *Judicia Greg. Pap. III 21;* quoted by D. Sherwin-Bailey in *Homosexuality and the Western Christian Tradition*, p. 106

6 John T. McNeill and Helen M. Gamer, *op. cit.*, p. 185

7 Quoted by Ernst Robert Curtius in *European Literature and the Latin Middle Ages*, trans. Willard R. Trask, p. 114

8 *Ibid.*, p. 117

9 Ordericus Vitalis, *Historiae Ecclesiasticae*, VIII, 10, trans. Marjorie Chibnall, vol. IV, p. 189

10 William of Malmesbury, *Chronicle of the Kings of England*, trans. J. A. Giles, p. 337

11 *Coutumes de Beauvaisis*, cap. XXX, para. 833

12 Iris Origo, *op. cit.*, p. 198

Chapter 8

1 Ammianus Marcellinus, *Res Gestae* XXI, 16

2 Gregory of Tours, *op. cit.*, trans. O. M. Dalton, vol. II, pp. 462–3

3 St Augustine, *City of God*, Book XVIII, cap. 53, trans. Henry Bettensen, p. 838

4 Bede, *A History of the English Church and People*, cap. 32, trans. Leo Sherley-Price, pp. 89–91

5 Guibert of Nogent, *op. cit.*, trans. C. C. Swinton Bland, pp. 205–8

6 Donald Attwater, *The Penguin Dictionary of Saints* (London 1965) p. 106

7 Petrus Cantor, *Verbum Abbreviatum*, in *Patrologia Latina*, ed. J-P. Migne (Paris 1844–64), vol. CCV, p. 230; trans. G. G. Coulton, *A Medieval Garner*, footnote to Extract No. 41, p. III

8 John of Winterthur, *Chronica*, in *Monumenta Germaniae Historica, Scriptores* (Hanover and Berlin 1826ff), vol. III, p. 278

9 Jean Froissart, *op. cit.*, trans. Geoffrey Brereton, p. III

10 *Concilium Lateranense IV*, cap. ii, in J. D. Mansi's *Sacra Conciliorum Collectio* (Paris and Leipzig 1902–13), vol. XXII, p. 986

11 William the Breton, *Gesta Philippi Augusti*, ed. Delaborde, in *Oeuvres de Rigord et de Guillaume le Breton* (Paris 1882), vol. I, p. 232

12 John of Durbheim, pastoral letter of 1317, quoted by Norman Cohn, *The Pursuit of the Millennium*, p. 182

13 St Augustine, *Confessions*, Book 13, XXXII, trans. F. J. Sheed, p. 287

14 St John Chrysostom, in *Patrologia Graeca*, ed. J-P. Migne (Paris 1857–66), vol. LIX, p. 346

Chapter 9

1 Bede, *op. cit.*, trans. Leo Sherley-Price, p. 86
2 St Augustine, *City of God*, Book X, cap. 12, trans. Henry Bettensen, p. 390
3 Bede, *op. cit.*, trans. Leo Sherley-Price, p. 272
4 Gregory of Tours, *op. cit.*, trans. O. M. Dalton, vol. II, pp. 265–6
5 Roger of Wendover, *Flowers of History*, trans. J. A. Giles, vol. I, pp. 526–7
6 Guillaume de Loris and Jean de Meun, *op. cit.*, trans. Charles Dahlberg, pp. 298–306

Chapter 10

1 *Codex Theodosianus* 16. 8. 9; quoted by J. Parkes in *The Jew in the Medieval Community*, p. 13
2 Gregory of Tours, *op. cit.*, trans. O. M. Dalton, vol. II, p. 125
3 Notker the Stammerer, *Charlemagne*, trans. Lewis Thorpe in *Two Lives of Charlemagne*, p. 109

4 Adhémar de Chabannes, *Historia*, in *Monumenta Germaniae Historica*, *Scriptores* (Hanover and Berlin 1826ff.), vol. IV, p. 139
5 *Chronicle of Prior Geoffrey*, trans. G. G. Coulton, *A Medieval Garner*, Extract No. 47, p. 118
6 Adhémar de Chabannes, *Chronicle*, ed. Chavanon, p. 175
7 Roger of Hoveden, *op. cit.*, trans. Henry T. Riley, vol. II, pp. 148–9
7A See G. Kisch, *The Jews in Medieval Germany*, pp. 107–9
8 Quoted by G. Kisch, *ibid.*, p. 128
9 Thomas of Monmouth, *The Life and Miracles of St William of Norwich*, trans. and ed. A. Jessop and M. R. James, p. 33
10 Matthew Paris, *op. cit.*, trans. J. A. Giles, vol. III, p. 138
11 *The Book of the Knight de la Tour Landry*, ed. G. S. Taylor, p. 126, and Matthew Paris, *op. cit.*, trans. J. A. Giles, vol. III, p. 333
12 Quoted by G. Kisch, *op. cit.*, p. 295
13 *Ibid.*, p. 293
14 Gregory of Tours, *op. cit.*, trans. O. M. Dalton, vol. II, pp. 302–3
15 Quoted by J. Parkes, *op. cit.*, p. 341

Select Bibliography of Original and Secondary Sources in English and French

H. P. J. M. Ahsmann, *Le culte de la Sainte Vierge et la littérature Française profane du Moyen Age*, Utrecht 1930.

Dante Alighieri, *The Inferno,* trans. Dorothy L. Sayers (Penguin Classics), London 1949.

The Anglo-Saxon Chronicle, trans. and ed. G. N. Garmonsway, London 1953.

St Thomas Aquinas, *Summa Theologica,* trans. by the Fathers of the English Dominican Province, 12 vols., London 1912–1917.

F. Artz, *The Mind of the Middle Ages* (2nd edition), New York 1953.

Isabel Aspin, *Anglo-Norman Political Songs*, Oxford 1953.

Yitzhak Baer, *A History of the Jews in Christian Spain*, 2 vols., Philadelphia 1971.

Geoffrey Barraclough, *The Medieval Papacy*, London 1968.

Geoffrey Barraclough, *The Origins of Modern Germany*, Oxford 1957.

Luijo Basserman, *The Oldest Profession*, trans. James Cleugh, London 1967.

M. Bateson (editor), *Borough Customs*, Selden Society, 18 and 21, London 1904–6.

Beaumanoir, *Coutumes de Beauvaisis*, ed. A. Salmon, 2 vols., Paris 1899.

Bede, *A History of the English Church and People*, trans. Leo Sherley-Price (Penguin Classics), London 1963.

J. G. Bellamy, *The Coterel Gang; an anatomy of a fourteenth-century band of criminals, English Historical Review,* LXXIX, 1964.

J. G. Bellamy, *Crime and Public Order in England in the Later Middle Ages*, London 1973.

J. G. Bellamy, *Justice under the Yorkist Kings, American Journal of Legal History,* IX, 1965.

M. L. B. Bloch, *Feudal Society*, trans. L. A. Manyon, London 1961.

Henry de Bracton, *De Legibus et Consuetudinibus Angliae*, trans. and ed. S. E. Thorne, Selden Society, 85, London 1968.

Jocelin of Brakelond, *Chronicle*, trans. H. E. Bulter, London 1949.

Adam of Bremen, *History of the Archbishops of Hamburg-Bremen*, trans. F. J. Tschan, Columbia New York 1959.

Britton, trans. F. M. Nichols, 2 vols., Oxford 1865.

P. Boissonade, *Life and Work in Medieval Europe*, trans. Eileen Power, London 1927.

Johann Burchard, *At the Court of the Borgia*, ed. and trans. Geoffrey Parker, London 1963.

C. J. Burford, *The Orrible Synne*, London 1973.

Chronicle of Bury St Edmunds (1212–1301), trans. Antonia Gransden, London 1964.

Calendar of Patent Rolls, 1327–1509 55 vols., Public Records Office, London 1891–1916.

C. Calisse, *A History of Italian Criminal Law*, Continental Legal History Society, VIII, 1928.

Cambridge Medieval History, 8 vols., Cambridge 1911–36.

G. A. Campbell, *The Knights Templar*, London 1957.

Norman F. Cantor and Samuel Berner (editors), *Ancient and Medieval Europe to 1500*, New York 1970.

E. Carus-Wilson, *Medieval Merchant Ventures*, London 1967.

Thomas of Celano, *The Lives of St Francis of Assisi*, trans. A. G. Ferrers-Howell, London 1908.

P. Champion, *Splendeurs et Misères de Paris, 1431–84*, Paris 1933.

Geoffrey Chaucer, *The Canterbury Tales* in *Complete Works*, ed. W. W. Skeat, vol. IV, OXford 1894

H. J. Chaytor, *The Troubadours*, Cambridge 1912.

St Bernard of Clairvaux, *Letters*, ed. and trans. B. S. James, London 1953.

J. M. Clark, *The Dance of Death in the Middle Ages and the Renaissance*, Glasgow 1950.

W. K. L. Clarke, *The Ascetic Works of St Basil*, London 1925.

R. M. Clay, *The Medieval Hospitals of England*, London 1909.

Norman Cohn, *Europe's Inner Demons*, Sussex 1975.

Norman Cohn, *The Pursuit of the Millennium* (Paladin), London 1970.

Philippe de Commynes, *Mémoires*, trans. Michael Jones (Penguin Classics), London 1972.

Anna Comnena, *The Alexiad*, trans. E. R. A. Sewter (Penguin Classics), London 1969.

G. G. Coulton, *Five Centuries of Religion*, 4 vols., Cambridge 1923–50.

G. G. Coulton, *From St Francis to Dante: a translation of all that is of primary interest in the Chronicle of Salimbene (1221–88), with notes etc. from other medieval sources*, London 1906.

G. G. Coulton (editor and translator), *A Medieval Garner. Human documents from the four centuries preceding the Reformation*, London 1910.

G. G. Coulton, *A Medieval Panorama*, 2 vols. (Collins/Fontana), London 1961.

G. G. Coulton, *Medieval Studies*, 1–16, London 1905–22.

J. C. Cox, *The Sanctuaries and Sanctuary Seekers of Medieval England*, London 1911.

Liutprand of Cremona, *Works*, trans. F. A. Wright, London 1930.

Ernst Robert Curtius, *European Literature and the Latin Middle Ages*, trans. Willard R. Trask, New York 1953.

Léopold Delisle, *Etudes sur la Condition de la Classe Agricole et l'Etat de l'Agriculture en Normandie au Moyen Age*, Paris 1903.

C. Delisle Burns, *The First Europe. A Study of the establishment of medieval Christendom 400–800*, London 1947.

Dialogus de Scaccario, trans. C. Johnson, London 1950.

David C. Douglas, *The Norman Achievement 1050–1100*, London 1969.

Mary Douglas (editor), *Witchcraft: Confessions and Accusations*, London 1970.

Eadmer, *History of Recent Events in England*, trans. G. Bosanquet, London 1964.

Einhard, *The Life of Charlemagne*, trans. Lewis Thorpe in *Two Lives of Charlemagne* (Penguin Classics), London 1969.

Joan Evans, *Life in Medieval France* (revised edition), London 1957.

Joan Evans (editor), *The Flowering of the Middle Ages*, London 1967.

R. C. Finucane, *Miracles and Pilgrims: popular beliefs in medieval England*, London 1977.

Fleta II, Prologue, Book I, Book II, ed. and trans. H. G. Richardson and G. O. Sayles, Selden Society, 72, London 1953.

Fleta III, Books III and IV, ed. and trans. H. G. Richardson and G. O. Sayles, Selden Society, 89, London 1972.

J. Fortescue, *The Governance of England*, ed. C. Plummer, Oxford 1926.

Otto of Friesing, *Deeds of Frederick Barbarossa by Otto of Friesing and his continuator Rahewin*, trans. C. C. Mierow and R. Emery, Columbia New York 1953.

Otto of Friesing, *The Two Cities*, trans. A. P. Evans and P. Knapp, Columbia New York 1928.

Jean Froissart, *Chronicles*, selected and trans. G. Brereton (Penguin Classics), London 1968.

Fr. Funck-Brentano, *Les Brigands*, Paris 1937.

Francesco Gabrielli (editor and translator), *Arab Historians of the Crusades*, trans. from the Italian by E. J. Costello, London 1969.

The Tale of Gamelyn, with notes etc. by W. W. Skeat, Oxford 1884.

Gesta Francorum, trans. R. Hill, London 1962.

Annalist of Ghent, *Annals of Ghent*, trans. Hilda Johnstone, London 1951.

Edward Gibbon, *The Decline and Fall of the Roman Empire*, 6 vols. (Everyman), London 1910.

J. Gilchrist, *The Church and Economic Activity in the Middle Ages*, London 1969.

E. Gilson, *Jean Duns Scot*, Paris 1952.

Ranulf de Glanville, *Treatise on the Laws and Customs of the realm of England commonly called Glanville*, ed. and trans. G. D. G. Hall, London 1965.

Sir Thomas Gray, *Scalacronica*, trans. Herbert Maxwell, Glasgow 1907.

S. Grayzell, *The Church and the Jews in the Thirteenth Century*, Philadelphia 1933.

V. H. H. Green, *Medieval Civilization in Western Europe*, London 1971.

'William Gregory's Chronicle': The Historical Collections of a Citizen of London in the Fifteenth Century, ed. J. Gairdner, Camden Society, New Series XVII, London 1876.

C. Gross, *The Gild Merchant*, Oxford 1890.

C. Gross (editor), *Select Cases from the Coroners Rolls, 1265–1413*, Selden Society, 9, London 1896.

Guide du Pèlerin de St Jacques de Compostelle, ed. J. Vielliard, (fourth edition) Mâcon 1969.

D. J. Hall, *English Medieval Pilgrimage*, London 1966.

R. A. R. Hartridge, *A History of Vicarages in the Middle Ages*, Cambridge 1930.

M. Hastings, *The Court of Common Pleas in the Fifteenth Century*, Ithaca 1947.

Sidney Heath, *Pilgrim Life in the Middle Ages*, London 1911.

F. Heer, *The Medieval World*, trans. J. Sondheimer, London 1962.

R. H. Hilton, *A Medieval Society*, London 1966.

St Augustine of Hippo, *City of God*, trans. Henry Bettenson (Pelican Classics), London 1972.

St Augustine of Hippo, *Confessions*, trans. F. J. Sheed, London 1945.

W. S. Holdsworth, *A History of English Law*, ed. A. C. Goodhart and H. G. Hanbury, 16 vols., London 1966.

Holinshed, *Chronicles of England, Scotland and Ireland*, 6 vols., London 1907–8.

Roger of Hoveden, *Annals*, trans. Henry T. Riley, 2 vols., London 1853.

J. Huizinga, *The Waning of the Middle Ages*, trans. F. Hopman, London 1924.

John Hus, *Letters*, ed. and trans. H. B. Workman and R. M. Pope, London 1904.

Paul Johnson, *A History of Christianity*, London 1976.

Jean de Joinville, *The Life of St Louis*, trans. M. R. B. Shaw in *Chronicles of the Crusades* (Penguin Classics), London 1963.

Philip E. Jones (editor), *Calendar of Plea and Memoranda Rolls of the City of London, 1437–1482*, 2 vols., Cambridge 1954, 1961.

J. J. Jusserand, *English Wayfaring Life in the Middle Ages*, trans. Lucy Toulmin Smith, London 1889.

S. Katz, *The Jews in the Visigothic and Frankish Kingdoms of Spain and Gaul*, Cambridge Mass. 1937.

Maurice Keen, *The Outlaws of Medieval Legend*, London 1961.

E. W. Kemp, *An Introduction to Canon Law*, London 1957.

Richard Kieckhefer, *European Witch Trials, their Foundations in Popular and Learned Culture 1300–1500*, London 1976.

P. D. King, *Law and Society in the Visigothic Kingdom*, Cambridge 1972.

G. Kisch, *The Jews in Medieval Germany: a study of their legal and social status*, Chicago 1949.

E. N. van Kleffens, *Hispanic Law until the End of the Middle Ages*, Edinburgh 1968.

David Knowles, *Christian Monasticism*, London 1969.

David Knowles, *Saints and Scholars*, Cambridge 1962.

Paul Lacroix, *Moeurs, Usages et Costumes au Moyen Age et à l'Epoque de la Renaissance*, Paris 1874.

The Lanercost Chronicle, trans. Herbert Maxwell, *Scottish Historical Review*, vol. VI, 1908–9.

The Book of the Knight de la Tour Landry, ed. G. S. Taylor, London 1930.

Lanfranc, *Monastic Constitutions*, trans. David Knowles, London 1953.

Langland, *Piers the Ploughman*, trans. J. F. Goodridge, London 1959.

H. C. Lea, *A History of the Inquisition of the Middle Ages*, 3 vols., New York 1888.

H. C. Lea, *Sacerdotal Celibacy*, 2 vols., London 1907.

H. C. Lea, *Superstition and Force*, Philadelphia 1892.

Gordon Leff, *Heresy in the Later Middle Ages*, 2 vols., Manchester 1967.

E. Leroy Ladurie, *Montaillou: Village occitan de 1294 à 1324*, Paris 1975.

P. S. Lewis, *Later Medieval France: the Polity*, London 1968.

Liber Albus [of the City of London, compiled, 1419, by J. Carpenter, Clerk]: The White Book of the City of London, trans. H. T. Riley, London 1861.

Alain de Lille, *Textes Inédites*, with an introduction by Marie-Therèse d'Alvernay, Paris 1965.

V. D. Lipman, *The Jews of Medieval Norwich*, Jewish History Society of England, 1967.

E. C. Lodge, *Gascony under English Rule 1152–1453*, London 1926.

Guillaume de Loris and Jean de Meun, *The Romance of the Rose*, trans. Charles Dahlberg, Princeton 1971.

A. Lukyn-Williams, *Adversus Judaeus*, Cambridge 1935.

John T. McNeill and Helen M. Gamer, *Medieval Handbooks of Penance,* Columbia New York 1938.

Loren C. McKinney, *Early Medieval Medicine,* Baltimore 1937.

William of Malmesbury, *Chronicle of the Kings of England from the earliest period to the reign of King Stephen,* trans. J. A. Giles, London 1847.

William of Malmesbury, *Historia Novella,* trans. K. R. Potter, London 1955.

Edward J. Martin, *The Trial of the Templars,* London 1928.

Le Menagier de Paris, trans. Eileen Power, London 1928.

R. Menéndez Pidal, *The Cid and his Spain,* trans. Harold Sunderland, London 1934.

J. R. H. Moorman, *The Franciscan Order to 1517,* Oxford 1968.

Thomas of Monmouth, *The Life and Miracles of St William of Norwich,* trans. and ed. A. Jessop and M. R. James, Cambridge 1896.

Don Ramon Muntaner, *Chronicle,* trans. Lady Goodenough, 2 vols., Hakluyt Society, London 1920.

John Myrc, *Instructions for Parish Priests,* ed. E. Peacock, Early English Text Society, 31, London 1868.

Guibert of Nogent, *Autobiography,* trans. C. C. Swinton Bland, London 1925.

J. T. Norman, *The Scholastic Analysis of Usury,* Cambridge Mass. 1957.

Notker the Stammerer, *Charlemagne,* trans. Lewis Thorpe in *Two Lives of Charlemagne* (Penguin Classics), London 1969.

Joseph F. O'Callaghan, *A History of Medieval Spain,* Ithaca and London 1975.

Zoé Oldenbourg, *Massacre at Montséjur,* trans. Peter Green, London 1961.

C. W. Oman, *The Art of War in the Middle Ages* (revised edition), London 1953.

Iris Origo, *The Merchant of Prato,* London 1957.

Iris Origo, *The World of San Bernardino,* London 1963.

R. Oursel, *Les Pèlerins du Moyen Age, les hommes, les chemins, les sanctuaries,* Paris 1963.

S. R. Owst, *Literature and Pulpit in Medieval England. A neglected chapter in the history of English letters and of the English people,* Oxford 1961.

S. Painter, *Medieval Society,* Ithaca 1951.

Matthew Paris, *English History,* trans. J. A. Giles, 3 vols., London 1852.

James Parkes, *The Conflict of the Church and the Synagogue,* London 1934.

James Parkes, *The Jew in the Medieval Community,* London 1938.

The Paston Letters, ed. J. Gairdner, Edinburgh 1910.

C. Petit-Dutaillis, *Studies and Notes supplementary to Stubbs' Constitutional History,* 2 vols., Manchester 1914.

L. O. Pike, *A History of Crime in England,* 2 vols., London 1873.

Colin Platt, *The English Medieval Town,* London 1976.

Charles Poncé, *Kabbalah,* London 1974.

A. L. Poole, *Obligations of Society in the XII and XIII Centuries,* Oxford 1946.

Eileen Power, *Medieval Women,* ed. M. M. Postan, Cambridge 1975.

Joshua Prawer, *The Latin Kingdom of Jerusalem; European Colonialism in the Middle Ages,* London 1972.

R. B. Pugh, *Imprisonment in Medieval England,* Cambridge 1968.

Brian Pullan (editor), *Sources for the History of Medieval Europe from the mid-Eighth Century to the mid-Fourteenth Century,* Oxford 1966.

B. H. Putnam, *Proceedings before the Justices of the Peace in the Fourteenth and Fifteenth Centuries, Edward III to Richard III,* Ames Foundation 1938.

H. Rashdall, *Universities of Europe in the Middle Ages*, 3 vols., Oxford 1895.

M. E. Reeves, *The Influence of Prophecy in the Later Middle Ages*, Oxford 1969.

Paul Riant, *Inventaire Critique des Lettres Historiques des Croisades*, Paris 1880.

H. G. Richardson, *English Jewry under the Angevin Kings*, London 1960.

H. T. Riley (editor and translator), *Memorials of London and London Life in the Thirteenth, Fourteenth and Fifteenth Centuries; being extracts from the early archives of the City, 1276–1419*, London 1868.

M. Roberts, *St Catherine of Siena and her Times*, London 1906.

Fritz Rörig, *The Medieval Town*, trans. D. Bryant, London 1967.

C. Roth, *The History of the Jews in England*, Oxford 1941.

C. Roth, *The History of the Jews in Italy*, Philadelphia 1946.

Rotuli Parliamentorum, 6 vols., Records Commission, London 1767–77.

Romain Roussel, *Les Pèlerinages à travers les Siècles*, Paris 1954.

Steven Runciman, *A History of the Crusades*, 3 vols., Cambridge 1951–4.

Steven Runciman, *The Medieval Manichee*, Cambridge 1947.

Jeffrey B. Russell, *Witchcraft in the Middle Ages*, Ithaca and London 1972.

George Ryley-Scott, *The History of Corporal Punishment*, London 1938.

George Ryley-Scott, *The History of Torture*, (Luxor Press) London 1967.

John of Salisbury, *Historia Pontificalis*, trans. Marjorie Chibnall, London 1956.

G. O. Sayles (editor), *Select Cases in the Court of the King's Bench*, Selden Society, 55, 57, 58, 74, 76, 82, London 1936–65.

R. A. Sharpe (editor), *Calendar of Letter Books of the City of London, 1275–1498*, Books A–L, II vols., London 1899–1912.

D. Sherwin-Bailey, *Homosexuality and the Western Christian Tradition*, London 1955.

Beryl Smalley, *Historians in the Middle Ages*, London 1974.

R. W. Southern, *The Making of the Middle Ages*, London 1958.

R. W. Southern, *Western Society and the Church in the Middle Ages*, London 1970.

M. Spinka, *John Hus*, Princeton 1969.

Jacob Sprenger and Henricus Institor, *Malleus Maleficarum*, trans. The Revd. Montague Summers, London 1948.

Statutes of the Realm, vols. I–III, Records Commission, London 1810–16.

E. L. G. Stones, *The Folvilles of Ashby-Folville, Leicestershire, and their associates in crime, 1326–1347*, Royal Historical Society Transactions, 5th Series, vol. 7, London 1957.

R. L. Storey, *The End of the House of Lancaster*, London 1966.

Jonathan Sumption, *Pilgrimage, an Image of Medieval Religion*, London 1975.

H. O. Taylor, *The Medieval Mind*, 2 vols., Cambridge Mass. (reprinted) 1949.

J. Taylor, *The Universal Chronicle of Ranulf Higden*, Oxford 1966.

A. H. Thomas (editor), *Calendar of Plea and Memoranda Rolls of The City of London, 1323–1437*, 4 vols., Cambridge 1926–43.

E. A. Thompson, *The Goths in Spain*, Oxford 1969.

Brian Tierney, *Medieval Poor Law*, Berkeley and Los Angeles 1959.

Arthur Tilley (editor), *Medieval France*, Cambridge 1922.

Gregory of Tours, *History of the Franks*, trans. O. M. Dalton, 2 vols., Oxford 1927.

T. F. Tout, *Collected Papers III*, Manchester 1934.

H. R. Trevor-Roper, *The Rise of Christian Europe*, London 1965.

G. A. Turner (editor), *Select Pleas of the Forest*, Selden Society, 13, London 1899.

Geoffrey Trease, *The Condottieri*, New York 1971.

William of Tyre, *History of the Deeds beyond the Sea by William, Archbishop of Tyre*, trans. E. A. Babcock, Columbia New York 1943.

Walter Ullmann, *The Growth of Papal Government in the Middle Ages*, London 1959.

Walter Ullmann, *The Individual and Society in the Middle Ages*, London 1967.

Walter Ullmann, *Public Welfare and Social Legislation in Early Medieval Councils, Studies in Church History*, Cambridge 1971.

Jean de Venette, *Chronicle*, trans. J. Birdsall, ed. Richard A. Newhall, Columbia New York 1953.

Giovanni Villani, *Chronicle*, trans. Rose E. Selfe, ed. Philip. H. Wicksteed, London 1906.

Geoffrey de Villehardouin, *The Conquest of Constantinople*, trans. M. R. B. Shaw in *Chronicles of the Crusades* (Penguin Classics), London 1963.

François Villon, *Oeuvres Complètes*, ed. Auguste Lorgnon, Paris 1892.

A. L. Vincent and Clare Binns, *Gilles de Rais: the original Bluebeard*, London 1926.

Paul Vinogradoff, *Roman Law in Medieval Europe*, London and New York 1909.

Ordericus Vitalis, *Ecclesiastical History*, Books III–X, trans. Marjorie Chibnall, 4 vols., Oxford 1969–75.

Jacques de Vitry, *The Exempla, or illustrated stories from the Sermones Vulgares of Jacques deVitry*, with Introduction and Notes by T. F. Crane, Folk-Lore Society, 26, London 1890.

Helen Waddell, *The Wandering Scholars*, London 1927.

Gerald of Wales, *Autobiography*, trans. H. E. Butler,London 1937.

O. D. Watkins, *A History of Penance*, London 1920.

William Way, *The Itineraries of William Way, Fellow of Eton College, to Jerusalem A. D. 1458 and 1462 to St James of Compostella*, Roxburghe Club, London 1857.

Roger of Wendover, *Flowers of History*, trans. J. A. Giles, 2 vols., London 1849.

James J. Whilhelm, *Medieval Song: an Anthology of Hymns and Lyrics*, London 1972.

Charles Williams, *The Figure of Beatrice*, London 1950.

Thomas Wright, *Narratives of Sorcery and Magic from the most authentic sources*, 2 vols., London 1851.

D. B. Wyndham-Lewis, *Francois Villon: a documented survey*, London 1928.

Year Books, Les Reports del Cases en Ley, London 1678–9.

K. Young, *The Drama of the Medieval Church, 2 vols., Oxford 1933*.

List of Illustrations

Index